Knowledge That Matters

Knowledge That Matters
A Feminist Theological Paradigm and Epistemology

Lucy Tatman

THE
PILGRIM
PRESS
Cleveland

BT
83.55
.T38
2001

The Pilgrim Press, 700 Prospect Avenue, Cleveland, Ohio 44115-1100, USA
pilgrimpress.com

Co-published with Sheffield Academic Press Ltd
The Tower Building, 11 York Road, London SE1 7NX
71 Lexington Avenue, New York, NY 10017-653

A Continuum imprint

Copyright © 2001 Sheffield Academic Press

All rights reserved. Published 2001

Printed and bound in Great Britain on acid free paper

06 05 04 03 02 01   5 4 3 2 1

A catalog record for this book is available from the British Library

Library of Congress Cataloging-in-Publication Data

ISBN 0-8298-1448-5

CONTENTS

Acknowledgments	7
Introduction	9
Chapter 1 WHAT IS A DISCIPLINARY PARADIGM?	17
Chapter 2 INFLUENCES ON THE FORMATION OF ONE FEMINIST CHRISTIAN THEOLOGICAL PARADIGM	40
Chapter 3 THE COMPONENTS OF ONE FEMINIST CHRISTIAN THEOLOGICAL PARADIGM	66
Chapter 4 FEMINIST EPISTEMOLOGY: TRANSFORMING UNDERSTANDINGS OF KNOWERS, KNOWING AND THE WORLD TO BE KNOWN	95
Chapter 5 EPISTEMOLOGICAL COMMUNITIES AND THEIR CONSEQUENCES	125
Chapter 6 PARADIGMATIC AND EPISTEMOLOGICAL ELEMENTS IN THE THEOLOGY OF ROSEMARY RADFORD RUETHER	152
Chapter 7 PARADIGMATIC AND EPISTEMOLOGICAL ELEMENTS IN THE THEOLOGY OF CARTER HEYWARD	182

Chapter 8
PARADIGMATIC AND EPISTEMOLOGICAL ELEMENTS IN
THE THEOLOGY OF SALLIE MCFAGUE   212

Chapter 9
AN EPISTEMOLOGY OF PARTICIPATORY DISCERNMENT   249

Bibliography   262
Index of Modern Authors   268

ACKNOWLEDGMENTS

It is impossible to name everyone who contributed their time, encouragement and support to this book. However, there were a few people without whom it would have been impossible, most especially Rosemary Radford Ruether, Carter Heyward and Sallie McFague. They receive my deepest thanks for doing what they do. Lorraine Code gave generously of her time and wisdom, providing me with an invaluable crash course in feminist epistemology, and my advisors at the Australian National University, Jan Jindy Pettman, Winifred Lamb and Natalie Stoljar, were always there when most needed. Joanne Carlson Brown and Dorothea McEwan provided me with much needed long-distance advice, even when they didn't have enough time to do their own work. Most of all there were those friends who stuck with me through all those years when I was not writing to them: Louise, Shelly and Beth, Jon and Shelley. My thanks to my mother for all those words of encouragement. I must also acknowledge Bear the Cat, who sat on, thereby blessing, many chapters, and bit my ankles when I seemed too distracted from important things like food. Finally, there was, and thankfully still is, Judith Ion...no words will do. To everyone, thank you.

INTRODUCTION

In the beginning, when I first encountered Christian theology as an academic subject, I had no idea that feminist Christian theology existed. It was 1983, and I was a student at Birmingham-Southern College (a United Methodist institution) in Birmingham, Alabama. I had lived in Mobile, Alabama, since 1977, and, as I had been born in Montgomery in 1965, I regarded the years my family had not lived in the state as something of an aberration. Alabama, while not the whole world, was definitely the centre of the universe. It was a slow, orderly universe, with a distant and distractedly aloof (in that reserved, Episcopalian way) God Above; it was made for and meant to be used by 'us'; and it was a universe sometimes threatened (but never seriously) by 'those sorts of people', those who, for some unfathomable and obviously sinful reason, were too uppity, or vocally discontent with their God-given place in the scheme of things. I was never taught these things explicitly, nonetheless these facts were in the very air I breathed, so learn them I did. For the next year or two nothing I would be taught at Birmingham-Southern College would threaten this understanding of the universe. And then my world turned upside-down and inside-out, simultaneously. The following book is, in part at least, my attempt to explain to myself, seventeen years and two continents later, what happened.[1]

What happened was a love affair—a tumultuous, charged and painful love affair with feminist Christian theology, of the sort written by White, highly educated and economically privileged women in North America.[2] In a matter of days, it seems in retrospect, I went from being

---

1. I was to move from Durham, North Carolina, to Canberra, Australia, in November of 1992, and to Budapest, Hungary, in January of 1999. The body of this text was written in Canberra, revised in Budapest, and introduced and concluded in Ann Arbor and Novi, Michigan.

2. Importantly, I believe strongly that it is only after I have a thorough understanding of my own specific theological heritage that I can begin to compare this

a dutiful (if a tad brash) daughter of traditional Christian theology to a mad woman given to making incomprehensible utterances in theology classes. The problem was that I had been a very good daughter, with a surprisingly clear if mostly intuitive understanding of the sons' systematic theologies and, especially, their most fundamental assumptions, those without which their theologies made no sense. When at last I was introduced to feminist Christian theology (in Professor Earl Gossett's seminar on contemporary Christian thought, in the fall of 1985), I simply 'got' the fact that here was a whole new set of assumptions about the world, humanity, and God—assumptions I had never before dreamt of. And they all made more sense to me than any I had learned before. So I purchased all the feminist theology texts I could find at that time and read them again and again and again, until I learned how to speak this new language. That's when I began to make incomprehensible utterances in class. Incomprehensible? Yes. For while I understood what I was trying to say, and Professor Gossett (to his great credit) understood that I was saying something that might, in the right circumstances, be intelligible, hardly anyone else in the classroom did; suddenly I was speaking, it seemed to my peers, in a foreign language about a foreign world. It was, to put it mildly, a difficult time, but oh I had lovers. I had texts by Ruether, Daly, Collins, Morton, Heyward, Harrison, McFague, Plaskow, Christ, Russell, Schüssler Fiorenza, Trible; I was never alone, and I was busy.

To put it in the language that will appear in this book, I was wrestling a blessing from a new worldview, one conveyed and revealed to me in a new language, a language composed of transformed metaphors and models, a language spoken by a small (but rapidly growing) epistemic community. I was diving into a new feminist Christian theological paradigm, and, in my excitement, I took it all for granted. I took it for granted that this was a body of knowledge that counted as knowledge, and it was knowledge I hungered for. I, probably arrogantly and certainly unthinkingly, took for granted my right to enter the epistemic community engaged in the making of this knowledge.

To be fair, that arrogance was born not only out of my Whiteness and my class privilege, but also the fact that I was living as a young 'out' lesbian in Birmingham, Alabama. In the mid-eighties young lesbians

---

body of thought with, for example, womanist theology or mujerista theology or feminist Christian theology being written in England or Germany or Australia.

there needed a bit of arrogance just to get by. As for the thoughtlessness, it too was no doubt a product of Whiteness and privilege, partly. But in part I was simply responding to my calling. Feminist Christian theology is my life's passion, my vocation and my joy; it is the sort of knowledge I still hunger for, still desire to co-create with others. Accordingly, when the time came to decide what to write about, the decision was easy—feminist Christian theology and feminist epistemology: the knowledge, both sacred and secular (and always both at once), that has so changed my life.

Chapter 1 consists of an explanation of what I take to be the fundamental components of a theological paradigm. Given that within the academic discipline of Christian theology the notion of theological paradigms in general and of the existence of several feminist Christian theological paradigms in particular is now commonplace, I was struck by the fact that no one had attempted to detail the ways in which this particular feminist Christian theological paradigm differed from the classical Christian theological paradigm. What I discovered was that it is actually much more difficult to describe a paradigm than I had thought. As Thomas Kuhn noted, entering a new paradigm is akin to going through a conversion experience;[3] words tend to fail one, although the experience itself is real indeed. This being the case, or at least having been my experience, I set out to understand why, when one is looking into (or speaking out of) a new paradigm, words fail in the ways they do. I conclude that it is because the metaphors and models of a new paradigm are so tied to the basic metaphysical assumptions (or worldview) and value judgments of the new paradigm that without a grasp of the whole the individual terms are, by themselves, practically meaningless—in that their possible meanings are too many.

In Chapter 1, I introduce as well the notions of 'epistemic communities' and 'rhetorical spaces', drawing on the work of feminist philosopher Lorraine Code in particular. The point I try to make is that a theoretical paradigm is created and sustained not by isolated individuals but by an epistemic community: a group of people who, while they never agree on everything, at least understand each other well enough to engage in what I term 'meaningful disagreement' with one

---

3. Thomas Kuhn, *The Structure of Scientific Revolutions* (Chicago: University of Chicago Press, 2nd edn, 1970), p. 151. 'The transfer of allegiance from paradigm to paradigm is a conversion experience that cannot be forced'.

another. Further, their words only make sense when they are spoken and heard within the rhetorical space specific to their epistemic community. One of the epistemological issues that follows from this is that access to such epistemic communities and rhetorical spaces is limited, limited in power-riddled, non-innocent ways.

In Chapter 2 I back up, all the way to the Enlightenment, seeking to trace what I consider to be some of the most important philosophical and theological influences on the formation of one feminist Christian theological paradigm. The point I try to make in this chapter is twofold. On the one hand, feminist Christian theology written by White, educationally and economically privileged North American women in the latter third of the twentieth century is an outgrowth (one among others) of post-Enlightenment Christian theology, thoroughly rooted in what has gone before. On the other hand, it is also a unique combination of ideas and neither the epistemic community to utter them nor the rhetorical space in which they could be uttered existed before the mid-1960s (in the US). Making no claim to being a historian, I need to stress that the themes I chose to focus on in this chapter are those that I hear echoed in early and current feminist Christian theological texts. Other ears would have listened for and no doubt heard themes I did not.

Having thus set the stage, in Chapter 3 I engage with feminist Christian theology proper, giving a close reading of three early and influential feminist Christian theological essays. Specifically, I seek to identify the underlying metaphysical assumptions (or worldview) presupposed within these texts, their accompanying value judgments, and the metaphors and models used to convey these assumptions. It is my hypothesis that these essays by Valerie Saiving, Rosemary Radford Ruether, and Mary Daly do not serve as a mere corrective to some of the dominant tradition's more blatant excesses or lacks as regards its understanding of 'women', but are instead written from an understanding of 'a different heaven and earth', to borrow a phrase from Sheila Collins.[4] I seek to make this new worldview explicit in order to compare these early fundamental assumptions and value judgments concerning the nature of things with (in Chapters 6, 7 and 8) the fundamental assumptions running throughout the work of Rosemary Ruether, Carter

---

4. *A Different Heaven and Earth* is the title of Sheila Collins' 1974 assessment of the shape and contours of feminist theology in the United States to that date. Sheila D. Collins, *A Different Heaven and Earth* (Valley Forge, PA: Judson Press, 1974).

Heyward, and Sallie McFague. Again, my hypothesis is that, if this sort of feminist Christian theology is indeed a theological paradigm, then the fundamental assumptions of this paradigm must be fairly stable and substantially unchanging, although open to different emphases. They should be as readily identifiable in the first instances of this feminist Christian theology as they are in the most recent.

In Chapter 4 I exchange the language of paradigms for that of feminist epistemology. I do so because paradigmatic assumptions concerning humanity and the world (or creation) are always interwoven with epistemological assumptions about humans as knowers (or epistemic agents) and the world as a place it is important to know. Needing a language with which to discuss the epistemological assumptions inherent within the feminist Christian theological paradigm I am examining, I turn to North American feminist epistemology for assistance. Specifically, in this chapter I provide a reading of feminist standpoint theory as presented by Nancy Hartsock, Donna Haraway, and Sandra Harding.

In Chapter 5 I delve further into several epistemological themes which I read as being present but not fully elaborated in feminist standpoint theory/ies. These include the notion of an epistemic (or epistemological) community as the creator of knowledge, rather than an understanding of individuals as knowledge-makers; the notion of different epistemic communities as being granted more or less 'cognitive authority' (Kathryn Pyne Addelson's phrase) by the wider society of which they are a part; and the notion of knowledge as being continually made and remade within specific times and contexts, or, knowledge as inescapably relative to different communities of knowledge-makers. I include as well within this chapter a reading of Lorraine Code's discussion of the relationship between knowledge and power.

Importantly, I want to acknowledge that my journey into the land of feminist epistemology was, is, and cannot help but be coloured by the theological lenses set so firmly upon my nose. In other words, my readings of feminist epistemological texts are readings from the 'outside', and I want to own the fact that my interpretations lack the subtlety of touch and the extensive familiarity with the background to this material that a feminist philosopher would bring to the same texts. For this I apologise to those philosophers whose work I used; I learned much from them, and could not have written this book without the tools they provided. Nonetheless I cannot shake the feeling that in places I might have, unwittingly, used a wrench as a hammer—hence the apology.

With this groundwork in place, in Chapters 6, 7 and 8 I finally put all the pieces together as I engage in close readings of the feminist Christian theology of Rosemary Radford Ruether, Carter Heyward, and Sallie McFague, respectively. I seek to identify their paradigmatic assumptions concerning humanity, creation, and God; the influences of post-Enlightenment theology and philosophy on their thought; and their accompanying epistemological presuppositions. In so doing I argue that, collectively, their work is representative of one particular feminist Christian theological paradigm; it is a body of knowledge in its own right, one that is (as all bodies of knowledge are) open to serious misinterpretation if the underlying assumptions that support the knowledge claims made by these feminist Christian theologians are not acknowledged and taken seriously. (Let me state from the outset, however, that while I believe serious misinterpretation is always a possibility, I do not affirm the possibility of there ever being one single correct interpretation of any theologian's work or any theological paradigm.)

Because Ruether, Heyward, and McFague are not the only three feminist Christian theologians whose work I could have examined, I need to explain why I chose their work in particular. In part my reasons were purely pragmatic. Rosemary Ruether, a historical theologian, is the most widely published (and prolific) feminist Christian theologian in the world. Her influence on the development of feminist Christian theology is immense, and I know of no feminist Christian theologian who does not draw upon, at a minimum, her early work. Carter Heyward's writings are also highly influential. I chose to examine her work in the context of this book primarily because it is, as I read it, the most creative theology of all the feminist Christian theology with which I am acquainted. While she is perhaps better known for being the first feminist Christian theologian to discuss openly her lesbian life-choice as an integral part of her theology, I am more concerned (within the context of this book) with the fact that, as a constructive, systematic feminist Christian theologian, Heyward is changing the way theology can be done. Lastly, I chose to examine Sallie McFague's work on metaphorical theology because she has devoted more attention to the world-shaping power of language than any other feminist Christian theologian. As Chapter 8 will make clear, her attention to the metaphysical and epistemological implications of theological words is, in my opinion, unparalleled amongst feminist Christian theologians.

Additionally, the fact that Ruether writes as a Roman Catholic, Heyward as an Episcopalian, and McFague as a (never specifically identified) Protestant theologian means that, collectively, their work is broadly representative of North American, White feminist Christian thought per se—of the non-Evangelical sort. Finally, I must admit that I chose to examine their work in part because each one of these theologians has had a formative (more accurately, formidable) influence on my own theological education. In studying their work in such detail, I am researching my own theological heritage in order to have a better understanding of the theological ground I stand upon, always with others. This notion of a theological ground brings me to Chapter 9, the conclusion of this book.

In Chapter 9 I reflect upon the possibilities provided by such a theological ground (or framework or paradigm) to those of us who have the privilege of doing this sort of feminist Christian theology. In essence, I suggest that rather than assuming that everything that can be said about this sort of theology has been said (and therefore it is time to move on), it is only now that we can begin to do the meticulous, detailed work of re-writing, re-imagining every single theological concept we can think of. We can do this work now because, finally, we need not concern ourselves with defining, explicitly, every general theological assumption we make. In addition, I reflect upon a troubling tendency I have perceived recently amongst some feminist Christian theologians—a tendency to interpret others' works without regard to the theoretical assumptions inherent within the paradigmatic context in which those works were written. Such a tendency, I suggest, points to the usefulness of the sort of project I undertake in this book.

It points as well to the need to be mindful of the language-worlds in which we speak and write. Perhaps because it has been years since I was able to take for granted or even to name the centre of my universe, I have grown increasingly attuned to the many, varied universes our words convey. I have come to the realisation that there will always be just a trace of a southern drawl in my words, a drawl accompanied by that curious, unshakeable southern certainty that stories which seem to be going nowhere are the ones which will surprise you most in the end. There will be traces as well of blunt Australian directness, and instances of extreme Australian understatement. Recently immersed in the language-world of English as a second (or third or fourth) language, the English of Central and Eastern Europe, I find it both gorgeous and bewilderingly dense: modifiers appear in the most unlikely places, and words are somehow made to mean things I never imagined they could. For whatever reasons, I seem to enjoy the challenge of translating (when possible, and it's not, always) the feminist Christian theology I know into the languages of the different worlds in which I find myself. It may be helpful to read this book, then, as a translation, as my attempt to translate one sort of feminist Christian theology into a language intelligible both to those who are and those who are not members of the epistemic community making this knowledge. It is also my hope that from now on I will be able to write feminist Christian theology, instead of write about it.

Chapter 1

WHAT IS A DISCIPLINARY PARADIGM?

Does the feminist Christian theology written in the United States of America in the last third of the twentieth century by White, economically and educationally privileged women comprise a unique and identifiable body of knowledge? If it does, if, that is, such a specifically located and limited use of the term 'feminist Christian theology' is at all meaningful, then how is it possible to identify this body of knowledge? What are its distinguishing characteristics? What are the theoretical components of this body of knowledge? These are the questions I seek to answer in this book. They are epistemological questions broadly conceived which will lead eventually to a point-by-point examination of the epistemological framework around which one feminist Christian theological paradigm is constructed.

But I have just exchanged the phrase 'body of knowledge' for the term 'paradigm', and must now explain my reasons for this shift in language. In part my reasons are pragmatic: I have chosen to use the term and explore the concept of a paradigm simply because this term is a theological commonplace. With regard to feminist Christian theology written by White, educationally and economically privileged women in the United States, since the early 1970s most of these women have either implicitly or explicitly accepted that they are working both within and from a new theological paradigm.[1] However, puzzlingly (given

---

1. The earliest use of the term 'paradigm' (with reference to feminist theology) that I have found is by Rita Gross, in her introduction to the 1977 book *Beyond Androcentrism*. She wrote there, 'This volume, which grows out of the 1975 meeting of the Women and Religion section of the American Academy of Religion, reflects the continuing paradigm shift that is occurring in the discipline of the Academic Study of Religion... This paradigm shift is the scholarly and philosophic dimension of the feminist transformation of culture.' Rita M. Gross (ed.), *Beyond Androcentrism: New Essays on Women and Religion* (Missoula, MT: Scholars Press, 1977), p. 1.

the number of times the fact of this paradigm is mentioned or assumed), the precise nature of this paradigm has remained tacit, understood but unspoken. It has been taken for granted that both the nature of a disciplinary paradigm in general and of this new paradigm in particular are somehow self-evident. While Thomas Kuhn's work on scientific paradigms has been cited and quoted in brief, a more comprehensive examination of the nature of disciplinary paradigms *in connection with* a feminist Christian theological paradigm has not yet occurred.[2] It is my contention that until the structure and components of this feminist Christian theological paradigm are explicitly identified, it will be impossible to perceive, let alone to examine, the epistemological framework of this new theological paradigm. Additionally, it will be most difficult for anyone not working from within this paradigm to perceive it as a paradigm in its own right, or as a body of knowledge unique within the overarching academic discipline of Christian theology. It is also my contention, although I will not attempt to make the case here, that within the discipline of Christian theology there are a number of emerging Christian theological paradigms (in the sense of conceptual frameworks), each of which is consistent within itself and each of which forms a whole, though not static, worldview. To complicate matters further, I suggest that *no one understands Christian theology (or any other discipline) from outside an existing paradigm of some sort*.[3] Unfortunately, to borrow a phrase from Wittgenstein, a disciplinary paradigm is 'like a pair of glasses on our nose through which we see whatever we look at. It never occurs to us to take them off.'[4] Therefore, before I investigate the nature of one particular feminist Christian theological paradigm I need to make a case for my understanding of disciplinary paradigms in general.

My understanding of the concept of a disciplinary paradigm has been

---

2. See Sallie McFague, *Metaphorical Theology: Models of God in Religious Language* (Philadelphia: Fortress Press, 1982), pp. 79-83, and Elisabeth Schüssler Fiorenza, *In Memory of Her: A Feminist Theological Reconstruction of Christian Origins* (New York: Crossroad, 1986), pp. xxi-xxii. Both authors discuss Kuhn's understanding of a paradigm, McFague quite extensively, but neither elaborates on the specifically paradigmatic elements of feminist Christian theology.

3. See Mary Midgley, *Wisdom, Information and Wonder: What is Knowledge For?* (London and New York: Routledge, 1989), p. 233: 'Some set of propositions...must occupy this base position.'

4. Ludwig Wittgenstein, *Philosophical Investigations* (trans. G.E.M. Anscombe; Oxford: Blackwell, 2nd edn, 1958), p. 45e, no. 103.

1. *What is a Disciplinary Paradigm?*

informed by a reading of Thomas Kuhn's (1970) *The Structure of Scientific Revolutions* as well as by various feminist philosophers' and epistemologists' thoughts on and critiques of the concept of a paradigm, in particular those of Lorraine Code, Mary Midgley, and Lynn Hankinson Nelson.[5] While Kuhn's work has shaped my understanding of the concept of a paradigm, I am consciously picking and choosing from his work those aspects of his thought that I find most convincing and/or useful to my own argument. I do not engage in a direct critique of his conception of a paradigm; instead I plunder his text for the treasures I find most valuable with regard to the nature of a theological, rather than scientific, paradigm. Regarding my own reformulation of the concept, I am most indebted to Lorraine Code: in part for her insistence on Wittgenstein's dictum, 'knowledge is in the end based on acknowledgement', and in part for providing the theoretical notion she terms 'rhetorical space'—a notion I will adapt (and adjust slightly) in order to provide a ground for my conception of a disciplinary paradigm.[6]

Accordingly, in this chapter I shall firstly present a broad discussion of the concepts 'disciplinary paradigm' and 'rhetorical space'. I shall follow each broad overview with a more detailed analysis of each of the significant terms I introduce in the initial discussion. By the end of this chapter I will have established that inherent in any given disciplinary paradigm are epistemological presuppositions concerning, broadly, humans as knowers (or epistemic agents), the world to be known, and processes for acquiring knowledge. As, again, I am ultimately concerned with making explicit the epistemological elements inherent in one feminist Christian theological paradigm, in the next chapters I will explore more fully certain influences upon the formation of this paradigm and then take up the notion of feminist epistemology, reviewing some of the recent developments in the area of feminist epistemology. At this point, though, the most pressing question is, what is a disciplinary paradigm?

---

5. See Midgley, *Wisdom, Information and Wonder*; Lynn Hankinson Nelson, *Who Knows: From Quine to a Feminist Empiricism* (Philadelphia: Temple University Press, 1990); Lorraine Code, *What Can She Know? Feminist Theory and the Construction of Knowledge* (Ithaca, NY: Cornell University Press, 1991); and *idem*, *Rhetorical Spaces: Essays on Gendered Locations* (New York and London: Routledge, 1995).

6. Code, *What Can She Know?*, p. 215. See also Code, *Rhetorical Spaces*.

As I conceive it, the very concept of a disciplinary paradigm is itself a *Gestalt*, a theoretical 'whole' greater than the sum of its parts. Focusing on any one element of a disciplinary paradigm leads to a distorted view of the whole. To begin with the whole, therefore, I define a discipline as a body of shared knowledge structured by a conceptual framework of some sort.[7] In the simplest terms, a disciplinary *paradigm* is that shared conceptual framework. More specifically, it is a framework shaped by a set of metaphysical assumptions *so taken for granted they are almost never questioned* by the member-participants within a given disciplinary paradigm.[8] It is on the basis of these *shared metaphysical assumptions* that member-participants in a specific discipline are able to discuss meaningfully their understandings of certain aspects of the world. Whether or not they reach complete agreement about any given aspect is irrelevant; what matters is that they share a particular focus on the world—about which they speak in 'a common language'. This 'common language' is composed of a set of *metaphors* that are combined in various ways to form *models* that are in turn elaborations upon and refinements of specific aspects of that *epistemic community's* core metaphysical assumptions. Running throughout all the shared metaphors, models and core metaphysical assumptions is yet another shared variable: shared *value judgments*.[9]

Thus far I have identified four components of a disciplinary paradigm: (1) a set of shared metaphysical assumptions; (2) shared metaphors; (3) shared models; and (4) shared value judgments. Additionally, I have introduced the notion of an epistemic community—by which I mean all those who work within a disciplinary paradigm and whose

---

7. I am assuming that all knowledge is mediated by a language of some sort; and I accept Elizabeth Potter's use of Wittgenstein's analysis of the impossibility of private language as the basis for my incessant use of the word 'shared'. See Elizabeth Potter, 'Gender and Epistemic Negotiation', in Linda Alcoff and Elizabeth Potter (eds.), *Feminist Epistemologies* (New York and London: Routledge, 1993), pp. 161-86.

8. See Thomas Kuhn, *The Structure of Scientific Revolutions* (Chicago: University of Chicago Press, 2nd edn, 1970), pp. 7, 46, 184.

9. Kuhn, *Structure*, pp. 182-85. In seeking to answer the question 'what do [a scientific community's] members share that accounts for the relative fullness of their professional communication and the relative unanimity of their professional judgments?' Kuhn names 'metaphysical parts of paradigms', as well as 'models', 'metaphors' and 'values'.

work sustains that discipline.[10] Although I need to discuss these separately, each one of the first four components is integrally related to the other three, and none of them makes sense in the absence of a community of disciplinary practitioners—people working within the same discipline and communicating with each other through common metaphors and models. Let me stress that a disciplinary paradigm is not a recipe for complete agreement among all the members of a particular epistemic community; rather a disciplinary paradigm *provides a blueprint for* a depth of comprehension not possible when the metaphysical assumptions, metaphors, models and basic value judgments are not shared. A disciplinary paradigm provides the basis for both meaningful agreement and meaningful disagreement within an epistemic community.

As an example, imagine two ordained Roman Catholic theologians at the Vatican disagreeing about the importance of mass in a parish. Now imagine two particle physicists disagreeing about the importance of mass in an equation. In this example it is obvious that these conversations, while both about 'mass', are about two completely different topics, topics comprehensible only when a host of related assumptions about the nature of the world are tacitly acknowledged and accepted as framing the context of each discussion. As I define it, a disciplinary paradigm is a conceptual framework inclusive of all those accepted assumptions as well as the discipline-specific metaphors and models that enable meaningful discussion to happen at all. But, and this may be the most important *but* I shall write in this study, *meaningful discussion can only take place in those locations where the 'cognitive authority' of each participant is acknowledged by the other participants in the discussion.*[11]

To put it another way, communication between member-participants of an epistemic community within a disciplinary paradigm is possible because all are speaking within the same *rhetorical space*. As Lorraine Code introduces the term, a rhetorical space is a 'fictive but not fanciful or fixed location, whose (tacit, rarely spoken) territorial imperatives structure and limit the kinds of utterances that can be voiced within [it] with a reasonable expectation of uptake and "choral support": an

10. See Midgley, *Wisdom, Information and Wonder*, p. 71.
11. The expression 'cognitive authority' is Kathryn Pyne Addelson's; see 'Knower/Doers and their Moral Problems', in Alcoff and Potter (eds.), *Feminist Epistemologies*, pp. 265-94.

expectation of being heard, understood, taken seriously'.[12] As I interpret this quotation, the 'rarely spoken territorial imperatives' comprising the boundaries of each rhetorical space are inclusive not only of all the components of an epistemic community's disciplinary paradigm, but also of the *communal, power-riddled process of granting and withholding epistemic credibility to individual speakers*. In her work, Code's emphasis is on 'explorations of rhetorical spaces where acknowledgement is readily achieved, or where it is thwarted; where cognitive authority is readily granted, or denied and silenced'.[13] Her primary concern is not with making explicit the different components of specific conceptual frameworks; rather, in *Rhetorical Spaces* she demonstrates why it is the case that in a given context a particular person's epistemic agency depends at least as much on the state of that person's communally determined cognitive authority as it does on that person's grasp of any given conceptual framework. In positing the concept of a rhetorical space as necessarily co-existent with a disciplinary paradigm, I am trying to move away from a reading of a disciplinary paradigm as a benign or innocent set of abstractions, able to be embraced by any individual at will. Instead, I deliberately want to ground my explication of the components of a disciplinary paradigm on a usually unacknowledged, yet critically important, foundation: the social, political and moral disposition of the epistemic community sustaining the disciplinary paradigm.

On the one hand, deeply ingrained stereotypes and prejudices, when shared (consciously or not) by a majority or a powerful minority of an epistemic community, directly influence who is allowed to speak and who can expect to be heard within a disciplinary paradigm.[14] Consider

---

12. Code, *Rhetorical Spaces*, pp. ix-x. She borrows the phrase 'choral support' from Patricinio Schweikart.

13. Code, *Rhetorical Spaces*, pp. x-xi.

14. See Code, *What Can She Know?*, especially pp. 188-203. Code compares the effect of stereotypes on people's lives with the 'entrenched institutional and disciplinary power of a paradigm'—asserting that the power of a paradigm 'can confer legitimacy on [an] aspiring scientific endeavor or relegate it to the limbo of unacceptability' (p. 194). Likewise, stereotypes grant and deny legitimacy to whole categories of individuals. My contention is that the stereotypes unquestioningly held by a number of participants in any epistemic community are able to remain unquestioned in part precisely because the other components of their disciplinary paradigm support the stereotypic assumptions. In other words, it is a mutually reinforcing circle. Embedded in disciplinary paradigms are the assumptions that confer

the following: if I, as a feminist lesbian theologian, tried to join in the conversation about mass with a group of physicists, my words would not be acknowledged, not because feminist lesbians per se cannot be physicists, but because I personally do not know the language, the metaphors and models of particle physics. If, however, I tried to join in a conversation at the Vatican about mass, my words would go unheard not because I do not know the metaphors, models and metaphysical assumptions associated with parish mass, but because I am a feminist lesbian. Among the 'territorial imperatives' guarding the Vatican are quite a few that explicitly exclude feminists and lesbians from that rhetorical space. As Kathryn Addelson succinctly puts it, '*who* makes knowledge makes a difference. Making knowledge is a political act.'[15] Only those who are privileged to be *communally acknowledged* epistemic agents get to play in the paradigm, to have their voices heard in that paradigm's rhetorical space.[16] On the other hand, the structures that enable knowledge to be made, disciplinary paradigms, are not the individual creations of solitary eccentrics, nor do they exist in a cultural vacuum. A change in the cultural *Zeitgeist* affects the attitudes and beliefs of the member-participants of the epistemic communities within that culture. Broad social movements such as (in the United States) the movements for the abolition of slavery and for women's suffrage, the civil rights movement, the women's liberation movement, and the movement for gay and lesbian rights, can, over time, influence and transform the assumptions of a society about entire categories of humanity. That is, views formerly held by a minority can come to be held by a majority, although of course dissenting voices will remain. When such a broad shift in thought or value happens, however, no epistemic community within that society can remain immune to the effects of this transformation. Either a particular discipline can resist such a shift, reinstating within its rhetorical space its own attitudes and beliefs in various ways (witness the Vatican *vis-à-vis* women) [17] or the

---

legitimacy to stereotypes. When stereotypes are challenged and dismantled, so too are disciplinary paradigms transformed.

15. Addelson, 'Knower/Doers', p. 267 (italics in original).

16. Thus in paying attention to the rhetorical space enveloping a disciplinary paradigm one finds answers to the following questions: who, in that space, is acknowledged to have cognitive authority, and who has the power and authority to do such acknowledging?

17. See Rosemary Radford Ruether, 'Women's Difference and Equal Rights in

components of a disciplinary paradigm operative within that society can shift (witness the Vatican *vis-à-vis* slavery).

A rhetorical space is thus integrally connected to an epistemic community's disciplinary paradigm. The relevance accorded an epistemic community by the wider society seems to depend to a large extent on whether or not that community is able, over time, to express within its rhetorical space the insights, attitude changes and mood swings felt by the wider society of which it is a part. And when expressions in a given rhetorical space are changed, so too are adjustments made to the components of the associated disciplinary paradigm. In short, a disciplinary paradigm is not an inviolable theoretical abstraction; rather, the usually implicit assumptions and value judgments which saturate each disciplinary paradigm are steadily being *negotiated* and either affirmed or, occasionally, transformed by the member-participants sustaining that disciplinary paradigm.[18] Nonetheless, it does seem to require a rather loud[19] social movement to provoke, within an epistemic community, the explicit examination of the core assumptions shaping that community's disciplinary paradigm. It is time now to look more closely at the notion of core metaphysical assumptions.

Metaphysical Assumptions

> [N]othing at all can be strongly affirmed unless a whole mass of truisms is taken for granted as a background for it.[20]

Metaphysical assumptions are assumptions about the nature of reality; broadly, they are assumptions about the world, about being itself,

---

the Church', in Elisabeth Schüssler Fiorenza (ed.), *The Power of Naming: A Concilium Reader in Feminist Liberation Theology* (Maryknoll, NY: Orbis Books, 1996), pp. 210-11, for a discussion of the Roman Catholic Church's modern reversal of classical Christian anthropology. In the classical tradition 'woman' was unequal to 'man' as a creaturely being, but equal to 'man' in the 'sacramental order of salvation' (p. 211). From 1976, however, the Church has declared that, while 'woman' is equal to 'man' as a creaturely being, 'she' is unable to represent the image of Christ at the sacramental level.

18. See Potter, 'Gender and Epistemic Negotiation', pp. 161-86, for a discussion of epistemic negotiation.

19. I use the word 'loud' rather than 'large' deliberately, for the power (to influence change) of the views expressed in a rhetorical space depends more on decibel level than on the number of individuals speaking within that space.

20. Midgley, *Wisdom, Information and Wonder*, p. 235.

1. *What is a Disciplinary Paradigm?* 25

including human beings. In Mary Midgley's words, quoted above, they are the 'mass of truisms taken for granted' by a given community. This mass of truisms is akin to what Thomas Kuhn describes as the 'symbolic generalisations' and 'shared commitments' according to which a scientific community structures its research.[21] For instance, no astronomer today would engage in a research project to determine how quickly the rest of the universe revolves around the earth. It would be unthinkable, for a core assumption concerning the nature of reality, one shared by all astronomers *acknowledged by their peers* to be astronomers, is that the earth is not the centre of the universe. This is a critical characteristic of metaphysical assumptions: they determine the extent of what is, to a given epistemic community, thinkable. One of the reasons Kuhn characterizes co-existent disciplinary paradigms as 'incommensurable', or unable to be compared with each other, is that each disciplinary paradigm is founded on a slightly or very different set of core metaphysical assumptions. What is thinkable in one paradigm is often not conceivable or even *imaginable* in another.[22] This is easily understood when one asks a question appropriate in one discipline to a member-participant of another discipline. For example, if I asked the particle physicists to show me where in their equation concerning mass they had factored in the ongoing salvation of creation, they would quickly agree that I was out of my mind. In fact, I would be utterly outside the disciplinary paradigm I call 'home'.[23] Within their meta-

---

21. Kuhn, *Structure*, pp. 182-83.
22. Kuhn, *Structure*, p. 94: 'Like the choice between competing political institutions, that between competing paradigms proves to be a choice between incompatible modes of community life.' See also Midgley, *Wisdom, Information and Wonder*, p. 138: 'For good or ill, metaphysics flows out of and acts directly upon the imagination, which shapes our lives. It is for instance often clear that conversion to or from a particular philosophical standpoint makes people view life itself quite differently... This change is not just some chance psychological side-effect, or the result of naïve errors in the philosopher or the convert. It is conceptually necessary.'
23. I use the term 'home' deliberately, not as poetic embellishment but as the most apt metaphor I could find to express an individual's relationship to a disciplinary paradigm. In a similar manner, using the term 'circles' to refer to the 'contexts, usable traditions, and sets of conceptual tools' needed by humans to communicate and live with each other, Mary Midgley suggests that 'we should regard the circles as our own homes, with gratitude and respect, not with the simple resent-

physical frame of reference as physicists, physical reality cannot be subjected to salvation; it is a nonsensical thought. If, however, I asked a feminist ecological theologian to show me where in her theology she discusses the ongoing salvation of creation, she could pick up a book and say 'Chapter Six'. It is likely (not certain, but likely) that she would assume, moreover, that my question did *not* refer to a transcendent, other-worldly, God-induced state of eternal unchanging perfection, but to the ongoing, uphill effort on the part of humans in different times and places to enable the interdependent, co-existent flourishing of as many diverse aspects of creation as possible; it is highly unlikely that two conservative Southern Baptist theologians would make a similar assumption. Within their disciplinary paradigm is a set of metaphysical assumptions concerning the relative agency of humans and the ultimate agency of a transcendent God. The salvation of creation, in their frame of reference, is simply not conceived of in relative terms, whether relative to a particular time and place or relative to a particular group of human actors. Instead, only the ultimate metaphysical reality within their disciplinary paradigm, God, can effect the once and for all salvation of physical reality.

This last example highlights the difficulty of writing about metaphysical assumptions in general; they are not free-floating abstractions, able to be plucked from thin air and examined at will. Instead, they are implicitly incorporated within the metaphors and models of a disciplinary paradigm. The dissonance between a disciplinary paradigm that includes a specific metaphysical assumption (and a model through which that assumption is expressed) and a disciplinary paradigm that does not include the same assumption is readily evident. No less real, though far more difficult to grasp, is the difference between two disciplinary paradigms both of which incorporate a metaphysical assumption about 'the same' topic, and both of which use a specific model to convey that assumption. When the models appear to be the same, as in the phrase 'the salvation of creation', the temptation is great to accept that the underlying metaphysical assumption is the same.[24] This issue, while complicating my discussion of metaphysical assumptions and thus necessary to identify at this point, will have to wait until my discussion of metaphors and models for further elaboration.

ment which romantic individualism inculcates towards "society"' (*Wisdom, Information and Wonder*, p. 237).

24. Midgley, *Wisdom, Information and Wonder*, p. 72.

1. *What is a Disciplinary Paradigm?*

I wish now to draw a distinction *in emphasis* between two sorts of metaphysical assumptions: *ontological* and *anthropological* assumptions. Ontological assumptions I define as having to do primarily with the nature of physical reality. That is, I am using the phrase 'ontological assumptions' to refer primarily (though not exclusively) to assumptions about non-human creation. In epistemological terms, ontological assumptions are assumptions about 'the world to be known'. Certainly assumptions about the nature of human beings (or human essence) are assumptions about the nature of being as well, but for clarity's sake I am calling these sorts of assumptions, particularly when they incorporate social, ethical, political and cultural aspects, *anthropological assumptions*. I want to emphasize that anthropological assumptions are at least as much assumptions about the nature of human social/political existence as they are assumptions about a state of being or essence. Again in epistemological terms, anthropological assumptions correspond to assumptions about 'knowers' or epistemic agents. In effect, both sorts of assumptions are sub-categories of metaphysical assumptions, sub-categories with overlapping boundaries. Anthropological assumptions are a particularly important sub-category, however, for an examination of the anthropological assumptions of a given disciplinary paradigm reveals the usually tacit guidelines used by that epistemic community to measure the potential 'cognitive worthiness' of any given individual. That is to say, the anthropological assumptions inherent in a given disciplinary paradigm comprise at least some of the 'territorial imperatives' governing entrance into the epistemic community practising within that paradigm. How is this the case?

Are men (in the non-generic sense of the term) inherently incapable of rational thought? Are white-skinned individuals fully human? Are heterosexuals genetically flawed? The answers to these sorts of questions constitute the anthropological assumptions of a disciplinary paradigm. If the answer to the first question is 'yes', men's high testosterone levels do result in mental impairment, then it is highly unlikely that one will find many men participating in an epistemic community sustaining a disciplinary paradigm imbued with rational thought, for the simple reason that men have been deemed incapable of rational activity. Likewise, if white-skinned individuals are, perhaps by virtue of their shocking melanin deficiency, not fully human, then it is hardly necessary to take their opinions of themselves into account when one is studying their habits. Their opinions and feelings do not count, for they are not fully human opinions or feelings. Are heterosexuals genetically flawed? Why bother even to ask this question? It is quite silly if not unthinkable—after all, everyone knows that heterosexuality is perfectly normal. Indeed, no less a figure than James D. Watson, Nobel laureate and former head of the US based portion of the Human Genome Project, accepts this assumption without question. What he also accepts without question is the assumption that homosexual individuals *are* genetically flawed.[25] Absent from Watson's set of anthropological assumptions is the idea that sexuality is as social as it is personal, that it has a history, or better, histories contingent to time and place, histories that change and whose changes can be traced by examining different societies' attitudes and responses to the issue (broadly conceived) of sexuality. Instead, he accepts the notion of sexuality as an inviolable, genetically determined fact specific to each individual regardless of society, culture, era. Further, he assumes that homosexual lives have less inherent value than heterosexual lives. On the basis of these assumptions he has said publicly that if 'the gene which determines sexuality' is identified, he would support a woman's right to abort a homosexual foetus.[26]

My point, starkly made for emphasis, is that anthropological assumptions matter, that they are as much moral and/or political as they are metaphysical. Not only do they separate the thinkable from the unthinkable, they also define and separate the 'normal' from the 'not normal'.[27] Anthropological assumptions define and sanction the limits of scientific, social, political and moral acceptability in their time and place. Furthermore, at the same time they define who does and who does not have the potential to be an acknowledged epistemic agent in a community sustaining a disciplinary paradigm. Helen Longino, using the phrase 'background assumptions' where I would write 'metaphysical assumptions', expresses the issue in this manner:

> Because background assumptions can be and most frequently are invisible to the members of the scientific community for which they are

---

25. See story in *Canberra Times*, Monday, 17 February 1997, 'Let mums abort gay babies: Nobel laureate'.
26. *Canberra Times* article.
27. See Evelyn Fox Keller, 'Nature, Nurture, and the Human Genome Project', in Daniel J. Kevles and Leroy E. Hood (eds.), *The Code of Codes: Scientific and Social Issues in the Human Genome Project* (Cambridge, MA: Harvard University Press, 1992), p. 298.

background and because un-reflective acceptance of such assumptions can come to define what it is to be a member of such a community (thus making criticism impossible), effective criticism of background assumptions requires the presence and expression of alternative points of view.[28]

I interpret her point to be that anthropological assumptions have profound (and profoundly power-riddled) epistemological ramifications—but then, so too do ontological assumptions.

Is physical reality composed entirely of discrete bits of matter, and is it able to be most fully known by the examination of each discrete bit, broken down to its smallest possible part? Or is physical reality an interdependent, integrally related whole, with no single aspect able to be fully known in isolation from its relation to the whole? These are *ontological* questions baldly stated; yet any answer to them, even a simple yes or no response, requires at a minimum an implicit affirmation of a corresponding set of anthropological assumptions and value judgments. This is a critical point; every ontological assumption is also, simultaneously, a value judgment. There are no value-neutral metaphysical assumptions. The following questions highlight the interdependence of value judgments, ontological and anthropological assumptions.

If physical reality can be most fully known by an examination of each discrete bit of matter in its most divisible form, then does the whole of physical reality *in itself* have any inherent value? If the 'whole' does have value, then do divided bits of matter have any inherent value? Is there *more value* to be gained by dividing a bit of physical reality into its smallest constituent parts than there is value in leaving it alone? Is the value of physical reality less than the value of human knowledge gained by dissecting and manipulating that reality? What is the relationship between human and non-human reality (or matter)? Is all non-human matter of value only insofar as it proves useful to humans? Which humans get to decide which non-human matter is useful/valuable and which is not? Are some humans of more value than other humans and therefore worthy of greater access to useful/valuable bits of non-human matter? If so, then which humans get to decide who is of more value and who is of less value? Are humans, as part of physical reality, simply the sum of their smallest,

---

28. Helen E. Longino, 'Subjects, Power, and Knowledge', in Alcoff and Potter (eds.), *Feminist Epistemologies*, pp. 111-12.

most divided parts? Does knowing an individual's smallest parts (considered at this time by molecular geneticists to be the base pairs of proteins which make up their genetic sequence) constitute knowing fully that individual? Which is of more value, knowing a particular human's genetic sequence, or knowing that embodied human?

These are some of the questions encompassed by a disciplinary paradigm's supporting metaphysical assumptions. And these metaphysical assumptions combine to create an epistemological framework roughly sketched; they provide the answers to the questions 'who is able to know?', 'what conceivably can be known about the world?', and 'how are those acknowledged to be knowers able to know the world?' In short, every disciplinary paradigm is necessarily imbued throughout with a set of ontological and anthropological assumptions, or 'a mass of background truisms', which combine to form the basis of a shared, value-laden worldview. Importantly, metaphysical assumptions and value judgments (unlike a discipline's metaphors and models) are never specific to a single disciplinary paradigm.[29] This is because no disciplinary paradigm is entirely isolated from what Lynn Nelson, following Quine, calls 'a network of other going theories'. Instead, Nelson argues, each disciplinary paradigm occupies a position in relation to a network of other disciplines, *and the metaphysical assumptions of an era permeate them all*.[30] Think, for instance, of theology and astronomy, two disciplines with only the most tenuous relation to each other: nonetheless, just as today no astronomer acknowledged to be an astronomer can examine the heavens from the perspective of a flat earth, neither can a theologian acknowledged to be a theologian posit heaven and hell to be located respectively above and below a flat earth. The 'going theory' inherent in the ontological assumptions of both disciplines is that the earth is not flat and, by implication, that the universe is not a hierarchically tiered structure—a theory with profound astronomical and theological consequences. Not all metaphysical assumptions of each discipline are shared by all the other disciplines of an era, but no discipline will be acknowledged in the wider society or culture to be a legitimate discipline if it does not share some of the assumptions of an era.

---

29. See Midgley, *Wisdom, Information, and Wonder*, p. 69.
30. See Nelson, *Who Knows*, pp. 82-83, 88-90.

1. *What is a Disciplinary Paradigm?* 31

Metaphors and Models

[O]ur words are surely [both] the open channels
through which we communicate with others,
[and] a wall that divides us from them.³¹

As mentioned above, within a disciplinary paradigm the member-participants communicate with each other by drawing from and contributing to a common pool of metaphors. More specifically, they share a set of metaphors, the meanings and uses of which are discipline-specific; as mentioned earlier, the metaphor 'mass' means one thing to a particle physicist and quite another to a Roman Catholic theologian,³² while the metaphor 'salvation' means one thing to a feminist Christian theologian and something else entirely to a Southern Baptist theologian. Knowing how a metaphor is used and understood within a given disciplinary paradigm is not, however, a matter of memorizing a simple definition. Instead, the metaphor can be understood only in the broader context of the metaphysical assumptions and accompanying value judgments inherent in that disciplinary paradigm, and in the narrower context of its relationship to the other discipline-specific metaphors with which it is layered to give shape to given disciplinary models.

Language: A Brief Segue
Thus far I have been using the terms 'metaphor' and 'model' as though their meanings are self-evident. Before I attempt to unpack or untangle my uses and intended meanings of these terms, however, I need to provide a ground for such uses and meanings by way of a brief explanation of the understanding of language that underpins this entire book. Debates concerning language rage on; the following is not a thorough survey of those debates, but a slender collection of scavenged insights chosen because they 'fit' within the concept of a disciplinary paradigm

---

31. Midgley, *Wisdom, Information and Wonder*, p. 223.
32. Janet Martin Soskice, *Metaphor and Religious Language* (Oxford: Clarendon Press, 1985), p. 83. I am aware that, strictly speaking, the priests' 'mass' and the physicists' 'mass' is an example of homonymy, or an instance where two words are spelled exactly alike but have completely different meanings. My point is simply that their meanings are entirely dependent upon the contexts in which they are used. See pp. 34-35 for further clarification regarding my understanding of metaphors.

I am proposing. Methodologically, this brief section is not a *justification* for my understanding of metaphors and models, but, following Nelson Goodman, an *invitation*.[33] That is, I invite the reader to be persuaded by the following depiction of language on the basis of its suitability or fittingness in relation to the rest of my study. If it helps to make sense of my discussion of metaphors and models then that is justification enough. I begin by paraphrasing Paul Tillich: 'all language points *beyond* itself while participating *in* that to which it points'.[34] After inserting human language-users into Tillich's words, I understand his point to be as follows: language is the swaddling cloth in which all of us are wrapped at birth. We are never nakedly, innocently 'in' the world, for we experience the world through the warp of the cloth so given.[35] Likewise never are we sent naked into the wilderness, nor are we able to choose so to go, for 'beyond' is always already known as the weft of the cloth enfolding. Though we tear at our garments our lives are ever clothed. Humans are born into language at the same time as we are born into the world (the physical world inclusive of non-linguistic relations with other humans). Though distinct, the two are, in our experience, inseparable, each 'mutually constitutive' of the other.[36] That is, our words structure our world(s) just as much as our world(s) give shape to our words. For example, although physically I have never

33. See Jerry H. Gill, *Wittgenstein and Metaphor* (Washington, DC: University Press of America, 1981), p. 53. Gill, discussing Nelson Goodman's epistemological criteria as presented in his book *Languages and Art*, writes the following: 'The truth of philosophical accounts of "how things are" in various worlds and in world-making, as well as the truth of metaphilosophical versions of the nature of such philosophical accounts, is dependent on a flexible and relative application of such non-absolute criteria as coherence, consistency, and fittingness. When pressed to offer a justification of these criteria themselves, and of his own advocacy of them, Goodman replies that at such a bedrock level justification consists more of *invitation* and *persuasion* than of traditional argumentation' (emphasis in original).

34. Paul Tillich, *Dynamics of Faith* (New York: Harper and Colophon, 1958), p. 45 (italics added). This was written in the context of a discussion of symbols as being distinct from signs, and religious language as being symbolic language.

35. I realize that newborn babies and wolf-children experience the world without language, but newborn babies and wolf-children are not acknowledged to have cognitive authority in any epistemic community whatsoever by virtue of the fact that they are unable to communicate what they have experienced.

36. See Gill, *Wittgenstein and Metaphor*, p. 60. Gill is discussing Ricoeur's understanding of the relationship between speech and reality as being 'mutually constitutive'.

been in a desert, though deserts are *beyond* my physical, embodied experience, nonetheless if I were to go to a desert one day I could experience it only through the categories and concepts I know already through language—hot, dry, dust, thirst, sand, camels, sunsets, wind, etcetera. The linguistic world I was born into includes the structure and character of 'desert', and my experiences of a desert would be mediated through—both made possible and constrained by—the linguistic categories and concepts I would carry with me into any place that fit, more or less, my pre-conceived understanding of a desert. To refer again to Tillich, the 'desert' words I know point beyond themselves, alluding to that which they are not. Simultaneously, they wrap themselves around that which they are not: smoothing, stacking, separating, joining, giving shape and texture and form. Humans live, move, and have our being in world(s) ceaselessly embraced by words. These words both enable or make possible and constrain human relations with the world. To quote Jerry Gill,

> At the primordial level words do not function as arbitrary and/or optional tags for various, ready-made, and isolated aspects of reality. Rather, they serve, along with our bodies, as our primary means of indwelling and participating in the world.[37]

The context from which I take this quotation is crucial. Gill is not saying that the world does not exist apart from language about the world. Instead, he is alluding to the fact that as soon as any aspect of reality is named it is also placed in a network of relationships with other aspects of reality—and with the people doing the naming. It ceases to exist, if it ever did, as a purely independent entity. Instead, it becomes woven into the warp and weft of some epistemic community's linguistically expressed understanding of the world. It is through that shared understanding of the whole world (including metaphysical assumptions and value judgments concerning the world) that members of that community are able to engage or participate with any particular aspect of reality. Yet naming the world is not simply a unidirectional process, tightly controlled by a linguistic community. There is a difference between a word and an object named by that word, a gap between the two, and different aspects of the world do not yield readily to the embrace of just any words upon them. For an utterance (or communication) to be understandable, there has to be some sort of 'fit' between the

---

37. Gill, *Wittgenstein and Metaphor*, p. 69.

thing or thought *as named* and its relations with other aspects of the world entangled/posited in the naming process. It may be a 'fit' made possible or plausible on the basis of empirical sense data (rocks are hard), or on the basis of a tightly held value judgment (everyone ought to want to get married to someone of the opposite sex), or on the basis of a set of spurious assumptions about the world ('women's uteruses wander around in their bodies when they take math courses'[38]), but there must be some sort of 'fit' in order for a meaningful relationship between word and referent to be proposed and acknowledged by an epistemic community.

Nonetheless, while there is a 'fit', there is also a gap between word and referent. And here, in the gap between the word and thing, in amongst all the possible relations between the word, the referent, and the rest of the world, lies metaphor. In short, 'all speech is metaphoric in that it affirms an identity between two material entities (word and thing) which are not metaphysically identical'.[39] At the most basic level, then, my use of the term 'metaphor' is broadly inclusive of every word used by member-participants of an epistemic community, for 'all speech is metaphoric'. This is not, however, an adequate account of metaphor in the context of a disciplinary paradigm, for most speech is composed of what Paul Ricoeur terms 'dead metaphors', or terms that have become absolutized and literalized. When this happens the gap between the word and its referent (the thing or idea it points toward) closes up, making only one relationship between word and thing possible. As I understand them, 'living' metaphors are those words evocative of more than one possible relationship between word and referent. When conversation or discourse occurs with living metaphors the speaker/writer and hearer/reader in that rhetorical space are necessarily participants in the relational matrix formed by those metaphors. Meaning is co-created as much by the hearer's interpretation of the relations between the words and that to which they refer as by the speaker's intended relations between the words, and by the influence of the world upon those words. In other words, living metaphors are profoundly relational terms. To understand them one must participate in the relational networks of which they are a part.

38. Example from Sandra Harding, 'Rethinking Standpoint Epistemology: What is "Strong Objectivity"?', in Alcoff and Potter (eds.), *Feminist Epistemologies*, pp. 49-82.

39. Gill, *Wittgenstein and Metaphor*, p. 44.

1. *What is a Disciplinary Paradigm?*

But there are potential problems with an account of metaphor in which individual terms are defined as metaphors, for some argue that single words are, by themselves, not metaphoric; or, more precisely, that 'metaphor is only meaningful in the context of a complete sentence'.[40] This is the case because one word apart from any context, such as the word 'salvation', can only hint at a host of possible, and possibly incompatible, relations with other words. A metaphorical expression narrows the range of those possible relations by relating one word directly to another. In the process, both words combine to create a new network of meaning. That is, together, the terms in a metaphorical expression both refer to something, some specific thing that is knowable, and simultaneously create that thing. A metaphorical expression evokes into being a set of relations that had not previously existed. Janet Martin Soskice speaks toward what I call the 'channelling' of potential meanings into one metaphoric utterance: 'plurality at the level of significance (a plurality of associative networks) is compatible with a unity of referential intent'.[41] While I am less certain than Soskice that a metaphorical expression is used to refer to one thing only, I believe she has named a critical factor concerning metaphors: single metaphors are inherently plural, so plural that they can be meaningful only insofar as they are related to other metaphors.

Within a given disciplinary paradigm, then, are certain metaphorical terms which collectively bear the weight of conveying meaning about the subject matter with which the discipline is concerned. Strictly speaking, these key metaphors are, by themselves, practically meaningless; or rather, alone, their possible meanings are too many: they hint at too many possible relationships in the gap between word and referent. For example, by itself the metaphor 'salvation' points beyond itself in a host of directions simultaneously. Because it is a vibrant metaphor it does evoke a range of possible models: perhaps a sense of salvation coming down to earth from a God above, or a momentary sense of healing and wholeness, or a struggle to put right that which is wrong, warped and twisted beyond recognition. By itself the metaphor 'salvation' is too rich in potential meaning to be an open channel through which communication can happen. Instead, in isolation it

---

40. Mara E. Donaldson, *Holy Places Are Dark Places: C.S. Lewis and Paul Ricoeur on Narrative Transformation* (Lanham, MD: University Press of America, 1988), p. 38.

41. Soskice, *Metaphor*, p. 88.

serves as a wall blocking communication between speaker and hearer. But metaphors are never used in isolation. They are combined with other metaphors to form models. And models, to quote Sallie McFague, 'give intelligibility to the unintelligible. Models, unlike discrete or passing metaphors, yield this intelligibility in a structural or comprehensive manner.'[42] Where a metaphor 'suggests a community of relations',[43] *a model posits a specific set of relations between different aspects of the world*; this relational network can be loosely or tightly presented, as with, loosely, 'justification by grace through faith alone' or, tightly, '$E = MC^2$'. Thus it is *the relations between the metaphors* that are paradigm-specific: the way the metaphors are layered into models to provide a framework of images (loosely or tightly) expressive of meaning. But again, these models must not contradict the metaphysical assumptions inherent throughout the disciplinary paradigm of which they are a part. Instead, they are the means through which those assumptions are made explicit.

At this point, in order to clarify my understanding of metaphors and models it will be helpful to examine in more detail concrete examples of what I am trying to describe. Already I have used the metaphor 'salvation' several times, and earlier used the expression 'the salvation of creation' as an example of a model whose meaning is paradigm-dependent. It should be evident by now that 'salvation' is a metaphor replete with a host of possible meanings; in other words, because different hearers or readers attribute to this metaphor vastly different meanings the metaphor salvation is necessarily entangled in a diverse range of associations with other metaphors. Which associations it is allowed depends on which paradigm it is uttered and heard in. Individual metaphors such as 'mass' or 'wave' or 'salvation' or 'sin' are all examples of vibrant, living metaphors. The possibilities they call to mind are numerous, and it is their very plurality that makes them so vibrant. Models, while evocative of fewer possible meanings, provide a depth of complexity and focus unattainable through single metaphors.

The model 'the salvation of creation' is, according to the schema I have sketched, more accurately defined as *approaching* the status of a model. I write 'approaching' deliberately, for whether it is appropriately understood as a model or not depends, again, on the context in

---

42. McFague, *Metaphorical Theology*, p. 73.
43. Soskice, *Metaphor*, p. 95.

1. What is a Disciplinary Paradigm?

which it is uttered or written. Context is everything for, waiting in the wings, just off to the side of the (potential) model 'the salvation of creation', are at least three other metaphors: 'God', 'creation' and 'humanity'. At a minimum, humanity waits there as a part of creation, subject to being affected somehow by salvation. Possibly, depending on the paradigm-context in which the phrase is uttered and heard, humanity is there to effect salvation, both the salvation of creation and of God. Likewise, God's role in this potential model is unclear. God could be hanging around to do the work of salvation, or God could be in as much need of salvation as the rest of creation. How much need creation has for salvation is yet another related issue. The answer to that question depends on the metaphysical assumptions supplied by specific disciplinary paradigms. Different paradigms supply different assumptions, different value judgments and, ultimately, provide the possibility of two 'identical' models positing drastically different relations between their 'shared' metaphors. Sallie McFague puts the point succinctly:

> Models are paradigm-dependent—there is no innocent eye; hence, the principal criterion for judging a model, even in science, is not whether it corresponds with 'facts', but whether it fits in the schema of 'facts' as understood by a given paradigm.[44]

To her words I would add that the principal criterion for interpreting a model is understanding *how it fits* in the paradigm of which it is a part. It is not possible to understand the relationship between the metaphors 'salvation' and 'creation' in the absence of an accompanying framework; the best one can do when faced with this expression out of context is to identify that there is some sort of relationship between the metaphors. Of course, a good model, in context, will not limit the possible relations between its metaphors to just one, but will evoke and hold in tension several possible relations simultaneously.

Unfortunately, just as metaphors can lose their metaphoricity over time, becoming literalized (or being understood to have only one fixed meaning), so too can models lose their flexibility, becoming rigid prescriptions of 'the way things are'. When this occurs the model is mistaken for the modelled and the distance or the gap between the model and that to which it points is denied.[45] And this is a critical

---

44. McFague, *Metaphorical Theology*, p. 138.
45. McFague, *Metaphorical Theology*, p. 74: 'The principal danger in the use of

issue: like all language, a model both points toward and participates in that to which it points. When the member-participants of any epistemic community confuse the model for the sum total of the reality it points toward they paradoxically participate in constricting the world about which they seek to know more. The model can become a tyrant, denying the existence of other equally valid models of the same subject matter. In theology the model 'God the Father' has functioned in just such a tyrannical manner, denying the illuminative capacity of other models such as 'God the sister' or 'God the wind'. The hegemonic status of the model God the Father is brought home when one looks to a different disciplinary paradigm, such as physics, where two distinct models of light peacefully co-exist: light as wave and light as particle. In this case each model is revelatory of different aspects of the same reality, light. Neither model is understood to reveal completely the nature of light, and because both are necessary to illumine some but not all aspects of light, they each seem to be able to maintain more easily their own internal distance, the distance between the model and the modelled. This is a critical epistemological issue: whenever one model dominates the imagination of an epistemic community it limits that community's knowledge to those 'facts' that are a reflection of the model's own image. The introduction of another model or models is necessary to re-establish the creative space in which disciplinary practitioners can ask a different set of 'what if' questions. And sometimes a new model will introduce or convey a new set of metaphysical assumptions and value judgments. If this new model is acknowledged to be of epistemic value by the member-participants of an epistemic community within a disciplinary paradigm, it can initiate a paradigm shift within that discipline. (Whether or not a new model is accepted, however, depends in part on the acknowledged epistemic agency or cognitive authority of those who propose and embrace the new model.)

To conclude, then, models, which are themselves layered metaphors, are the means by which the metaphysical assumptions and underlying value judgments of a discipline are expressed. Epistemologically, knowledge of different aspects of reality is conveyed through models, but this knowledge is always paradigm-dependent. Returning to the quote from Wittgenstein with which I began this discussion of

models is…the loss of tension between model and modeled. When that distance is collapsed, we become imprisoned by dogmatic, absolutistic, literalistic patterns of thought.'

disciplinary paradigms, humans cannot help but view the world through 'a pair of glasses on our nose'. Another name for those glasses which, carefully ground and shaped and polished, do enable us to see some things clearly while blinding us to other aspects of the world, is 'disciplinary paradigm'. It is time now to look more closely at the theological and philosophical influences upon the formation of one disciplinary paradigm—that of feminist Christian theology written by White, economically and educationally privileged women in North America.

Chapter 2

INFLUENCES ON THE FORMATION OF ONE FEMINIST
CHRISTIAN THEOLOGICAL PARADIGM

The purpose of this chapter is to identify certain formative theological and philosophical influences on the structure and components of one feminist Christian theological paradigm—that formed in the United States by White, educationally and economically privileged women throughout the late 1960s, 1970s and 1980s. In theological terms I intend to establish that this feminist Christian theology is neither a creation *ex nihilo* nor the development of a single insight peculiar to a few isolated middle class White women. Instead, it is one outgrowth of approximately two centuries of theological and philosophical, not to mention scientific, political, and social upheaval in the United States and Europe—a time which saw the classical Christian paradigm rejected, replaced, resurrected, again refuted and ultimately refused by a diverse assortment of Christian theologians.[1] Here I will not be identifying every new Christian theological development since the Enlightenment, nor will I be exploring in detail every social and political influence upon the development of the feminist Christian theological paradigm I will be examining.[2] What I intend to do instead is to paint a

---

1. Robert H. King, 'Introduction: The Task of Theology', in Peter C. Hodgson and Robert H. King (eds.), *Christian Theology: An Introduction to its Traditions and Tasks* (Philadelphia: Fortress Press, 2nd edn, 1985), p. 2.
2. In particular I will not be tracing the development of Marxist thought, although feminist Christian theology is highly influenced by it. My reason for this is that the influence of Marxist thought on feminist Christian theology is, arguably, explicitly named more often than any other philosophical or ideological influence. In this chapter I want to focus on those influences which I perceive to be just as critical as Marxist thought but less often named as such. See, for example, Sheila D. Collins, *A Different Heaven and Earth* (Valley Forge, PA: Judson), p. 116; Beverly Wildung Harrison, 'The Role of Social Theory in Religious Social Ethics: Reconsidering the Case for Marxian Political Economy', in *idem*, *Making the Connections:*

picture in broad strokes, to trace the outlines of those theological and philosophical themes and historical occurrences I consider to have been particularly important and particularly influential in the development of this feminist Christian theological paradigm—as will be evident especially in the work of Rosemary Radford Ruether, Carter Heyward and Sallie McFague.

Methodologically, while following a chronological outline I shall be naming and lifting out (of context) a wide smattering of theological and philosophical developments. The issues I shall discuss are, I am well aware, far more complicated (in their contexts) than my analyses of them will convey. However, what I am trying to accomplish by the end of this chapter is to give the reader a rich sense of the theological, philosophical and social chaos out of which feminist Christian theology was born. One of the implicit assumptions permeating this chapter is that, theologically, two hundred years is not a long time; the dust raised by the Enlightenment has not yet settled. Nonetheless, to put it metaphorically, a number of other earthquakes have already rocked the Western Christian theological establishment. One of those earthquakes is feminist Christian theology, and its epicentre is located at the convergence of several pre-existing fault-lines. In this chapter I identify these intellectual 'fault-lines', thereby contextualizing feminist Christian theology within the academic discipline of theology. Importantly, my concern in this chapter is primarily with identifying those theological and philosophical developments that feminist Christian theologians have appropriated and transformed in the context of one feminist Christian theological paradigm. I am *not* attempting to trace either the development of the rhetorical space that accompanies this feminist Christian theological paradigm or the historical development of second-wave feminism. That is a task for a historian, which I am not. However, I do want to acknowledge that the development of the rhetorical space in which feminist Christian theologians could speak to each other with a 'reasonable expectation of being heard, understood, taken seriously' (to quote Lorraine Code) was, epistemologically, the most vital element in the formation of the feminist Christian theological

Essays in Feminist Social Ethics (ed. Carol S. Robb; Boston: Beacon Press, 1985, pp. 54-80; Rosemary Radford Ruether, 'Communitarian Socialism and the Radical Church Tradition: Building the Community of Liberation', in *Liberation Theology: Human Hope Confronts Christian History and American Power* (New York: Paulist Press, 1972), pp. 145-55.

paradigm. Within this 'space' a number of feminist Christian theologians acknowledged the epistemic agency of each other, and insisted that the abstract category 'woman' had been the *object* of theological pronouncements for long enough. Within the rhetorical space enveloping the feminist Christian theological paradigm, real live women became theological *subjects*. They did not, however, begin to do theology from scratch.

As with the majority of contemporary North American and Western European Christian theological developments, feminist Christian theology is an outgrowth of the Enlightenment, one of the heirs, albeit a pessimistic heir, to the liberal Protestant theology that arose in response to the philosophical demise of an objective, transcendent, sovereign deity. Briefly, the eighteenth century saw the philosophy of David Hume (1711–76) and Immanuel Kant (1724–1804) combine to call into question, indeed to reject, the possibility of any *purely objective knowledge* of God. While this statement seems a commonplace here and now, at the time it shook the epistemological foundations of the classical Christian theological paradigm.[3] If, as according to Hume, all knowledge of facts must be drawn from the sense-data of concrete experiences, then one cannot reasonably connect knowledge of the existence of the world with or to knowledge of a God beyond the world. The assumption of a God beyond the world can be an assumption or belief, but it cannot properly be called knowledge.[4] Kant's arguments against objective knowledge of God went even further. Kant proposed that

> knowledge of God could only be established if either God himself were immediately accessible to our awareness, or 'God' were a category demonstrably necessary, like those of space and time, to the ordering and shaping of our understanding.[5]

Because God is neither 'immediately accessible' to our physical senses nor 'demonstrably necessary' to human conceptions of the existence of the world, no objective knowledge of God is possible, according to Kant.

---

3. See below for a description of the beliefs integral to the classical Christian paradigm.
4. Alasdair Heron, *A Century of Protestant Theology* (Philadelphia: Westminster Press, 1980), pp. 14-16.
5. Heron, *Protestant Theology*, p. 17.

2. Influences on the Formation

Simply put, in rejecting the objectivity of 'God' Hume and Kant also undermined the rational basis or foundation of any theological assertion having to do with God (and most of them do). But the implications of their work went even further; not only were the gates of Reason temporarily closed to theologians, but also the realm of practical action. An objective God had been 'proven' rationally to be no longer a pure necessity in day-to-day existence; and although Kant in particular was exceedingly clear that *faith* in God and, he asserted, belief in immortality were practically necessary to direct human affairs,[6] one long-term consequence of his epistemological bombshell was to collapse the distinction between theology and ethics, 'in effect reducing theology to ethics'.[7] Consequently morality and ethics were able to stand alone, no longer intimately associated with theology. The question became, where is there room for religion? About what can theologians speak and on what grounds can they make their claims? Is there a difference between theology and ethics? Enter the German theologian Friedrich Schleiermacher (1768–1834), according to Deane Ferm the 'most important forerunner of religious liberalism'.[8]

In 1799 Schleiermacher published a slender (by German theological standards) volume entitled *On Religion: Speeches to its Cultured Despisers*.[9] In it he identified and claimed for 'religion' a space neither rational nor experiential (in the sense of direct physical experience). According to Schleiermacher, 'religion's essence is neither thinking nor acting, but intuition and feeling'.[10] 'To have religion means to intuit the universe....'[11] In a brilliant move, Schleiermacher accepted (on one level) Kant's separation of metaphysics and ethics from 'God'; he tacitly accepted that 'metaphysics and morals' were not divine

---

6. Heron, *Protestant Theology*, p. 18.
7. King, 'Introduction: The Task of Theology', p. 11.
8. Deane William Ferm, *Contemporary American Theologies: A Critical Survey* (San Francisco: Harper & Row, 1981), p. 3.
9. Friedrich Schleiermacher, *On Religion: Speeches to its Cultured Despisers* (ed. and trans. Richard Crouter; Cambridge: Cambridge University Press, 1988 [1799]). I am focusing on Schleiermacher's early work rather than on his later theology because in it the disjunction between Schleiermacher's thought and the thought of the reformers is more immediately evident. However, Schleiermacher believed that his later theology was in continuity with what he proposed in *On Religion*.
10. Schleiermacher, *On Religion*, p. 22.
11. Schleiermacher, *On Religion*, p. 52.

creations. In the next breath, however, he located finite humans *within the infinite totality* of all that is:

> Metaphysics and morals see in the whole universe only humanity as the center of all relatedness, as the condition of all being and the cause of all becoming; religion wishes to see the infinite, its imprint and its manifestations, in humanity no less than in all other individual and finite forms.[12]

Schleiermacher side-stepped the question of a rational epistemological *foundation* for knowledge of an objective God by insisting that 'the idea of God adapts itself to each intuition of the universe', and that 'whether we have a God as part of our intuition depends on the direction of our imagination'.[13] Because intuition or feeling simply cannot be empirically tested, the effect of Schleiermacher's proposal was to remove theology entirely from the scientific realm. In other words, in his attempt to save theology as a viable intellectual pursuit, Schleiermacher had to admit that theology was no longer 'queen of the sciences'. Put epistemologically, Schleiermacher made it possible for theologians to continue writing about the affect of God, but he made it much more difficult for theologians to be considered the final arbiters of *truth* claims about God or anything else.

To return to his theological proposals: finite human participation in the universe was, for Schleiermacher, participation in the infinite, in the totality of all that is. Equally important, neither the universe nor humanity was dependent on an *objective*, transcendent deity. Humans were, however, intimately bound up in the universe as 'finite manifestations of the infinite'; further, human existence was utterly dependent on the universe, over which humans had no absolute control. This is not to say that humans did not have the freedom to act or control parts of the earth, but this lived freedom was a consequence of finite existence and did not alter the fact of humans' absolute dependence on the totality of all that is, or the infinite.

In his later work (*The Christian Faith*)[14] Schleiermacher characterized human awareness of this absolute dependence as 'God-consciousness'. In contrast to God-consciousness, he characterized 'world-consciousness' as an awareness of lived interdependence, or

---

12. Schleiermacher, *On Religion*, p. 23.
13. Schleiermacher, *On Religion*, pp. 52-53.
14. Friedrich Schleiermacher, *The Christian Faith* (ed. H.R. Mackintosh and J.S. Stewart; Edinburgh: T. & T. Clark, 2nd edn, 1956 [1830]).

'the feeling of relative freedom and dependence that one has over against the world'.[15] Schleiermacher was wary that world-consciousness without God-consciousness could lead to decidedly immoral human actions; but, he believed, the ethical consequences of acknowledging the ultimate unity of all that is (interpreting, as he did, the totality of all that is as a single whole) would lead to ever more just and equitable societies, for people would realize that their actions mattered in the far grander scheme of things. In other words, for Schleiermacher it was the awareness that individuals were always in relation to the whole, and that their always relational participation mattered to or affected the course of finite instances in the infinite, that made ethics an integral aspect of theology.[16] Accordingly, he rejected Kant's second 'postulate of practical reason', the need for belief in individual immortality.[17] Neither the threat of punishment nor the lure of heavenly reward was, for Schleiermacher, an adequate fulcrum upon which to place an ethical lever. Furthermore, in one astonishing sentence he dispensed with the traditional understanding of immortality altogether. 'To be one with the infinite in the midst of the finite and to be eternal in a moment, that is the immortality of religion.'[18] In short, Schleiermacher suggested that to 'intuit the universe' leads one to live in it rightly or ethically, with the awareness that finite moments are a gift of the infinite, and that immortality as participation in the infinite occurs in every here and now.

Theologically there are (at least) two extraordinary developments in Schleiermacher's thought. To begin with, he stepped outside the bounds of the classical Christian paradigm initially formulated by Augustine and upheld, with varying emphases, by Aquinas, Luther and Calvin. Briefly, within the classical paradigm God is a wholly other, transcendent, omniscient, omnipotent, absolutely sovereign deity. In relation to this God humans are a 'damned mass', *non posse non pecarre*, or not able not to sin. There is a gulf between God and humanity—caused by sinful human actions—that humans cannot overcome; nonetheless God can and does bridge this gulf, revealing Godself to humanity through

---

15. King, 'Introduction: The Task of Theology', p. 13.
16. See Schleiermacher, *On Religion*, p. 77: 'Insofar as everyone stands only in contact with the closest person, but also has a closest person on all sides and in all directions, each is, in fact, inseparably bound up with the whole.'
17. Heron, *Protestant Theology*, p. 18.
18. Schleiermacher, *On Religion*, p. 54.

Jesus Christ and acting in history to effect salvation—through the saving death and resurrection of Jesus Christ, by establishing the Christian church, by bestowing undeserved eternal life on a select few, and ultimately by bringing to an end the world as it is and restoring it to a state of perfection.

On the one hand Schleiermacher relinquished the notion of an absolutely sovereign deity, opting instead for a God whose existence could be intuited but was not demanded; and on the other hand he rejected the notion that humanity was inevitably nothing more than a damned mass. Deeply influenced by the German Romanticism of his day,[19] Schleiermacher had an optimistic opinion of human nature. Human beings could, through the judicious use of scientific and technological developments, change the course of history, alleviating misery and moving towards ever more just social relations.[20] In incorporating these beliefs throughout his theology he initiated a major Christian theological paradigm shift. His theology was infused throughout with a different set of metaphysical assumptions than those first put forward by Augustine over a millennium earlier. Two points are critical. He accepted implicitly the scientific view of the universe voiced by Galileo and established by Copernicus, Kepler and Newton. Rather than positing creation (the earth) as being in the centre of the universe and humanity as being the culmination of creation, he accepted simply that the earth was one small part of an infinitely vast whole, and that humans were but a tiny aspect of the universe.[21] Similarly, rather than

---

19. See Richard Crouter, 'Introduction', in Schleiermacher, *On Religion*, p. xi.

20. See Crouter, 'Introduction', p. xxxviii, and Schleiermacher, *On Religion*, p. 93. Schleiermacher writes, 'There is no greater hindrance to religion than that we must be our own slaves, for everyone is a slave who performs something that should be accomplished by dead forces. One thing we hope for from the perfection of the sciences and arts is that they will make these dead forces subject to us, that they might turn the corporeal world and everything of the spiritual world that can be regulated into a fairy palace where the god of the earth needs only to utter a magic word or to press a button to have his commands done. Then, for the first time, everyone will be freeborn...'

21. Schleiermacher, *On Religion*, p. 51: 'But now I have told you clearly enough that humanity is not everything to me, that my religion strives for a universe of which humanity, with all that belongs to it, is only an infinitely small part, only one particular transient form.' It is worth noting that it was not until 2 November 1992 that the Roman Catholic Church officially admitted that Galileo had been correct. Personal correspondence with Dorothea McEwan, 14 October 1997.

2. Influences on the Formation

locate god directly above or over creation, he defined God as that which humanity is dependent *upon*. His emphasis was not on humanity standing in judgment under God, but on humanity enjoying finite existence because of God. Drawing no sharp distinction between humanity, the universe, and God, Schleiermacher was able to see, in the natural world and in human creations, e.g. science and the arts, glimpses of the infinite.[22] Furthermore, he acknowledged that these glimpses were visible to the non-Christian as well as to the Christian, although he did assert that Christianity was the highest form of ethical monotheism.[23]

In the nineteenth century these tendencies in Schleiermacher's thought were taken up and emphasized to varying degrees by Albrecht Ritschl (1822–89), Adolf von Harnack (1851–1930) and Ernst Troeltsch (1865–1923), among others. Collectively, their theology came to be known as Liberal Protestantism.[24] Receptivity to current scientific truths and an openness to future scientific revelations, rejection of creeds, dogmas and miracle stories that contradict rational (empirical) knowledge of the world, respect for the truths of other religions, acceptance of historical-critical methods, and an insistence on the practical ethical implications of theology/Christianity: these are the characteristics of Liberal Protestantism. When applied to the 'doing' of theology, these presuppositions resulted in the radical revisioning of a number of theological concepts. Sin and salvation in particular were transformed.

Rather than understanding sin, both personal and systemic, as the bondage into which all humans are born and from which salvation is provided by God alone, there was a tendency in liberal theology to emphasize sin as the result of a lack of understanding or knowledge. Provided with an opportunity, individuals could improve themselves and, collectively, society.[25] Furthermore, the ethical imperative inherent

---

22. Schleiermacher, *On Religion*, p. 58: 'For religious works of art are always exhibited everywhere; the whole world is a gallery of religious views...' Also p. 63: 'Being born and dying are such points, when they are perceived, at which it cannot escape us how our own self is universally surrounded by the infinite and which always arouse a quiet longing and a holy awe.'

23. Schleiermacher, *On Religion*, pp. 113-17.

24. See James Richmond, 'Liberal Protestantism', in Richardson and Bowden (eds.), *The Westminster Dictionary of Christian Theology*, pp. 325-28.

25. See Ferm, *Contemporary American Theologies*, pp. 4-9. See also Richmond, 'Liberal Protestantism', pp. 327-28.

in Jesus' proclamation of the kingdom of God made it one's Christian duty to strive to bring about the 'salvation' of society. Instead of having an individualistic, otherworldly focus, liberal theologians turned their attention to influencing the historical developments of this world.[26] The kingdom of God was to be realized through human actions on earth.[27] In other words, the kingdom of God was understood to be 'the realm of ideal human relations'.[28] But with no objective foundation (God) for these faith/knowledge claims, on what grounds could theologians speak of the kingdom of God?

In answering this question Albrecht Ritschl contributed greatly not only to the development of what would become one of the central models of the feminist Christian theological paradigm, but also to the re-establishment of an epistemological foundation for theological assertions. Following Kant's distinction between 'judgments of fact' and 'judgments of value', Ritschl located all theological endeavours in the realm of 'value'. He 'believed that religious and theological statements are essentially judgments of value-for-us'.[29] While understandings of the world (or creation) were quite properly informed by scientific research,[30] and understandings of humankind were quite properly informed by critical-historical research, Ritschl believed it was the task of the theologian to posit the value of human existence. For the Christian theologian, this meant turning to the work, deeds,

---

26. See Schleiermacher, *On Religion*, p. 16. Schleiermacher in particular seems to have been deeply offended by the idea of a heavenly hereafter and the classical emphasis on individual, eternal salvation. He wrote, '[T]hose who make a distinction between this world and the world beyond delude themselves; at least all who have religion believe in only one world.'

27. Within Liberal Protestantism it was Albrecht Ritschl who took up Kant's identification of the kingdom of God with 'the ethical organisation of human society' (Heron, *Protestant Theology*, p. 35). See also King, 'Introduction: The Task of Theology', p. 19, and Donald Miller, 'Liberalism', in Richardson and Bowden (eds.), *The Westminster Dictionary of Christian Theology*, p. 324.

28. Eric J. Sharpe, 'The Kingdom of God', in Richardson and Bowden (eds.), *The Westminster Dictionary of Christian Theology*, p. 317.

29. Heron, *Protestant Theology*, p. 35. See also Richmond, 'Liberal Protestantism', p. 326.

30. In fact Ritschl had a negative view of the physical world; he accepted a mechanical view of nature and proposed that 'each individual has more value than the whole of nature' (personal communication with Dr Earl Gossett, 27 February 1985).

teachings and parables of Jesus—for in the Gospels was the historical record of the faith claims of the Christian church, more precisely, a record of the response of a faithful community to the values revealed to that community through the work and words of Jesus. Those values were found in the ethical demands of the kingdom of God as preached and lived by Jesus, which Ritschl interpreted to be 'the organisation of humanity through action inspired by love'.[31] Instead of relying on individual God-consciousness, or awareness of absolute dependence, as a ground for theological claims, Ritschl turned to the ethical imperative of love as the theological (and simultaneously epistemological) norm.[32] Practically, his emphasis on love of God and neighbour meant paying attention to the actual welfare of one's neighbour, which meant that love had to have at least something to do with social justice.[33]

The Social Gospel movement of the late nineteenth and early twentieth centuries took up this notion of the kingdom of God as a historical goal to be corporately realized on earth. In Social Gospel theology the emphasis was on the systemic nature of sin and evil. Injustices, or occasions when the possibility of human becoming was thwarted, were perceived to be a part of the social fabric of life. Consequently, institutional transformations were seen as the solution. Only by changing the social, economic and political structures ('the greedy ethics of capitalism and militarism'[34]) in which whole communities live, move and have their being, could the kingdom of God be realized. Walter Rauschenbusch, a leading figure in the Social Gospel movement, stated the tenets of Social Gospel theology in this way:

> Since Christ revealed the divine worth of life and personality, and since his salvation seeks the restoration and fulfillment of even the least, it follows that the kingdom of God, at every stage of human development, tends toward the social order which will best guarantee to all personalities their freest and highest development. This involves the redemption

---

31. Personal communication with Dr Earl Gossett, 27 February 1985.
32. Ritschl rejected what he considered to be Schleiermacher's de-personalized characterization of God; instead, he asserted that God must be a personality perfectly embodying the personal characteristic of love.
33. This understanding of the integral relationship between love and justice will be strongly echoed in feminist Christian theology. See in particular, Isabel Carter Heyward, *The Redemption of God: A Theology of Mutual Relation* (Lanham, MD: University Press of America, 1982).
34. Eric J. Sharpe, 'Social Gospel', in Richardson and Bowden (eds.), *The Westminster Dictionary of Christian Theology*, pp. 540-41.

of social life from the cramping influence of religious bigotry, from the repression of self-assertion in the relation of upper and lower classes, and from all forms of slavery in which human beings are treated as merely means to serve the ends of others... Since love is the supreme law of Christ, the kingdom of God implies a progressive reign of love in human affairs.[35]

Importantly, the ideal of the kingdom of God was both a future goal and a prophetic judgment upon existing injustices. If the kingdom was to be brought about, repentance and conversion would have to be collective processes, resulting in communal social and political changes. However, although the kingdom of God was understood to stand in judgment of the status quo, the Social Gospel movement was underpinned with a sense of optimism. Historical progress, while requiring great effort, was believed to be achievable. The kingdom of God could be 'man-made'.

Two factors, one scholarly and one political, combined to call into question the progressive optimism of the Liberal theologians and their reliance on the ethical ideal of the kingdom of God. In 1906 Albert Schweitzer published *The Quest for the Historical Jesus*, a survey work in which he analysed the attempts (to that date) by New Testament scholars to discover what could be known about Jesus of Nazareth. He concluded that very little could be said about the historical figure of Jesus with any degree of certainty at all, and furthermore, what New Testament scholars were most certain of was that Jesus' message concerning the kingdom of God had a decidedly eschatalogical, indeed, apocalyptic focus. In simplest terms, critical readings of the Gospels, in particular the Synoptic Gospels (Matthew, Mark and Luke), revealed, according to Schweitzer, that Jesus was not primarily concerned with establishing ongoing just social relations on earth, but with preparing people's hearts and minds for the imminent arrival of the kingdom of God, that is, for life in the world to come as heralded by the end of all existing earthly relations.[36]

---

35. Quoted from an excerpt of *A Theology for the Social Gospel*, by Walter Rauschenbusch, originally published in 1917. Walter Rauschenbusch, 'A Theology for the Social Gospel', in Peter C. Hodgson and Robert H. King (eds.), *Readings in Christian Theology* (Philadelphia: Fortress Press, 1985), p. 319.

36. See Heron, *Protestant Theology*, pp. 51-54. Regarding the eschatalogical focus (concerning the 'end time' or 'last times') of Jesus' preaching, it was Albrecht Ritschl's son-in-law, Johannes Weiss, with his 1892 *The Preaching of Jesus*

2. Influences on the Formation 51

Although the basis for the ethical interpretation of the gospel message as put forward by Liberal theologians was thus seriously challenged by historical and biblical scholars, it is possible that they could have countered this challenge successfully by reminding those scholars that Jesus' vision of the imminent coming of the kingdom of God did not in fact eventuate. Just as Paul had had to adjust his teachings to accommodate the fact that the end of the world was not at hand, so too was it still appropriate to do theology responsive to the ongoing existence of humanity, taking into account historical developments (scientific and cultural) undreamed of in Jesus' time. However, in 1914 the optimistic sense of humanity's progress toward eradicating social sins and evils was almost completely destroyed by the advent of the First World War. Suddenly it was evident that humans were just as capable of being inhumane as they ever had been.

In response to the shortcomings of Liberal theology as he perceived them, Karl Barth, a Swiss pastor and professor, returned to the classical Christian paradigm.[37] He reasserted the notion of an unbridgeable gulf between God and humanity, insisting on God's nature as 'wholly other'; he insisted that the Word of God was unknowable to 'man' except through God's revelation of that Word, and lastly, he insisted that the Word of God was Jesus Christ. Human beings were sinners, judged by God and completely dependent on God's mercy. Nothing in creation could lead one to God;[38] only God could reveal Godself, which God did in Jesus Christ. For Barth the *only* subject of theology was the Word of God, Jesus Christ. The theologian ought to speak of *nothing* apart from its relationship to Jesus Christ. Barth thus reversed the liberal trend to speak of Christianity as one religion among others (his faith allowing him to posit no saviour other than Jesus Christ); he believed Christian theologians had no business doing theology in conversation with scientists or artists; and he insisted that the only

---

Concerning the Kingdom of God, who significantly challenged the notion of the kingdom as a human ideal.

37. His first work, *Commentary on the Epistle to the Romans*, was published in 1918, while he was still a 'virtually unknown pastor' in Safenwil, Switzerland (Heron, *Protestant Theology*, p. 73).

38. Barth was vehemently opposed to any form of natural theology, or the attempt to discern God in any manifestation of creation, for example, through the universal laws of nature or through contemplation of particular, awe-inspiring aspects of creation. Barth insisted that God was wholly-other-than God's creation.

foundation (epistemological, ethical or otherwise) of Christian theology was the faithful reception of God's revelation of the Word of God, which always and only came from God above.[39]

In order to understand why Barth asserted the views he did as sharply as he did it is important to note what he was trying to achieve or, perhaps more accurately, to combat. The nineteenth-century Liberal accommodation of contemporary scientific 'truths' and support of state-sanctioned social improvements had led to a feeling, among theologians and within Christian churches, that a more perfect human realm could and would be brought about through cultural advancements. For Barth, who witnessed before and during the First World War the churches' complicity in the German government's political and military actions, such an alliance between church and state or faith and culture became untenable, indeed idolatrous. His response was a vehement 'No' to every attempt by 'man' to reach toward 'God'. Further, he wished for there never to be any confusion between human actions and divine actions.[40] He insisted that all social, political, economic and scientific achievements or programmes were human programmes, and as such they were inevitably flawed. To his credit, Barth took with utmost seriousness human capacity for sin. He believed, furthermore, that reinstating an unbridgeable gulf between humanity and God actually 'freed man to be man'; it could lead to an acceptance and appreciation of imperfect, finite existence, and to humility and thanksgiving in the face of an almighty God.

Barth's was the last great attempt to resurrect the classical Christian paradigm. Widely acknowledged to be the most important Christian theologian of the first half of the twentieth century, his words reverberated throughout the rhetorical space surrounding Christian theology in Western Europe and North America, muffling less certain, less triumphal voices. Ironically, just as the First World War had slowed the progress of Liberal theology, the Second World War and the Nazi Holocaust contributed greatly to the ensuing diminishment of Barth's

---

39. See John Bowden, 'Word of God', in Richardson and Bowden (eds.), *The Westminster Dictionary of Christian Theology*, pp. 603-604.

40. In 1934 he helped to draft the Barmen Declaration, a sharp criticism of those German Christians supportive of Hitler. At the time he was a university professor in Bonn, but when he refused to take the oath to Hitler he was dismissed and moved back to Switzerland (Heron, *Protestant Theology*, p. 86 and p. 74).

'neo-orthodox' position.[41] In allowing such incomprehensible suffering, Barth's all-powerful God had, it seemed to many, proven Godself to be too far removed, too far above human affairs. Such a God simply was not worthy of worship. However, Barth's answer to Liberal theology was not the only influential theological development in the first half of the twentieth century, although it was for some time the benchmark against which other perspectives were measured.

To conclude this review of the (pre-1960) influences on the feminist Christian theological paradigm I shall examine briefly two other theological approaches, theological existentialism and process theology—both of which echo themes found in Schleiermacher's thought.[42] Again, I shall do no more than sketch the outlines of these complex areas, emphasizing themes rather than particulars. I am trying to convey not the fine details of particular theological approaches, but a sense of how it was that Christian theology came apart at the seams in the latter half of the twentieth century, with more and more theologians expressing growing dissatisfaction with traditional understandings of theological concepts. This was a time when the old wine skins simply could not hold the new wine.[43]

Concerning existentialist theology, I wish to highlight three points. First, whereas Barth had insisted that the proper subject for theology was the Word of God as known to 'man' by faith through revelation, one of his contemporaries, Rudolph Bultmann, asserted instead that the proper subject of theology was 'the clarification of the content of faith'.[44] Adopting the existential philosophy of Martin Heidegger,

---

41. See Ferm, *Contemporary American Theologies*, p. 20.

42. See Schleiermacher, *On Religion*, p. 108 and p. 116, where Schleiermacher insists that humans are inescapably dwellers in the world and describes humanity as straining against the universe, 'ever vacillating, ever halting at the particular and accidental...' This description resonates with the existentialists' understanding of humans' location in the world of objects, and with the risk of defining one's existence solely on the basis of those objects. Similarly, on p. 77 he describes his view of the universe as a whole, with each individual aspect of the universe integrated into the whole and only separated 'forcibly and arbitrarily'. Within this overarching schema, however, he also insists on individuation in order for participation in the universe (p. 67)—a belief integral to process thought.

43. It was not until the 1960s, however, that the question of who was allowed to be a wine-maker was raised.

44. John MacQuarrie, *An Existentialist Theology* (London: SCM Press, 1955), p. 6. See also pp. 234-325 in the same volume, in which MacQuarrie discusses

Bultmann insisted on making explicit the 'pre-theological' underpinnings of his assertion, namely, *the ontological understanding of the existence of 'man', whose faith can only be known insofar as it is a part of 'his' human existence*.[45] In other words, before one can speak of the *content* of faith one must make clear the *context* of faith, and that context is human existence, human being-in-the-world.[46] Furthermore, all understandings of human existence *are a part of* human existence. The argument was, therefore, that existentialism was 'not a speculative philosophy, but an analysis of that understanding of human existence which is given with existence'.[47] Thus while Barth argued that any extraneous philosophical system could only cloud or weaken the Christian message, Bultmann (and Paul Tillich, among others) argued that one must understand the character of lived human existence in order to understand the Christian faith as a part of that existence.[48]

Secondly, both existentialist philosophers and theologians were deeply concerned with halting the modern trend according to which only scientific knowledge of 'man' and the world was worthy of the name 'knowledge'. Scientific knowledge, they argued, was only one special sub-species of the knowledge and understanding that humans need to live in the world.[49] They insisted that questions such as 'of what is sea water composed?' simply cannot replace questions such as 'what is the nature of my being?' According to the existentialists, practical, concrete existence is positively rife with situations in which

---

Bultmann's theology gaining prominence after the Second World War, when Barth's theological programme came to be seen by many as 'curiously irrelevant to the modern mind'.

45. MacQuarrie, *An Existentialist Theology*, pp. 6-7 and p. 237.

46. MacQuarrie, *An Existentialist Theology*, p. 39. The expression 'being-in-the-world' is the English translation of Heidegger's term, 'in-der-Welt-sein', which he used to stress the point that human existence is only possible *somewhere*, in a context surrounded by other things, and that human existence is shaped by what 'we' do or do not do with those other things.

47. MacQuarrie, *An Existentialist Theology*, p. 8.

48. This is one aspect of existentialism that has been taken up in a lively fashion by feminist Christian theologians, no doubt causing Bultmann, Tillich and many others to roll over in their graves. It is safe to say that they did not foresee the consequences of their perfectly reasonable assertion.

49. See MacQuarrie, *An Existentialist Theology*, pp. 54-56. See also James Richmond, 'Existentialism', in Allan Richardson and John Bowden (eds.), *The Westminster Dictionary of Christian Theology*, pp. 201-204.

discerning how I can participate meaningfully in the world (as opposed to losing myself in it) requires a radically different sort of knowledge than the knowledge of the chemical composition of sea water. Importantly, in making this argument the existentialist theologians reinserted into the theological enterprise *an epistemological component based on lived experiences* rather than on revelation breaking in from God above. With their emphasis on *what knowledge is primarily for*, theological existentialists called attention to the fact of embodied, incarnate, concrete, relational existence in-the-world,[50] and they insisted that interpreting understandings of existence is as theological a task as it is philosophical, for faith apart from existence is simply nonsensical.

Thirdly, instead of speaking of God almost exclusively in terms of the Word of God, as Barth did, the existentialists tended to speak of God as the 'ground of Being'. In order to grasp the implications of this shift in symbolic language (and for Paul Tillich in particular language about God was symbolic, participatory language) it is necessary to explore what they meant by the term 'being'. According to Alasdair Heron, 'when Existentialists spoke of "Being" they were not treating it as an entity, but using it in order to draw attention to the mysterious reality of existence itself, to the wonder of the fact that anything "is" at all...'[51] The phrase 'ground of Being' is thus an allusion to the source or 'author' of all being, human and non-human being alike.[52] In terms reminiscent of Schleiermacher's characterization of a feeling of absolute dependence (as God-consciousness), the existentialists asserted that all being (human and non-human alike) is dependent upon a ground of being—which does not necessarily have to be a personal

---

50. The Jewish existentialist (sometimes considered personalist) philosopher Martin Buber in particular posited the relational character of existence, declaring, in *I and Thou*, 'In the beginning is relation' (p. 18). In this poetic work he contrasted I–Thou relationships, in which I and Thou (whether person, place or thing) are mutually enriched through our relationship, with I–It relationships, in which I seek to make It (whether person, place or thing) into an object for my own ends, and in so doing also objectify and thus diminish myself. See Martin Buber, *I and Thou*, (trans. Ronald G. Smith; Edinburgh: T. & T. Clark, 2nd edn, 1958 [original German edn 1923]).

51. Heron, *Protestant Theology*, p. 144, paraphrasing a statement made by Heidegger in which he was trying to clarify his own use of the term.

52. See MacQuarrie, *An Existentialist Theology*, p. 74. 'he can seek a ground of being, which means simply a Creator who is author both of man's being and of the being of nature'.

deity. Again let me stress that here I am trying to describe briefly only some of those themes which are taken up and developed in feminist Christian theology. Consequently I am not concerned with setting out, in the body of this chapter, the existentialists' conception of the fundamental condition of human existence—alienation or estrangement. However, it is important to note that a core metaphysical presupposition upheld by the existentialists, namely that human being is utterly distinct from and alien to non-human being (or, theologically, that humans are in the world but not of it) is *not* a component in the feminist Christian theological paradigm.

Earlier I mentioned that the feminist Christian theological paradigm is one of the inheritors of the scientific developments of the nineteenth and twentieth centuries. Specifically, the metaphysical presuppositions inherent in the feminist Christian theological paradigm are, as will become clear in future chapters, in accordance with the basic tenets of the theory of relativity and quantum rather than classical (or Newtonian) physics—briefly, interdependent relationality, rather than independence, isolation and self-sufficiency, is posited as being fundamentally characteristic of all that is. However, the first thorough-going incorporation of the assumptions of the 'new' physics into a systematic philosophical/theological approach was carried out by Alfred North Whitehead in his monumental work, *Process and Reality* (1929).[53] Strictly speaking, what came to be known as process theology is a distinct theological paradigm unto itself by virtue of its numerous unique metaphors and models. In order to convey his thoughts Whitehead created, to quote Thomas Kuhn, 'a new universe of discourse', and it is impossible to convey the depth and intricacy of his ideas without recourse to his metaphors. Broadly, what he attempted was to propose a general metaphysical description applicable to *every* 'entity' in the universe as the universe is experienced in *this* 'cosmic epoch'.[54] There are two points I need to clarify immediately. First, Whitehead insisted that metaphysical presuppositions lurked behind all statements

---

53. Alfred North Whitehead, *Process and Reality: An Essay in Cosmology* (New York: MacMillan, 1929). I am not here concerned with whether or not it was his deliberate intention to start with recent developments in physics and move to philosophy and theology, although I do not believe it was, or that he in fact did so. However, intentional or not, his thought was very much in line with the then newly developing scientific paradigm shift.

54. Whitehead, *Process and Reality*, pp. 148-50.

of fact: '[E]very proposition proposing a fact must, in its complete analysis, propose the general character of the universe required for that fact. There are no self-sustained facts, floating in nonentity.'[55] Secondly, he did not believe that any cosmic epoch was eternal in a temporal sense, and he assumed that two or more cosmic epochs could exist simultaneously.[56] (To understand this statement imagine a universe composed of anti-matter existing at the same time as our universe composed of matter—the 'general character' of that universe would be utterly distinct from ours.) The point is that he deliberately constructed his metaphysical scheme relative to 'this' epoch in 'this' universe, and he consistently carried the notion of 'relativity' throughout his work. He thus rejected the notion of any 'once and for all' description of reality.

According to Whitehead 'entities' are not to be conceived of as substances, but as processes. That is, an 'actual entity' is to be conceived as an *event becoming* rather than as a *state of being*. When an entity ceases becoming, or in his terms, achieves satisfaction, it 'perishes'. However, no entity can 'become' in isolation and no entity perishes without a trace. In Whitehead's words, 'the primary stage in the concrescence [becoming] of an actual entity is the way in which the antecedent universe enters into the constitution of the entity in question, so as to constitute the basis of its nascent individuality'.[57] In other words, every present actual occasion (another term for 'actual entity') is indelibly shaped by the processes/events that lead up to its 'becoming'. The weight of the past presses inexorably into the present, imposing a limited range of possibilities on the potential range of 'becoming' experienced or felt by each actual entity. Because of this, some order is maintained in the universe. The past is never lost, but as it is re-membered in each present it shapes and limits the form the present can take.

Whitehead describes each perished actual entity as achieving 'objective immortality'—immortal in the sense that it continues to be felt, remembered and incorporated into present actual entities, and objective in the sense that past actual occasions are objectified by present actual

---

55. Alfred North Whitehead, 'In Defence of Speculative Philosophy', in Donald W. Sherburne (ed.), *A Key to Whitehead's Process and Reality* (New York: MacMillan, 1966), p. 199.
56. See Sherburne, *A Key to Whitehead's Process and Reality*, pp. 80-81.
57. Whitehead, *Process and Reality*, p. 230.

occasions. Which is to say the subjective fulness or entirety of the perished actual occasion is lost to the temporal world because only some aspects of it are 'positively prehended' by concrescing (becoming) actual occasions. Those aspects of the perished actual occasion which are 'negatively prehended' are not incorporated into the physical/temporal present. However, in Whitehead's description of God he posits the view that each perished actual occasion is remembered in its subjective fulness in the consequent nature of God. Briefly, Whitehead's 'God' has three natures: the primordial, the consequent and the superjective. These can be understood as corresponding respectively to divine imagination, eternal memory and future vision. God 'works' in the universe in three ways. Initially God perfectly imagined the most harmonious and most perfect relationships possible in a universe of pure potentiality. Our universe, however, is an actual, not a potential universe. Hence God's consequent nature: continually apprehending and remembering perfectly every single actual entity and every society of entities (enduring objects like rocks and humans). In God's superjective nature a possible future is envisioned in which each actual entity achieves as valuable a 'satisfaction' as possible. This vision or 'lure' becomes a part of the present universe of each actual entity, able to be positively or negatively prehended by it. In the process view of God, nothing is ever forgotten or lost, nor is anything ever forced or demanded.

As noted above, present reality is never merely the unchanged repetition of the past. With each new actual occasion comes novelty and change as well as a memory of the past. That is, every actual entity integrates its feelings of the past in a manner unique to itself; thus every actual entity is entirely new at the same time as it is entirely dependent upon the past. Again, once it has achieved satisfaction (or perished) it becomes available as a resource for the becoming of future actual entities.[58] Whether speaking of a single actual entity or a society of actual occasions (e.g. a human), the basic process remains the same: every entity seeks to feel through or experience its 'antecedent universe' in a singular, integrated fashion—or as a whole. It does so by

---

58. Whitehead, *Process and Reality*, p. 130 and p. 233: 'In the conception of the actual entity in its phase of satisfaction, the entity has attained its individual separation from other things; it has absorbed the datum, and it has not yet lost itself in the swing back whereby its appetition becomes an element in the data of other entities superseding it.'

bringing 'the many into one' and it then adds itself to that 'one'. In Whitehead's words, 'the many become one and are increased by one.'[59] This is the basic rhythm of the universe in process thought: integration, individuation, integration—order and novelty and order, simultaneously and ceaselessly.

I have described Whitehead's thought in considerable detail for three reasons. First, I find process thought to be hauntingly beautiful, a harmony composed of hope and tragedy in equal measure. In process thought, as in feminist Christian theology, it is impossible to transform quickly any history of systematic oppression or injustice. Every time anyone's life (in process terms, any enduring society of actual occasions) is distorted, diminished or denied, the temporal present and future are impoverished to an unknowable degree. What has been lost (a person's life or hopes or dreams, a culture's memories, a community's way of being...) is lost to this world forever. However, it is equally true that the present and the course of the future are affected by every becoming occasion of love (or justice or harmony or right relationship). In process thought little things matter greatly. Second, the affinities between these aspects of process thought and feminist Christian theology are strong, and in my opinion, extremely important to name. Lastly, Alfred North Whitehead and, later, Charles Hartshorne and Henry Nelson Wieman had the audacity to reject or radically reconceptualize any theological notion they felt was untenable in relation to the metaphysical presuppositions they embraced. They proved (as Schleiermacher had done earlier) that neither the *how* nor the *what* of theology was fixed, unalterable.[60] By the 1960s, the decade in which the feminist Christian theological paradigm has its immediate social and political roots, the *what* of Christian theology was revealed to be indivisible from the *who* of Christian theology. In other words,

---

59. Whitehead, *Process and Reality*, p. 32.

60. They called into question and rejected such bedrock theological assumptions as divine omnipotence and omniscience, not to mention the concepts of predestination, the salvation of the elect, and eternal damnation. See Charles Hartshorne, *Omnipotence and Other Theological Mistakes* (Albany, NY: State University of New York Press, 1984). I include this reference because the title is so delightfully apt; my point, however, is that these theological notions had to be rejected (at least implicitly) even in the initial writings in process thought because they contradict basic assumptions about the nature of the universe and of God posited in process theology.

some theologians (feminist and otherwise) increasingly asserted that theological content was closely related to theological authorship.[61]

It is not possible, within the context of this chapter, to identify all of the social, political, scientific/technological, and ethical factors leading to the historical event known as the 1960s. However, here I must at least name two of those factors which were to be of particular importance to Christian theologians. The dropping of the atomic bomb on Hiroshima and Nagasaki by the US made it impossible for any theologian to consider scientific achievements as inevitably 'progressive' or for the good of all humanity. The development and use of nuclear weapons also prompted a re-examination of the ethical dimension of Christian theology. Similarly, the fact of the Holocaust prompted an examination of the role of Christian anti-Semitism in creating a social and political climate in which such genocide was not only considered but carried out. The sheer scale of such senseless death and destruction was (and remains) simultaneously unbearable yet mandatory to consider. As Barth had been confronted by an enormous human capacity for sin that he witnessed first in the First World War, so too were Christian theologians in confronted, in the aftermath of the Second World War, with human sins of a magnitude that had previously seemed impossible.

With this legacy it is perhaps not surprising that in the 1960s in the US the civil rights movement, massive demonstrations against US involvement in the war in Vietnam, and, by the end of the decade, the increasingly visible women's liberation movement[62] collectively called into question the structure of society. Who had the power to decide that one race was superior to another? Who had the power to send US

---

61. In 1988, in the fifteenth anniversary introduction to *A Theology of Liberation*, Gustavo Gutiérrez wrote: 'Although theology is a language for communicating God, in every place it must display the inflections given it by those who formulate it and those to whom it is directed. Every language has a number of dialects... Our theological language is subject to the same rule; it takes its coloring from our peoples, cultures, and racial groupings... This accent may not be to the liking of those who until now have regarded themselves the proprietors of theology and are not conscious of their own accent (to which, of course, they have every right) when they speak of God' Gustavo Gutiérrez, *A Theology of Liberation* (trans. and ed. Sister Caridad Inda and John Eagleson; Maryknoll, NY: Orbis Books, 1988), p. xxxv.

62. For example, Betty Friedan's revolutionary book, *The Feminine Mystique*, was originally published in 1964 (New York: Dell).

troops to kill and be killed in a small Asian country? Who was excluded from the country's economic and political and military strongholds? The 1960s were a time when fundamental presuppositions governing the structure of society were openly challenged. The 1960s were also, not incidentally, a time of tremendous theological upheaval. A growing number of theologians were of the opinion that, in the face of the Nazi Holocaust, Hiroshima, Nagasaki and napalm, to speak or write of an immutable, omniscient, omnipotent and benevolent deity was rationally untenable and morally unconscionable. According to them, God—literally—was dead.[63] With Dietrich Bonhoeffer's words as a rallying cry, the death-of-God theologians proclaimed it was time for 'man to come of age', to live in the absence of God. Concretely, what this meant, at least in part, was for 'man' to live knowing that 'for good or ill he bears responsibility for what he makes of his life and the life of the world'.[64] For the death-of-God theologians there simply was no longer an omnipotent God prepared to come to the rescue of 'man'. The focus of their theological attention was on this world as it is 'here' and 'now'. A similar 'this-worldly' focus was also prominent in the work of a number of theologians concerned with secular society, in particular Harvey Cox.[65] However, in much secular theology God remained alive and well, and very much wholly-other-than any aspect of God's creation.

Meanwhile, in the Roman Catholic Church there were two momentous developments: in the early 1960s Pope John XXIII, cardinals, bishops and the laity were preparing for the Second Vatican Council, during the course of which the active participation of the laity in the affairs of the Church was encouraged,[66] while in Peru (1968) Gustavo Gutiérrez was insisting that all theology is shaped by the context in which it is developed, and that theology developed by economically

---

63. See Thomas J.J. Altizer and William Hamilton, *Radical Theology and the Death of God* (New York: Bobs-Merrill, 1966). I realize that not all the death-of-God theologians would describe God as literally dead; Paul van Buren in particular was concerned with the bankruptcy of traditional god-language rather than with the literal death of a transcendent deity. However, Hamilton and Altizer certainly felt that there had been such a transcendent God and that now such a God was dead.

64. Heron, *Protestant Theology*, p. 155.

65. Harvey Cox, *The Secular City* (New York: Macmillan, 1968).

66. The Second Vatican Council was concluded (after John XXIII's death) in Rome in 1965.

privileged Western Europeans or North Americans was not appropriate to the context of the poor in Latin America. The God of the gospels is a God with a preferential option for the poor, said Gutiérrez, and liberation theology was voiced for the first time.[67]

At the same time as White, middle-class men were burying God or turning to the 'secular city' and liberation theology was beginning to take shape in Latin America, in the US a number of Black churchmen (and they were primarily men) were meeting and beginning to relate Black Power to theology. In the summer of 1966 the underlying foundation of Black theology was established with the publication of a full-page advertisement in the *New York Times*, entitled 'Black Power: Statement by the National Committee of Negro Churchmen, July 31, 1966'.[68] Signed by forty-seven Black churchmen and one woman, it was clear that from where they stood God was fully alive and sustaining the struggle of Black communities to liberate themselves from the racist, violent and oppressive conditions imposed upon them by White America(ns). In 1969 this vision was cogently expressed in the opening paragraph of 'Black Theology', a statement written by the Theological Commission of the National Committee of Black Churchmen (NCBC). Importantly, James Cone, who was also to publish his first book, *Black Theology and Black Power* in 1969, was the 'key member' of the NCBC Theological Commission which drafted the statement.[69] The statement begins:

> Black people affirm their being. This affirmation is made in the whole experience of being black in the hostile American society. Black Theology is not a gift of the Christian gospel dispensed to slaves; rather it is an *appropriation* which black slaves made of the gospel given by their

---

67. See Gustavo Gutiérrez, 'Expanding the View', in Marc H. Ellis and Otto Maduro (eds.), *Expanding the View* (Maryknoll, NY: Orbis Books, 1988), p. 4. 'The name and reality of "liberation theology" came into existence at Chimbote, Peru, in July 1968.' For the moment I ignore the simultaneous development of feminist Christian theology. However, I do want to note that, as I will discuss further in the next chapter, the development of feminist Christian theology, Black theology and liberation theology occurred simultaneously, with at least one leading feminist theologian (Rosemary Ruether) engaged with ongoing developments in both Black and liberation theology.

68. Gayraud S. Wilmore and James H. Cone (eds.), *Black Theology: A Documentary History, 1966–1979* (Maryknoll, NY: Orbis Books, 1979), pp. 23-30. See also pp. 17-18.

69. Wilmore and Cone, *Black Theology*, p. 77.

2. Influences on the Formation 63

> white oppressors. Black Theology has been nurtured, sustained and passed on in the black churches in their various ways of expression. Black Theology has dealt with all the ultimate and violent issues of life and death for a people despised and degraded. The black church has not only nurtured black people but enabled them to survive brutalities that ought not to have been inflicted on any community of men. Black Theology is the product of black Christian experience and reflection. It comes out of the past. It is strong in the present. And we believe it is redemptive for the future [italics in original].[70]

This paragraph is rich with metaphysical presuppositions (e.g. 'black people affirm their being', 'the ultimate and violent issues of life and death'), with metaphors (e.g. 'black', 'slaves', 'gospel', 'white'), with models (e.g. 'the black church', 'black Christian experience'). And it is from beginning to end a value judgment; it is simultaneously a condemnation of the treatment of Black people in America by White Americans and a positive affirmation of the goodness (although the term 'good' does not appear in the paragraph, 'gospel' is literally translated as 'good news') of Black lives and Black 'being'. In marked contrast to most theology written by White male authors, the emphasis on Black churches and the Black community is coupled with the *absence* of any reference to individual lives, thus whatever is 'redemptive' about Black theology is redemptive in a collective, corporate sense. It is clear from this brief excerpt that Black Theology is based upon a host of presuppositions, and a way of talking about those presuppositions, that are, taken together, unique to Black theology. In other words, Black theology is a theological paradigm unto itself: a paradigm formed at the same time as the feminist Christian theological paradigm and the Latin American liberation theological paradigm.

These distinct theological paradigms multiplied during and following the 1960s, and rather than attempt to deny the validity of all other paradigms, they each sought instead to bear witness to the lived truths and faith-claims of particular, *theretofore epistemically silenced*, communities.[71] This is a critical point. What happened in the 1960s was

---

70. Wilmore and Cone, *Black Theology*, p. 100.
71. See Gutiérrez, *A Theology of Liberation*, p. xxxvi: 'I mentioned earlier the dialogue between the theologies of the Third World, in which the theologies emerging from minorities in different countries all participate on an equal footing. But this further dialogue does not stop at the borders of the Third World. There have also been very profitable meetings with representatives of types of theological thinking that originate in Europe and North America. Then there is the encounter with

that *groups* of people who had previously been denied entrance into the rhetorical space surrounding the discipline of Christian theology came together and created the rhetorical spaces in which they could speak and write and piece together their own theological paradigms. Those who had previously been ignored or made the objects of theological reflection became active theological subjects. However, again, they did not start from scratch. As the 'Black Theology' statement baldly declares, they appropriated models and metaphors from the gospel and from any source they found valuable. Thus it is not surprising that different theological paradigms share what seem to be 'the same' metaphors and models, e.g. redemption, sin, liberation, the kingdom of God. What differs with each paradigm, however, is the underlying metaphysical presuppositions and value judgements.

Having gone on a somewhat lengthy tour to arrive at this point, let me review it briefly. In roughly chronological order: Hume and Kant deny the objective existence of God, leaving future theologians with a not insignificant epistemological issue on their hands. Schleiermacher defines religion as an 'intuition of the universe' and radically depersonalises God, suggesting that 'God' be understood instead as the 'whence' of every aspect of the universe, from the greatest to the least. Ritschl insists that the kingdom of God is to be created on earth by the power of loving human endeavours. The Social Gospel movement understands and expresses systemic sins in social, political and economic terms. The 'real' intentions and concerns of Jesus of Nazareth are called into question. Faced with the horror of the First World War, Barth seeks refuge in a familiar figure, an omnipotent, wholly-other deity who promises eventual salvation in a better realm. After the Second World War, and with it yet more humanly created horror in the form of the Holocaust and the dropping of the atomic bomb, the existentialists refuse Barth's turn to a personal God-above. Like Schleiermacher earlier, they put their faith in the fact that anything is at all. Process theologians too reject the omnipotence and otherness of God, and insist on the relationality (for good and ill) of all

---

the feminist perspective in theology and with the new and challenging contribution this is making. My impression is that the deeper importance of this dialogue is to be found, not in the coming together of theologians, but in the communication established among Christian communities and their respective historical, social, and cultural contexts, *for these communities are the real subjects who are actively engaged in these discourses of faith*' (italics added).

that is, was, and ever will be. The 1960s erupt, and initially there is much theological talk of taking responsibility for one's actions. In the US peace is demanded; love is celebrated; students, activists and a president are shot; race riots spread from city to city. The power of an elite few (primarily White) men to name God, to direct the affairs of the world, and to define the lives of entire categories of humanity is challenged and rejected by the laity in the Roman Catholic Church, by the poor in Latin America, and by Black (primarily male) theologians in the US. This is the theological inheritance and, combined with the emergence of second-wave feminism, the historical setting for the development of feminist Christian theology.

Chapter 3

THE COMPONENTS OF ONE FEMINIST CHRISTIAN
THEOLOGICAL PARADIGM

Having identified the formative theological influences upon the feminist Christian theological paradigm I wish to examine, in this chapter I shall identify and make explicit the metaphysical presuppositions, the underlying value judgments, and (some of) the metaphors and models that make up this paradigm. To do this I shall engage in a close reading of three early and deeply influential essays: 'The Human Situation: A Feminine View', first published by Valerie Saiving in April 1960 in *The Journal of Religion*; 'Motherearth and the Megamachine: A Theology of Liberation in a Feminine, Somatic and Ecological Perspective', first published by Rosemary Radford Ruether in *Christianity and Crisis* (12 April 1972); and 'After the Death of God the Father', first published by Mary Daly in *Commonweal* (12 March 1971). These three essays all appear in the first section (entitled 'The Essential Challenge') of the first anthology of constructive feminist theological texts, *Womanspirit Rising: A Feminist Reader in Religion*, edited by Carol P. Christ and Judith Plaskow and first published in 1979.[1] I accept Christ and Plaskow's designation of these essays as formative feminist Christian theological texts, and in the course of this chapter I shall

---

1. Carol P. Christ and Judith Plaskow (eds.), *Womanspirit Rising: A Feminist Reader in Religion* (San Francisco: Harper & Row, 1979). While published five years earlier, the 1974 text *Religion and Sexism: Images of Women in the Jewish and Christian Traditions*, edited by Rosemary Radford Ruether, is a compilation of essays written specifically to examine the role of religion (in the Jewish and Christian traditions) in shaping traditional cultural images that are degrading to women. As such it is not explicitly concerned with constructive feminist theological efforts; rather, in it the authors highlight misogynist thoughts from the traditions' pasts and in so doing put forward the necessity to engage in non-misogynist constructive efforts.

3. *Components of One Feminist*

demonstrate how it is that collectively they do represent 'the essential challenge' of one feminist Christian theological paradigm. In addition to them I shall refer to Daly's *The Church and the Second Sex* (1968), as well as to *Beyond God the Father* (1973), to Ruether's *Liberation Theology* (1972), and, lastly, to Sheila Collins's *A Different Heaven and Earth* (1974).

Because, as I suggested in Chapter 1, a paradigm is composed of metaphysical presuppositions and value judgments as these are conveyed through the use of various metaphors and models, I shall seek to identify the metaphysical presuppositions and value judgements within this feminist Christian theological paradigm through an examination of the following key theological metaphors, each of which is used in one or more of the essays I examine: sin, love, revelation, salvation, incarnation, reconciliation, and messiah/messianic. Additionally, I shall discuss the following models as they are used in the texts: the cultivation of the garden, the body of God, and the second coming of God. Lastly, I shall refer again to Thomas Kuhn's understanding of the process of creating a paradigm, in particular to his emphasis on the necessary formation of a new universe of discourse with which to speak of a new world(view).

In 1960 Valerie Saiving published 'The Human Situation: A Feminine View',[2] the essay now considered to mark the beginnings of (White, North American) feminist Christian theology. The essay did not, however, have an immediately transformative impact on the theological world. Rather, it was discovered by women studying theology in the late 1960s and has come to be considered to be something which it was not when it was first published, i.e., *the* landmark feminist theological text.[3] Saiving's central hypothesis was that, theologically, the 'human condition' or the 'human situation' (she used the terms interchangeably) had been characterized inadequately because it had been defined exclusively on the basis of 'masculine experience'. Further, she proposed that this inadequacy was particularly evident when one examined contemporary theological characterizations of love and

---

2. Originally published in *The Journal of Religion* (April, 1960) by the University of Chicago Press, all citations in this book are from Valerie Saiving, 'The Human Situation: A Feminine View', in Christ and Plaskow (eds.), *Womanspirit Rising*, pp. 25-42.

3. Christ and Plaskow, 'Introduction', in *Womanspirit Rising*, p. 21.

sin.[4] Specifically, she chose to look at the theological metaphors of sin and love because their contemporary characterisations (by males) as self-assertion and selflessness respectively seemed to Saiving to be related to 'a widespread tendency in contemporary theology to describe man's predicament as arising from his separateness and anxiety occasioned by it…'[5] In other words, Saiving believed that characterizations of sin and love were dependent on this specific understanding of 'the human condition'. If separateness and anxiety did not characterize the experience of all humans, then these conceptualizations of the metaphors of sin and love were inadequate. In short, Saiving questioned a primary metaphysical (in this instance *anthropological*) *presupposition*, the assumption that the human situation is always and everywhere that of alienation and estrangement, and two fundamental theological *metaphors*—love as entirely self-giving and self-sacrificial and sin as self-assertion. Importantly, she was aware that 'analys[es] of the human situation and the definitions of love and sin which accompany [them] are mutually dependent concepts'.[6] That is, she interpreted theology to be a whole composed of interrelated parts. Whenever one of the parts is altered so too are the other parts affected. This insight matches the understanding of the components of a disciplinary paradigm proposed in the first chapter.

Basing her analysis on her own 'experience and observation'[7] she noted that *as mothers* women have been expected to give almost all of themselves to their infants and children. If contemporary male theologians (in particular she was responding to the work of Anders Nygren and Reinhold Niebuhr) were correct, this would imply that women as mothers were the most loving (self-giving) and least sinful (self-asserting) members of humankind. However, Saiving went on to state her observation that 'a woman can give too much of herself, so that nothing remains of her own uniqueness; she can become merely an

---

4. Saiving, 'The Human Situation', pp. 25-27.
5. Saiving, 'The Human Situation', pp. 25-26.
6. Saiving, 'The Human Situation', p. 27.
7. In 'The Human Situation', Saiving acknowledged (p. 29) that she was writing out of her 'own experience and observation as it [had] been clarified and substantiated' by the anthropological accounts of Margaret Mead, Ruth Benedict and Ashley Montagu and the psychoanalytic perspectives of Helene Deutsch, Erich Fromm and Theodor Reik, as well as the sociological insights of Talcott Parsons.

emptiness, almost a zero, without value to herself, to her fellow men, or, perhaps, even to God'.[8] While contemporary (male) theological considerations of sin were grounded on the assumption that 'man' pays too much self-referential attention to the 'I' aspect of the 'I–Thou' relationship, Saiving approached the subject from her own experience and detected a peculiarly 'feminine' distortion of the I–Thou relationship—the 'feminine' sin of self-negation rather than the 'masculine' sin of self-elevation.

Saiving drew her characterization of 'feminine sin' from her description of a mother's relationship to her child. Her analysis was based on a description of the undivided attention infants and children require in order to thrive. To the extent that infants and children do require an astonishing amount of care and attention in order to survive Saiving's description was also prescriptive—a prescription based it seems on her belief that a society that encourages women 'to despise the functions of childbearing and nurture...is in grave danger of bringing about its own destruction'.[9] Yet her *judgment* of self-giving, self-transcending love differed radically from that of her contemporaries. While Saiving evaluated positively a mother's *occasional* experience of self-transcending love she also denied this experience be-all and end-all status. In her words, the attempt to 'sustain a perpetual I–Thou relationship...can be deadly. The moments, hours, and days of self-giving must be balanced by moments, hours, and days of withdrawal into, and enrichment of, her individual selfhood *if she is to remain a whole person*'[10] (italics added). Saiving accepted as a given the fact that most women in all cultures are or become or have been mothers, but she refused to accept 'motherhood' as exclusively definitive of women's situation or condition, in other words, of women's nature or being. She thus rejected the limits placed on 'woman' by previous theological anthropologies, e.g. that a woman was fit by nature *only* to be 'for birth and children' (the view of Jerome),[11] and she rejected also the notion

---

8. Saiving, 'The Human Situation', p. 37.
9. Saiving, 'The Human Situation', p. 33.
10. Saiving, 'The Human Situation', p.37.
11. See Mary Daly, *The Church and The Second Sex* (Boston: Beacon Press, rev. edn, 1985), p. 85. In 1964 Rosemary Ruether also publicly rejected the limits inherently placed on women by the Roman Catholic Church's refusal to approve of the use of artificial birth control. In an essay appearing in William Birmingham (ed.), *What Modern Catholics Think about Birth Control* (New York: New

that 'woman's' being (physical, emotional, and spiritual) was inferior, of less worth and dignity (or, as Barth insisted, of a second ontological order)[12] than 'man's'. Instead, she based her statements on an anthropological presupposition which I term 'the full, unqualified humanity of women'. This anthropological presupposition was a necessary corollary to her (value) judgment that a woman's life can and *ought to be* the life of '*a whole person*'. That this presupposition and accompanying value judgment were strange and novel is evident by the implicit assumption in the following quotation, to the effect that at the time Saiving was writing, women had to choose between being women or being fully human. Writing of the few women she knew who were questioning the adequacy of the then current conception of the universal 'human' situation, Saiving said, 'they want, in other words, to be both women *and* full human beings'.[13]

Regarding women's situation, her description highlighted the fact that many women's *experience as mothers* was not that of separation, alienation, and estrangement, as the human situation had been defined by contemporary theologians, but very often that of enmeshment and utter involvement. She did not claim that women were incapable of the sin of pride or self-assertion, but that women's lived experiences were more likely to put women at the risk of a different sort of sin altogether, and that this different sort of sin was the logical extension of what had been characterized by male theologians as the epitome of love. In short, Saiving proposed that 'woman's' tendency toward self-underdevelopment is as sinful and harmful to self, humanity and God as is 'man's' temptation toward misplaced pride of self and will to power. She thus transformed the metaphors sin and love, enlarging their scope and range of applicability. Rather than presenting a rigid contrast between them, her more open understanding of the metaphors

---

American Library, 1964), pp. 233-40, 'A Question of Dignity, A Question of Freedom', Ruether wrote, 'Such a request is simply a demand that I scuttle my interests, my training, and in the last analysis, my soul'. Quoted in Daly, *The Church and the Second Sex*, p. 133.

12. See Karl Barth, 'The Doctrine of Creation', in *Church Dogmatics*, III, sec. 4 (ed. G.W. Bromily and T.F. Torrance; Edinburgh: T. & T. Clark, 1961): 'in order she is woman, and therefore B, and therefore behind and subordinate to man [who is A]... She, too, has to realise that she is ordered, related and directed to man and has thus to follow the initiative which he must take'.

13. Saiving, 'The Human Situation', p. 36 (italics in original).

sin and love was based on her recognition that, as regards their meaning, they are in a mutually interdependent relationship with 'sinners' and 'lovers'. She assumed that *who* was doing the sinning or the loving was a theologically significant issue. As a consequence, when she looked at the lived experiences of the women she knew[14] she realized that they were at risk of a different sort of sin than that defined by Nygren and Niebuhr.

By beginning from this assumption Saiving argued that theology written from the perspective of male/masculine experience, although previously taken as normative and universally true, was in fact neither normative nor universal. Her point was that contemporary theologians had accepted as universal truth an understanding of the human situation based on the experiences of only half of the human race, the male half, *which tended not to experience enmeshment and involvement with another's life to the same degree as women-as-mothers*. Saiving exposed a fundamental anthropological assumption regarding humanity to be erroneously narrow, i.e., that 'the human condition' was always and everywhere that of alienation and estrangement, and she showed *how* this error was sustained in the theological metaphors of love (as self-sacrifice) and sin (as self-assertion) that had been constructed to reflect and support this narrow view of 'the universal condition of humanity'.

Methodologically, Saiving's approach involved examining and describing her own experience, exploring her interpretation of women's 'condition' 'in dialogue with other women', and using interdisciplinary sources in order to 'clarify and substantiate' her knowledge claims.[15] Before she could write 'The Human Situation', Saiving

---

14. Importantly, Saiving wrote this essay in the context of a Western, industrialized, capitalist society, as a relatively privileged member of that society. Her reflections applied specifically to White, middle- or upper-class Western women and men and, as such, were devoid of any race or class analysis (not to mention her presumption of heterosexuality and motherhood as the norm for all women). See Judith Plaskow, *Sex, Sin and Grace: Women's Experience and the Theologies of Rheinhold Niebuhr and Paul Tillich* (Lanham, MD: University Press of America, 1980), p. 2.

15. Saiving has written elsewhere: 'From…personal history I draw two conclusions relevant to any exploration of the relations between feminism and process thought. On the one hand, not even an intimate acquaintance with Whitehead's ideas is capable of *creating* feminist consciousness; such consciousness arises out of a certain kinds [*sic*] of life experience, explored in dialogue with other women.

had first of all to question within herself the assumption that contemporary theologians' description of the human situation was accurate. Importantly, the theological paradigm within which she worked at the time neither questioned this assumption nor provided the impetus to question it. The universal nature of the human situation was a fundamental 'given', an implicit anthropological assumption grounding and pervading the Christian theological paradigm within which she worked. When, within this paradigm, real, embodied women were occasionally noticed to be something of a problem or anomaly, the concept 'woman' was categorically 'adjusted' to fit within the 'universal' understanding of 'man'.[16] In Thomas Kuhn's words, the 'body of intertwined theoretical and methodological belief that permit[ted] selection, evaluation and criticism'[17] (or paradigm) within which Saiving worked accepted as a given the universality of the human condition. That 'given' regarding theological selection (a 'choice' of one universal understanding of humanity) in turn determined what could be evaluated: one universal understanding of the human situation. How then did Saiving come to step outside the theological paradigm of her time and question this universal theoretical premise?

On the other hand, feminist consciousness, once awakened, seeks a conceptual framework for self-understanding, and process philosophy may provide such a framework' [italics in original]. Valerie C. Saiving, 'Androgynous Life: A Feminist Appropriation of Process Thought', in Sheila Greeve Davaney (ed.), *Feminism and Process Thought* (Lewiston, NY: Edwin Mellen Press, 1981), pp. 12-13. Her epistemological assumptions are more evident in this quote than they are in 'The Human Situation', and include the following: making knowledge claims on the basis of lived experience, verifying these knowledge claims through discussion with others, and elaborating them through the process of dialogue instead of through solitary reflection.

16. Aquinas 'adjusted' woman by assigning to 'her' Aristotle's biological definition of woman as 'misbegotten male'; Jerome was willing for women to be women when involved with 'birth and children'; however, '...when she wishes to serve Christ more than the world, then she will cease to be a woman and will be called man (*vir*)' (quoted in Daly, *The Church and the Second Sex*, p. 85). Ambrose wrote: 'she who does not believe is a woman and should be designated by the name of her sex, whereas she who believes progresses to perfect manhood...' (quoted in Daly, *The Church and the Second Sex*, p. 85). And Karl Barth believed that, ontologically, 'man' was super-ordinate to 'woman' and 'woman' was sub-ordinate to 'man'.

17. Kuhn, *Structure*, pp. 16-17.

3. *Components of One Feminist* 73

Kuhn posits the presence of an anomaly as a critical instigating factor in a paradigm shift, so perhaps Saiving's personal situation as an anomaly, that is, as a female theologian in a field dominated and defined primarily by White men, meant that she was not as committed to maintaining the worldview of the old paradigm—a worldview which did not include her existence as fully human subject. This is only speculation on my part; however, Mary Daly's experience in 1966 of being called 'Miss Daly' by her colleagues at Boston College—when she possessed not one but three doctorates—lends credence to my supposition that Dr Saiving was probably not perceived to fit seamlessly within the theological worldview of the 1950s.[18]

Importantly, Saiving's analysis of the human situation included (1) a criticism of what had been presented as the universal human condition, (2) a transformation of the theological understanding of the human condition, and (3) a reformulation of the metaphors sin and love in accordance with the new anthropological presupposition. This mirrors precisely three aspects of paradigm formation. Kuhn repeatedly states that 'assimilating a new sort of fact demands a more than additive adjustment of theory':[19] that in fact a new paradigm requires changing 'the meaning of established and familiar concepts',[20] and that 'a new theory is always announced together with applications to some concrete range of natural phenomena'.[21]

To conclude, Saiving set about transforming Christian theological knowledge of the human situation by presenting a new anthropological presupposition (that of the full, unqualified humanity of women) through two revised metaphors, sin and love. Additionally, the values that informed her approach were significantly different from the values undergirding the old paradigm. For instance, Saiving considered that maintaining a 'self' was both a necessary aspect of full humanity and of greater value than giving all of one's self away. Epistemologically, she assumed that her interpretation of her own experiences and observations (an interpretation made in dialogue with others) was sufficient to base a knowledge claim on, and, having made this epistemological shift, she exposed the fact that the consequence of denying the diver-

---

18. Mary Daly, *Outercourse: The Be-Dazzling Voyage* (San Francisco: HarperCollins, 1992), p. 89.
19. Kuhn, *Structure*, p. 53.
20. Kuhn, *Structure*, p. 108.
21. Kuhn, *Structure*, p. 46.

sity of lived experience is found in the partiality of supposedly universal statements.[22]

Rosemary Radford Ruether's essay, 'Motherearth and the Megamachine', published in 1972 in *Christianity and Crisis* as well as in her book *Liberation Theology*, is an extended reflection on 'a set of dualities that still profoundly condition the modern worldview'.[23] Her thesis was that Christianity had inherited strands of Jewish apocalyptic thought which in turn had joined with and been reinforced by certain aspects of Platonic and neo-platonic thought. When combined, this inheritance proved to be profoundly 'world-negating' and to make itself felt in particular on the bodies of women and the earth itself.

> All the basic dualities—the alienation of the mind from the body; the alienation of the subjective self from the objective world; the subjective retreat of the individual, alienated from the social community; the domination or rejection of nature by spirit—these all have roots in the apocalyptic-Platonic religious heritage of classical Christianity. But the alienation of the masculine from the feminine is the primary sexual symbolism that sums up all these alienations. The psychic traits of intellectuality, transcendent spirit, and autonomous will that were identified with the male left the woman with the contrary traits of bodiliness, sensuality, and subjugation. Society, through the centuries, has in every way profoundly conditioned men and women to play out their lives and find their capacities within this basic antithesis.[24]

As she traces the origins of these dualities, Ruether identifies in the Jewish tradition a shift away from an earth-based religion, like that of the Canaanites, towards a historical faith. In other words, she suggests that as Jewish thought developed, the religious concept of 'the renewal of life' was more and more cut off from the earth or from any natural processes. Instead, such renewal was understood to come *with* the future as opposed to *from* the earth. Increasingly, this future hope was then identified not with any actual historical possibility but with 'the apocalyptic negation of history itself, [with] a cataclysmic world destruction and angelic new creation'.[25] This shift in emphasis from

---

22. See n. 14.
23. Rosemary Radford Ruether, 'Motherearth and the Megamachine: A Theology of Liberation in a Feminine, Somatic and Ecological Perspective', in Christ and Plaskow (eds.), *Womanspirit Rising*, p. 43.
24. Ruether, 'Motherearth', p. 44.
25. Ruether, 'Motherearth', p. 44.

this world to a hoped for future world was accompanied by a value judgment: this material world was considered inferior to that which was to come. Unfortunately, this judgment of the earth as an inferior place resonated with two closely related strands of Platonic thought: Plato's insistence on the absolute distinction between bodies and souls and his characterization of the female body as an inferior home (when compared with the male body) for the soul. While the soul's desired home was in the heavens, that is, the *ideal* was the soul freed from any body at all (described by Ruether in terms of 'liberation [as] a flight from the earth to a changeless, infinite world beyond'[26]), on the earth it was far better to be incarnate in male than in female form. In Ruether's words, 'Christianity brought together both of these myths—the myth of world cataclysm and the myth of the flight of the soul to heaven'.[27] Instead of treating them as myths, however, in Christian thought they were accepted as fundamental metaphysical presuppositions.

Ruether's two-sentence description of the effect of these presuppositions on 'man's' psyche served to identify the 'why' behind the ecological crisis (with which she was and remains deeply concerned), sexism, racism, classism and colonization:

> What we see in this development is a one-sided expression of the ego, claiming its transcendental autonomy *by negating the finite matrix of existence*. This antithesis is projected socially by identifying woman as the incarnation of this debasing threat of bodily existence, while the same polarized model of the psyche is projected politically upon suppressed or conquered social groups [italics added].[28]

In accepting *as descriptive of reality itself* an understanding of the material stuff of this earth as being of less inherent value and worth than the 'stuff' of a future earth (an entirely new creation) and in accepting *as descriptive of reality itself* an understanding of all human bodies (but female bodies most of all) as being of less inherent value and worth than a distinct and separable soul that seeks eternal life in a place not of this world, i.e., heaven, the early Church Fathers contributed to the establishment of a dualistic worldview integral to which was the denigration and devaluation of this world and this-worldly, especially female, bodies. For two millennia (in the Christian West, at least) social reality has been constructed on the basis of this dualistic

---

26. Ruether, 'Motherearth', p. 48.
27. Ruether, 'Motherearth', p. 49.
28. Ruether, 'Motherearth', p. 49.

worldview. As a result, noted Ruether, at this time a woman 'literally finds *reality itself* stacked against her, making the combination of maternal and masculine occupations all but impossible without extraordinary energy or enough wealth to hire domestic help' (italics in original). She went on to say that 'women simply cannot be persons within the present system of work and family, and they can only rise to liberated personhood by the most radical and fundamental reshaping of the entire human environment...'[29]

Ruether's point was that the 'modern technological environment' had been constructed to keep all but the most extraordinary (and generally elite) women firmly in their 'place', that is, living according to the roles assigned to women—as wife and mother and homemaker.[30] Accordingly, she understood the physical (as in physically created) structure of Western culture, particularly urban centres, to have been constructed on the basis of a set of erroneous metaphysical presuppositions and their accompanying value judgments, i.e., that female bodies are of less inherent worth and value than male bodies, that separable souls exist and are of more value than mortal bodies, and that this earth is of less inherent worth and value than a future creation. Importantly, while implicitly rejecting these metaphysical presuppositions as factually erroneous (and rejecting their accompanying value judgments as morally untenable), Ruether contended that any society constructed on the basis of them in effect turned them into reality. In other words, these metaphysical presuppositions became so embedded in the social fabric and the psyches of the men and women constructing that society that they *did* shape reality: the subjugation of women as a category influenced the construction of the physical environments in which we all live and work, as well as the reality of the global oppression of the poor and the destruction of the earth's natural resources. Accordingly, she recognized a pressing need to name alternative meta-

---

29. Ruether, 'Motherearth', p. 44.

30. Ruether, 'Motherearth', p. 44. 'The plan of our cities is made in this image: The sphere of domesticity, rest, and childrearing where women are segregated is clearly separated from those corridors down which men advance in assault upon the world of "work"'. There is in this essay an implicit assumption that a 'wife' and 'mother' would never *have* to work outside the 'home' in order to support herself, her children, or her male partner. There is thus a class- and race-bias running throughout this piece, and Ruether's interpretation of modern social reality is incomplete, focused as it is almost exclusively on the corridors of power.

physical presuppositions, and to base the structure of a new social reality upon them. However, in order to express these new metaphysical presuppositions she needed to use new (or, more accurately, transformed) metaphors and models.

Therefore, using the familiar metaphors 'humanity', 'reconciliation', 'salvation', 'messianic', and 'earth', she tells a new story, a story in which she introduces the model of 'the cultivation of the garden' and radically transforms the model of 'the body of God'. Above all else her story is based on a set of metaphysical presuppositions radically different from the ones she outlined in the first part of her essay. 'Reconciliation' is the most prominent metaphor in this new story, appearing when she describes the 'new humanity' she envisions: 'a new humanity arising out of the reconciliation of spirit and body'.[31] 'Reconciliation' appears again when she describes what she is writing toward: 'a post-technological religion of reconciliation with the body, the woman and the world', and yet again when she writes about this religion: 'its salvation myth will not be one of divinization and flight from the body but of humanization and reconciliation with the earth'.[32] Finally, in describing 'the new earth' she writes that 'the new earth must be one where people are reconciled with their labor...a world where people are reconciled to their own finitude...'.[33]

Theologically Ruether is making an extraordinary shift when she uses the metaphor 'reconciliation' in these sentences, for it is evident that she is not presupposing a God as the active reconciling agent in her 'salvation myth'. Traditionally, 'reconciliation' is understood to be accomplished by God and God alone. That is, humanity was (after the fall) metaphysically characterised as separate from and in need of reconciliation with God, but only God could do the reconciling. Humans, in the traditional account of reconciliation, are individual, passive recipients of God's grace. As Ruether uses the metaphor however, *people working together* are the ones who must accomplish

---

31. Ruether, 'Motherearth', p. 51. The 'humanity' she envisions is thus never disembodied, not even (perhaps especially not) theoretically or in the abstract. Descartes' famous pronouncement concerning his existence, 'cogito ergo sum', or 'I think therefore I am', is literally nonsensical when the fact of human bodies is accepted as inseparable from the fact of human existence.
32. Ruether, 'Motherearth', p. 52.
33. Ruether, 'Motherearth', p. 52.

their own reconciliation, who must reacquaint themselves with their own bodies, must stop trying to separate their own (or others') bodies and souls and intellects, and must acknowledge their dependent relationship upon this earth and all the creatures who inhabit it, including each other. The 'new humanity' she envisions is thus comprised of a reconciled people forming a society (in the largest sense of that term) that does not structure any lives on the bases of hierarchical dualities but that does acknowledge the embodied limits and finitude of humankind as well as the double-edged character of human intellectual and technological abilities.[34] Ruether's conception of 'reconciliation' is thus a careful acknowledgment that, individually, 'full personhood' has a communal, participatory component *and* involves the embodiment of intellect and spirit, and that, collectively, social reality is inextricably both technological (or humanly created) and natural.[35] Reconciliation, as she envisions it, leads to the possibility of salvation.

Not surprisingly, 'salvation' in this schema refers to a collective, ongoing process, expressed by Ruether through the model of 'the cultivation of the garden': 'Our model is neither the romanticized primitive jungle nor the modern technological wasteland. Rather it expresses itself in a new command to learn to cultivate the garden...'[36] Within

---

34. Ruether, 'Motherearth', p. 50. Ruether discusses the situation where, in the West, 'alienated members of the dominant society are seeking new communal, egalitarian life-styles, ecological living patterns, and the redirection of psychic energy toward reconciliation with the body' but amongst 'insurgent Third World peoples, [their] aspirations rise along the lines of the traditional rise of civilization through group pride, technological domination of nature and antagonistic, competitive relationships between peoples'. Ruether notes that Western human potential movements are 'elitist, privatistic, esthetic and devoid of a profound covenant with the poor and oppressed of the earth'. And she notes also that, as regards the Third World, 'such tendencies might be deplored by those who so far have monopolized technology and now believe they have seen the end of its fruitfulness, but they must be recognized as still relevant to the liberation of the poor and oppressed from material necessity and psychological dependency'. Hers is thus not a facile embrace of the body and rejection of technology. Instead, she is attempting a 'both/and' rather than an 'either/or' theological approach. Which aspect she emphasizes at any one time is always relative to the context about which she is writing at that time.

35. Regarding the communal element of personhood, see Ruether, 'Motherearth', p. 51, where she writes of a 'communal personhood that could participate in the successes of others rather than seeing these as merely a threat to one's own success'.

36. Ruether, 'Motherearth', p. 52.

this model 'salvation' is not the sole prerogative of a God above; it is neither an eternal state nor concerned with bodiless souls. Instead it is brought down to earth and reconnected to the soil, to physical matter, while simultaneously allowed a historical aspect. Rather than a one-off event, 'the cultivation of the garden' is a process that takes place in history and must be continually enacted by finite historical agents. Salvation is thus a communal process, one firmly rooted in 'the finite matrix of existence'. To put it another way, whether salvation happens or not is up to constantly changing communities, whose members are constantly being born and dying, each one with a unique relationship to and dependency upon the earth. For the communities to endure (in history) the earth must be cultivated with extreme care. Therefore *the site of salvation, or the cultivation of the garden, is this earth*. Again, salvation is the work, not of a God above or a God-on-earth-for-a-little-minute, but of reconciled humanity, which is inspired by *a value judgment* in the form of 'a polylinguistic appreciativeness that can redeem local space, time, and identity'.[37] Practically speaking, this means that non-human creation no less than humanity is acknowledged to be diverse, and accompanying this acknowledgment is an appreciation of diversity, of plurality. Finally, in the garden 'the powers of rational consciousness come together with the harmonies of nature in partnership'.[38]

As Ruether envisions it, 'in the garden' humanity is totally reconciled with the earth, but this involves more than acknowledging human dependency for life on the rest of creation. Humans are that part of the earth able to contemplate and direct the effects of their actions upon the rest of creation. Salvation therefore involves the careful redirection of human actions that have been perceived to be harmful to other aspects of creation. Salvation, in short, is about enabling the renewal of life, and not simply human lives. It is not about preserving individual lives or personalities, but is about enabling the possibility of life itself. In other words, salvation is about caring for 'the finite matrix of existence'. This is, I suggest, what Ruether meant when she named her essay 'a theology of liberation in a feminine, somatic and *ecological* perspective'. Salvation, as expressed through the model of 'the cultivation of the garden', is an ongoing, active and always partial and

---

37. Ruether, 'Motherearth', p. 52.
38. Ruether, 'Motherearth', p. 52.

incomplete process. It is realized (and not realized) on earth in history through human actions. Importantly, underlying and supporting Ruether's 'salvation myth' is an implicit metaphysical presupposition, that of *the inherent integrity of non-human creation*. By this expression I mean to point toward Ruether's affirmation of the value of creation apart from humankind. This affirmation, which is simultaneously a value judgment and a metaphysical presupposition, is a central tenet in her thought. Put positively, 'the finite matrix of existence' is blessed and good in and of itself. Put negatively, non-human creation is *not* to be perceived solely as a resource for humankind to use until it runs out. The earth and the creatures of the earth *do not* exist merely as 'means' to human 'ends', but are inherently worthy in and of themselves.

Another model for the reconciled humanity whose work is the cultivation of the garden (or the ongoing process of salvation) is 'the body of God'. When Ruether writes of a 'messianic appearing of the body of God', the 'body' of which she writes is clearly communal. As community(ies), the body of God (reconciled humanity) makes incarnate 'a living pattern of mutuality between men and women, between parents and children, among people in their social, economic, and political relationships and, finally, between mankind [*sic*] and the organic harmonies of nature'.[39] Further, the 'messianic' (meaning, as she uses the term, salvific—but not tied in any way to an individual saviour) aim of the body of God 'must be the total abolition of the social pattern of domination and subjugation and the erection of a new communal social ethic. We need to build a new cooperative social order out beyond the principles of hierarchy, rule, and competitiveness'.[40] In keeping with the language of this quotation, which is strikingly reminiscent of that of the Social Gospel movement, the task of the 'body of God' (or reconciled humanity) about which Ruether writes is to bring about the kingdom of God on earth.

To summarize, where there once was a transcendent God, there is in Ruether's thought a reconciled humanity. What was formerly God's work, the work of reconciliation and salvation, is in Ruether's thought humanity's work. Where there once was a heaven above, there is in

---

39. Ruether, 'Motherearth', p. 52. In the 'body of God' model I also read the merest hint of a possibility that non-human earth creatures as well as the physical soil, rock, water, and air of the earth are an integral part of the body of God, but to be truthful I am probably projecting later Ruether back into this early essay.

40. Ruether, 'Motherearth', p. 51.

Ruether's thought a 'finite matrix of existence'. Where there once were souls temporarily housed in more or less satisfactory bodies, in Ruether's thought there are finite persons, each embodied and each endowed with the capacity to participate for a limited time in the thoughtful, ongoing, communal creation of salvation on earth. To repeat, there is no transcendent God in Ruether's 'Motherearth and the Megamachine' essay.[41] She does not posit on the part of humankind a need for a single saviour figure or for eternal individual salvation, and she likewise rejects the metaphysical presupposition of a heaven above. She affirms the full, unqualified humanity of women, but asserts that the traditional Christian metaphysical presupposition denying the full humanity of women has caused social reality to be constructed in such a way as to make almost impossible the full, living personhood of any but 'an elite few' women.[42] Likewise, she acknowledges that the same set of metaphysical dualities has been used to deny the full humanity of non-elite men of all races and classes, as well as to justify the domination of the earth and the creatures of the earth. She replaces the metaphysical presupposition/value judgment that ranked humankind but a little lower than angels (and much higher than the earth or the creatures of the earth) with the metaphysical presupposition of the inherent integrity of all non-human creation, and she judges harshly the lived consequences of the previous dualistic metaphysical presuppositions. She presents a new worldview through the transformed metaphors of 'reconciliation', 'salvation', 'humanity', 'messianic' (transformed in that she does not associate that which is 'messianic' or salvific with a single saviour figure) and 'earth' (a transformed metaphor because Ruether tacitly accepts the earth as a part of the finite matrix of existence and does not denigrate or devalue it as mere matter). She also

---

41. Just exactly how Ruether does characterize God is a critical question, and one I that shall take up and explore in Chapter 6. This essay is typical Ruether, however, in that usually she writes of God not at all, other than to identify how past (elite male) theologians have characterised 'him'.

42. Ruether, 'Motherearth', p. 44. Ruether never denies the full humanity of anyone—male or female, oppressor or oppressed—but with her use of the expression 'full personhood' she indicates that human lives can be thwarted or not allowed to develop to their fullest potential, something that is enabled precisely when the 'full, unqualified humanity' of any category of people is disallowed by the prevailing metaphysical presuppositions. It is noteworthy that she criticizes Karl Barth precisely for perpetuating an understanding of 'woman' as subordinate to 'man'. See above.

expands on the metaphor of 'salvation' via the model of 'the cultivation of the garden', and lastly she completely recreates the model of 'the body of God', applying it in a communal sense to her vision of a new, reconciled humanity.

In short, in 'Motherearth and the Megamachine' Ruether writes from a whole new *set* of metaphysical presuppositions. Whereas Saiving had proposed one new anthropological presupposition through two transformed metaphors, Ruether introduces two new models and at least five transformed metaphors in order to express a new theological worldview. Saiving's anthropological presupposition (that of the full, unqualified humanity of women) and metaphors (sin and love as both self- and other-negating and self- and other-affirming) are implicit within this new worldview. But Ruether presents an entire (at least in rudimentary form) metaphysical outlook when she denies the existence of a future new creation wholly other than this earth and insists that 'salvation' involves, at a minimum, the ongoing renewal of non-human creation and is the responsibility of humankind.[43] Additionally, she expresses the vast scope of one feminist Christian theological endeavour when she presents (through her identification of those hierarchical dualisms in which all that is spiritual, intellectual, rational, good, holy, pure, light, above, etc. is identified with men—and in particular with elite males—and all that is physical, earthly, emotional, bad, evil, dirty, dark, below, etc. is identified with women and/or non-elite males, depending on context) the means for other feminist theologians to discern how reality as known in Western culture has been ordered through the ages by elite males. For Ruether, feminist Christian theology was and is about nothing less than the re-ordering of reality itself.[44]

Along with Ruether, Mary Daly was one of the first to grasp the nature and extent of this task. In her essay, 'After the Death of God the

---

43. Ruether thus also implicitly embraces a transformed understanding of eschatology (the study of end or last times).

44. See also Collins, *A Different Heaven and Earth*, pp. 16 and 189. Collins describes as a 'predominant theme' amongst early feminist theologians the attempt 'to find new criteria by which to order reality'. She also names as a fundamental feminist theological issue the effort 'to enable others to see through the cracks of the present reality system...' This supports my contention that feminist Christian theology involved, from its inception, a metaphysical component. Not incidentally, Collins continues by asserting that a 'new language' is needed to convey a different reality.

3. *Components of One Feminist* 83

Father', Daly begins by noting that the women's liberation movement had by that time already identified 'the oppressive character of our cultural institutions' as well as a long history of misogyny in 'the Judaic-Christian tradition'. She goes on to say that 'we now have to ask how the women's revolution can and should change our whole vision of reality'.[45] Immediately, then, Daly makes explicit the fact that positing new metaphysical assumptions, or a new vision of reality, is a central element in her work. Strikingly, Daly begins to answer her own question, how can the women's revolution change reality, by discussing 'values'. Continuous with this emphasis she later discusses what she terms 'the transvaluation of values', a process she believes is propelled by the 'becoming of women', which is in turn only possible when the pre-existing, constrictive metaphysical presuppositions concerning 'woman' have been called into question.[46] To understand why 'values' are so important in her thought it is necessary to note that throughout this essay Daly inextricably links 'values' with 'culture', repeatedly implying that the structures, ideologies and symbol systems of a culture are the outward manifestations of that culture's values. According to Daly, religion, or a 'belief system', plays a significant role in this process.

> What is happening, of course, is the familiar mechanism by which the images and values of a given society are projected into a realm of beliefs, which in turn justify the social infrastructure. The belief system becomes hardened and objectified, seeming to have an unchangeable independent existence and validity of its own. It resists social change which would

---

45. Mary Daly, 'After the Death of God the Father', in Christ and Plaskow (eds.), *Womanspirit Rising: A Feminist Reader in Religion* (San Francisco: Harper & Row, 1979), pp. 53-54.

46. Daly, 'After the Death', p. 60. Daly writes, 'The becoming of women implies also a transvaluation of values in Christian morality. As the old order is challenged and as men and women become freed to experience a wholeness of personality which the old polarizations impeded, the potentiality will be awakened for a change in moral consciousness which will go far beyond Nietzsche's merely reactionary rejection of Christian values'. See also Mary Daly, *Beyond God the Father* (Boston: Beacon Press, 1973), p. 36, where she writes that '[women's] exclusion from identity within patriarchy has had a totality about it which, when faced, calls forth an ontological self-affirmation'. Metaphysics and ethics are thus distinct but inseparable (better, they are two sides of the same coin) in Daly's thought. Values and metaphysical presuppositions support and sanction (justify) each other, and to challenge one is to call into question the other as well.

rob it of its plausibility. Nonetheless, despite the vicious circle, change does occur in society, and ideologies die, though they die hard.[47]

Daly implies that in order for social change to occur on a widespread scale the values and images supporting the status quo must first be questioned. Accordingly, she asserts that the 'women's revolution' calls into question at least two fundamental cultural images, that of 'masculinity' and its inherently less worthy counterpart, 'femininity'. Daly describes 'the eternal masculine stereotype' as connoting 'hyper-rationality, "objectivity", aggressivity, the possession of dominating and manipulative attitudes toward persons and environment, and the tendency to construct boundaries between the self (and those identified with the self) and the "other"'. She then describes 'the eternal feminine' as 'hyperemotional, passive, self-abasing, etc.'.[48]

She characterizes these images as partial 'caricatures' of human beings, and goes on to say that 'by becoming whole persons, women can generate a counterforce to the stereotype...as they challenge the artificial polarization of human characteristics'.[49] The notion of 'becoming' is critical in this essay; unfortunately, it is also complicated, for with the one term or metaphor Daly is alluding to both the ontological potential of an individual (or category of humanity) and that individual's (or category's) anthropological actualization of her or his (or its) potential. Like Saiving and Ruether, Daly envisions a social reality, or a culture, in which women are able to become 'whole persons' (Saiving and Daly) or to achieve 'full, liberated personhood' (Ruether). She values human 'wholeness' rather than prescribed (that is, metaphysically defined and sanctioned) partiality. Once again linking the metaphysical notion of 'wholeness' with values, she writes that

47. Daly, 'After the Death', p. 54. Presumably by the terms 'familiar mechanism' and 'projected' Daly is referring to the thought of Ludwig Feuerbach, Karl Marx, and Sigmund Freud, each of whom, albeit differently, posited God as a human creation onto whom humans continually projected their own hopes and fears and fantasies.

48. Daly, 'After the Death', p. 55. There are a few problematic elements in her account of the 'eternal' masculine and feminine stereotypes, most particularly the way in which she applies them to all cultures in the world since time immemorial. (Saiving's description of 'women's experience of motherhood' was similarly sweeping.) However, as descriptive of White, North American images of masculinity and femininity prevalent at the very least in the latter third of the twentieth century, I take her descriptions to be quite accurate.

49. Daly, 'After the Death', p. 55.

3. *Components of One Feminist* 85

'this becoming of *whole* human beings will affect the values of our society, for it will involve a change in the fabric of human consciousness'.[50] As in Ruether's essay, the implication in Daly's thought is that social reality is physically constructed on the basis of those values and metaphysical presuppositions that constitute the prevailing 'fabric of human consciousness'. Like Saiving and Ruether, Daly suggests that the full potential of women's and men's lives has been thwarted because 'woman' and 'man' (and by implication real live women and men) have been assigned only a limited range of supposedly suitable metaphysical characteristics.[51] In her words, she 'wishes to foster the evolution of consciousness beyond the oppressiveness and imbalance reflected and justified by symbols and doctrines throughout the millennia of patriarchy'.[52] And, again like Ruether, Daly suggests that human beings are thoroughly communal, or are in some way dependent on a supportive community in order to become ever more wholly who they are: 'human beings are called to self-actualization and to the creation of a community that fosters the becoming of women and men'.[53] Thus her self-proclaimed goal of 'the evolution of consciousness' beyond

50. Daly, 'After the Death', p. 55 (italics in original).
51. To a much greater extent in *The Church and the Second Sex*, *Beyond God the Father* and *Gyn/Ecology* than in 'After the Death of God the Father', Daly traces male thought patterns that justified, sanctioned and sometimes initiated social 'policing' of women's lives, or women's 'becoming'. I do not wish to imply that Daly's gift to feminist theology is her ability as a historian. What is remarkable about her work, however, is her ability to discern underlying metaphysical presuppositions and value judgments that deny the full, unqualified humanity of women-as-a-category, or women-in-the-abstract. Above all else Daly is concerned to liberate the *image* or the *symbol* 'woman' from several millennia of devalued confinement, for example, as only virgin, wife or whore. I believe that her whole body of work can be interpreted as an effort to create a theoretical 'space' in which real live (and diverse numbers of) women can explore their ontological potentialities. A close reading of Daly indicates that she wishes women's ontological potential never again to be limited by inhibiting metaphysical presuppositions. This is, at any rate, how I interpret Daly, and I believe it makes sense of her apparent confusion when real live women suggest to her that they are not represented in her work; indeed they are not, nor did she ever intend to write them in. Instead, she invites her readers to live their own lives in the absence (or at least with the awareness of the shadow) of centuries of debilitating, misogynist metaphysical presuppositions.
52. Daly, 'After the Death', p. 56.
53. Daly, 'After the Death', p. 59.

constricting metaphysical presuppositions regarding 'woman' and 'man' is dependent for its realization upon a widespread, cultural metanoia (conversion). That is, unless one is a member of a community (and, she would probably agree, society) that supports one's full, unqualified humanity, one's potential 'becoming' will inevitably be hindered because one cannot actualize any potential that one is a priori deemed not to possess.[54]

Beginning, then, with the metaphysical presupposition of the full, unqualified humanity of women, and linking this presupposition with the large-scale transformation of cultural images, symbols and value judgments concerning the relative worth of women and men, with what models and metaphors does Daly attempt to 'remythologize' Christianity?[55] In this essay Daly presents one revised model, that of 'the Second Coming of God', and she presents a transformed account of the metaphors of 'incarnation', 'revelation', and 'sin'. In order to understand Daly's revised account of 'incarnation' (and following from it, her account of 'the Second Coming of God') it is necessary to begin with her preferred model for 'God', which she borrows directly from Paul Tillich; that is, God as the power and ground of being. Daly acknowledges that 'Tillich's language of transcendence' is not the only language adequate to the task of representing or alluding to that which is of ultimate concern; she notes that '[the language] of Whitehead, James, Jaspers—or an entirely new language—may do as well or better'.[56] Nonetheless in this essay she does insist that 'authentic religious consciousness' is possible only when 'courage in the face of

---

54. In this regard Daly noted that Karl Barth posited 'woman' as 'ontologically subordinate to man', which makes it impossible for any woman to be perceived as an equal to any man ('After the Death', p. 54).

55. Daly, 'After the Death', p. 59. Regarding a perceived need to 'remythologize' Western religions, see also Collins, *A Different Heaven and Earth*, p. 21. It is notable also that Ruether wrote of a new 'salvation myth' rather than insisting on the eternal truth of one version of 'salvation'. I suggest that all of these writers are aware of the transitory nature of human understanding or 'truth' claims, but are simultaneously aware of a human need to 'myth' the point in order to understand at all.

56. Daly, 'After the Death', p. 58. This statement is significant (in that it supports my contention in the previous chapter of the influence of existentialist and process thought on feminist Christian theology) because here Daly takes up an existentialist approach to god-talk while explicitly acknowledging the plausibility of Whitehead's process approach.

anxiety' is embraced by an individual. She thus, for no apparent reason, ties herself to Tillich's very individualistic notion of 'the courage to be', which means, roughly, to affirm continually one's existence in the face of non-being, and in so doing she contradicts her earlier emphasis on the necessarily communal element of an individual's 'whole' personhood. Within her own expressed metaphysical presuppositions this notion does not fit. She uses Tillich's God-language, however, because she believes that his model, 'god' as the power and ground of all being, is almost impossible to use to sanction the subordination or oppression of any aspect of reality, human or non-human. On the level of image, 'the power and ground of being' supports and indeed suffuses all that is, which does fit within her metaphysical presuppositions, and which thought leads directly to Daly's transformed understanding of the metaphor 'incarnation'.

Rather than accepting the traditional understanding of 'incarnation' as limited to Jesus of Nazareth being fully divine and fully human, Daly extends the notion to include all of humanity.

> As a uniquely masculine divinity loses credibility, so also the idea of a unique divine incarnation in a human being of the male sex may give way in the religious consciousness to an increased awareness of the divine presence in all human beings, understood as expressing and in a real sense incarnating—although always inadequately—the power of being.[57]

Just as Ruether described a reconciled humanity as being 'the body of God', Daly describes the communal awakening of women 'to their human potential' in terms of God being made manifest in themselves, that is, in the lives of women living *into* their full potential rather than *according to* a restrictive set of alienating stereotypes. She calls this development 'the Second Coming of God incarnate', which is, not incidentally, the theological equivalent of waving a red flag at a wounded bull.[58] However, when read through the lens provided by her earlier comments on incarnation this statement cannot be interpreted as

---

57. Daly, 'After the Death', p. 59.
58. Daly, 'After the Death', p. 60. Traditionally (at least since 150 CE and Justin's *Apology*) the parousia, or the second coming, has been conceived as the triumphant return to earth of Christ, expressed in the Nicene Creed through the words 'He will come again in glory to judge the living and the dead'. To characterize the second coming as happening in ordinary women's lives is thus quite a theological shift.

poetic embellishment, but must be taken literally. She sees women, via the women's liberation movement, as both embodying and expressing the power of being (which is God) in a manner *heretofore unknown*.[59] 'The Second Coming of God' is thus a model expressive of both God as the power and ground of being and Daly's understanding of the category 'women' as participating in making God incarnate, or making actual that which is, without the full participation of *womankind* no less than mankind, only potential.

One of the more profound theological implications of Daly's assertion that the ground and power of being (God) is made incarnate in human lives is that, in so characterizing God, she must deny the notion of divine aseity, or self-sufficiency. In other words, implicit in her claim that humanity makes 'god' incarnate is the idea that, at least to some degree, God *needs* humanity in order to be made incarnate in that particular manner. Or, to put it another way, humanity makes actual a part of God which is, without humanity, only potential. If, as Daly implies, the ground and power of being can only exist in conjunction *with* and be known *through* being-itself, then insofar as humankind is a unique aspect of being, individual humans make incarnate unique aspects of God. Practically expressed, as babies are born into the world, so too is God born anew; as people die, so too do different incarnations of God die. God, far from being self-sufficient and immutable (or unchanging), needs humankind to make actual aspects of the power of being. This means, though, that God is constantly changing just as humans are constantly changing—physically, insofar as they are physically incarnate, and experientially, insofar as they incorporate new experiences into their lives and are affected by those experiences.

This implication, that the power and ground of being is ever-changing because being-itself is ever-changing, is not explicitly named

---

59. Daly, 'After the Death', pp. 54-55. Daly describes the 'women's revolution' as 'transforming the fabric of society from patriarchy into something that never existed before—into a diarchical situation that is radically new'. She says also, 'What I am discussing here is an emergence of women such as has never taken place before'. I take her comments to mean that she believes that at this time the 'emergence of women' is happening on such a scale as to bring about the cultural transformation of those metaphysical presuppositions that had equated 'woman' with 'feminine'. In other words, she perceives the women's revolution as having the strength to alter 'society's' prevailing assumptions about men and women. Unfortunately, which society she is talking about she never indicates, although she does discuss Western religion.

by Daly in this essay.⁶⁰ Nonetheless in order for her one sentence description of 'revelation' to make sense, the idea that being-itself as well as the ground and power of being is ever-changing is a necessary metaphysical presupposition. This is the case because when Daly asserts that she is critical of what she terms 'idolatry' that is often disguised as 'faith' or 'revelation', she explains herself by stating that 'revelation is an ongoing experience'.⁶¹ She says nothing more about revelation, but to posit it as ongoing is to reject the idea that 'revelation' could ever be contained in the life-event of a particular individual or in a set of writings about a past historical figure. If 'revelation' has something to do with the expression of that which is of ultimate concern (her understanding, again following Tillich, of 'faith'), and if 'revelation' is ongoing, then what is of ultimate concern cannot be static and immutable, but must change as being-itself changes. Thus no single revelation could ever be sufficient or expressive of the entire 'truth' of being, and to suggest otherwise would indeed be idolatrous.⁶² To put it another way, because being-itself is unfinished, to latch onto any one manifestation of it as completely revelatory of God or the whole ground and power of being (which is also mutable and, by implication, incomplete) is to participate in idol worship.

From this metaphysical ground it is but a short step to Daly's understanding of 'sin', which, although she does not expressly define it, can be stated as anything that inhibits or renders impossible the 'becoming'

---

60. It is noteworthy that this implication resonates strongly with process thought, more so, in fact, than with an existentialist approach.

61. Daly, 'After the Death', p. 60.

62. In Chapter 12 of *Liberation Theology* (entitled 'Latin American Liberation Theology and the Birth of a Planetary Humanity', which indicates her stance toward the full, unqualified humanity of all) Rosemary Ruether defines 'revelation' as 'that redeeming and liberating insight which makes people aware of the social contradictions that define their lives, and thrusts them toward a process of liberation from dependency and oppression'. Ruether, *Liberation Theology*, p. 183. Like Daly, she thus understands 'revelation' as ongoing, but Ruether explicitly relates revelation with the liberation of real lives from situations of oppression. She thus links revelation and action (or practical concern) in a way that Daly does not and cannot insofar as Daly links revelation with ultimate concern and allows a distinction to seep into her thought regarding that which is of ultimate and that which is of practical concern. Daly does, however, associate 'sin' with practical concerns, specifically, occasions of oppression. In this regard she and Ruether are in complete agreement.

(again a term best understood as the anthropological actualization of ontological potential) of any body or category of bodies. Or, to turn it around, that which is oppressive is sinful. What Daly stresses, however, is that beneath outward manifestations of sin, or actual instances of the oppression of (an)other(s), there are underlying beliefs and structures that promote and enable the oppression of entire categories of 'others'.[63] Traditional Christian conceptualizations of sin as an individual's action against God or God's commandments are described by Daly as examples of 'a privatized morality'.[64] Such a 'privatized morality' can neither acknowledge nor condemn the fact of *structures* of oppression, such as laws, public policies, unspoken practices and traditions that discriminate against entire categories of humanity. Further, such a 'privatized morality' can in no way be used as an analytical tool to discern the underlying metaphysical presuppositions that justify and cause to seem 'natural' the 'structures themselves of oppression'.[65] In moving the discussion of 'sin' away from an exclusive focus on individual actions, then, Daly is able to name as 'sinful' social structures and practices that have seemed, to those whose lives are not oppressed by them, perfectly 'natural' and/or ordained by God. Such a revised understanding of 'sin' is ultimately dependent, however, on a prior metaphysical presupposition, and that is the assertion of the full, unqualified humanity of *all*. In Daly's case, however, like Rosemary Ruether, she is explicitly concerned not only with the oppression of some categories of humanity by others but also with the degradation of the wider environment. Thus she understands that non-human creation can be sinned against.

---

63. Daly, 'After the Death', p. 61: 'It is well known that Christians under the spell of the jealous God who represents the collective power of his chosen people can use religion to justify that "us and them" attitude which is disastrous in its consequences for the powerless. It is less widely understood that the projection of "the other"—easily adaptable to national, racial and class differences—has basically and primordially been directed against women'.

64. Daly, 'After the Death', p. 61. Daly notes, in terms reminiscent of Saiving, that 'there has been theoretical emphasis upon charity, meekness, obedience, humility, self-abnegation, sacrifice, service. Part of the problem with this moral ideology is that it became generally accepted not by men but by women, who have hardly been helped by an ethic which reinforces their abject situation'.

65. Daly, 'After the Death', p. 61. Daly's emphasis on the structures of oppression as being sinful is, like Ruether's, closely related to the understanding of sinful social structures expressed in the Social Gospel movement.

> The consciousness raising which is beginning among women is evoking a qualitatively new understanding of the subtle mechanisms which produce and destroy 'the other', and a consequent empathy with all of the oppressed. This gives ground for the hope that their emergence can generate a counterforce to the exploitative mentality which is destroying persons and the environment.[66]

And underlying her contention that the environment can be sinned against is the metaphysical presupposition (and, simultaneously, value judgment) introduced in Ruether's essay, that of the inherent integrity of non-human creation.

To summarize, in 'After the Death of God the Father' Mary Daly writes from two fundamental metaphysical presuppositions, that of the full, unqualified humanity of women and men, and that of the inherent integrity of non-human creation. She identifies a necessarily communal or social aspect to the 'becoming' of women and men, and she stresses that the actual 'becoming' of entire categories of humanity is inextricably linked to the metaphysical potential associated with that category of humanity within the prevailing social order. To put it another way, she proposes that the limits inherent in the understanding of 'being' associated with a specific category or class of humankind directly affect the ability of individuals within that category to actualize their full potential. To realize oneself in any way 'outside' of one's *assumed* potential is almost impossible in that one is not perceived within the wider society as being capable of stepping outside one's pre-determined, symbolically conveyed, metaphysical limits. In order to convey her own metaphysical presuppositions Daly adopts Tillich's model of God as ground and power of being and reconceptualizses the metaphors 'incarnation', 'revelation', and 'sin'. She develops her notion of 'incarnation' through the transformed model of 'the Second Coming of God'—a model strikingly consonant with Ruether's transformed model of reconciled humanity as 'the body of God'. Like Ruether (yet again), within Daly's theological worldview there is no need for a solitary saviour figure.[67]

---

66. Daly, 'After the Death', p. 61.
67. Daly, 'After the Death', p. 58. Daly writes, 'An effect of the liberation of women will very likely be the loss of plausibility of Christological formulas which come close to reflecting a kind of idolatry in regard to the person of Jesus. As it becomes better understood that God is transcendent and unobjectifiable—or else not at all—it will become less plausible to speak of Jesus as the Second Person of the

Taken together, what do my readings of these three essays indicate concerning the paradigmatic aspects of feminist Christian theology? In Thomas Kuhn's essay, 'Reflections on My Critics', he delves into two aspects of paradigm formation that seem to be inextricably interlinked. He says that 'in the absence of a neutral language, the choice of a new theory is a decision to adopt *a different native language* and to deploy it *in a correspondingly different world*' (italics added).[68] While Saiving's essay is now considered to be a landmark feminist theological text, in fact neither the 'language' nor the 'world' in which it is now discussed and understood 'existed' when she first published it. To quote from Christ and Plaskow, 'Her article was reprinted once, and then, like [Elizabeth Cady Stanton's] *The Woman's Bible*, was forgotten'.[69] However, when Saiving's essay is read together with Ruether's 'Motherearth and the Megamachine' and Daly's 'After the Death of God the Father', I suggest that both the 'different native language' and the 'different world' Kuhn names begin to be revealed. Taking the language of Christian theology and transforming it completely—by linking it with a set of metaphysical presuppositions that had never been combined before—these women established the basic vocabulary necessary to comprehend and discuss feminist Christian theology. Together they redefined the metaphors 'sin', 'love', 'reconciliation', 'salvation', 'messiah/messianic', 'incarnation' and 'revelation', and introduced or reconceptualized the models 'the cultivation of the garden', 'the body of God', and 'the Second Coming of God'.[70]

Regarding 'the world' in and of which they wrote, underlying this feminist Christian theological paradigm are three primary metaphysical presuppositions: that of the full, unqualified and embodied humanity of all women, men and children without exception; that of the inherent

---

Trinity who 'assumed' a human nature. Indeed, the prevalent emphasis upon the total uniqueness and supereminence of Jesus will, I think, become less meaningful'. It is also worth noting that Saiving simply never mentioned Jesus at all in 'The Human Situation'.

68. Thomas Kuhn, 'Reflections on My Critics', in Imre Lakatos and Alan Musgrave (eds.), *Criticism and the Growth of Knowledge* (Cambridge: Cambridge University Press, 1970), p. 277.

69. Christ and Plaskow, 'Introduction', in *Womanspirit Rising*, p. 21.

70. Importantly, the models for God introduced by these women, 'the body of God' and the 'Second Coming of God', have everything to do with their understandings of humanity, and terribly little to do with a deity removed in any way from humanity.

integrity of all non-human creation; and that of the finite character of all human and all earthly existence. Associated with this last supposition is the rejection of the notion of eternal life, a heaven above, and the idea of a new creation brought into being by an omnipotent, transcendent, wholly-other deity. Above all else, in this paradigm the finite matrix of existence is valued for its own sake. Following on from this value judgment is the value accorded each distinct aspect of existence (meaning, in this instance, the whole of earthly creation). Because each aspect of this creation (including individual humans) is inherently valuable, there is no hierarchical ranking scheme associated with the feminist Christian theological paradigm. There is instead an acknowledgment of the intricate, interdependent web of life, to the effect that in order for Life to endure on earth for as long as it can, humankind must come to understand and abide by the limits of creaturely existence. Within the worldview of this feminist Christian paradigm the power of those who rule the state and church to define reality is fully acknowledged, as is the structurally embedded and metaphysically justified oppression of numerous categories of 'others'. So too is the extent of the task facing feminist Christian theologians well understood. In Mary Daly's words,

> We have been foreigners not only to the fortresses of political power but also to those citadels in which thought processes have been spun out, creating a net of meaning to capture reality. In a sexist world, symbol systems and conceptual apparatuses have been male creations... Therefore, the various ideological constructs cannot be imagined to reflect a balanced or adequate vision. Instead, they distort reality and destroy human potential, female and male. What is required of women at this point in history is *a firm and deep refusal to limit our perspectives, questioning, and creativity to any of the preconceived patterns of male-dominated culture.*[71]

In the chapters to follow I shall explore the extent to which Rosemary Ruether, Carter Heyward and Sallie McFague 'refuse to limit their perspectives' while continuing to engage with and refine the foundational propositions of this feminist Christian theological paradigm. But in order to talk in greater detail about the *knowledge claims* they are making I need first of all to make a crucial side-step; I need to delve into the subject of epistemology. Specifically, I need to ascertain what theory or theories of knowledge coexist with the feminist Christian

---

71. Daly, *Beyond God the Father*, pp. 6-7 (italics added).

theological paradigm. As discussed in the introduction, an underlying assumption in this work is that an epistemological framework is a necessary element in any endeavour that purports to represent truths about 'humanity', 'the world', and 'God'—however those metaphors are understood. Therefore, I turn now to an examination of recent feminist epistemological developments.

Chapter 4

FEMINIST EPISTEMOLOGY: TRANSFORMING UNDERSTANDINGS
OF KNOWERS, KNOWING AND THE WORLD TO BE KNOWN

Up to this point I have written almost exclusively in terms of metaphysical presuppositions, value judgments, metaphors and models, focusing specifically on the development of the paradigmatic aspects of (a specific type of) feminist Christian theology. In this chapter I am going to begin to change the terms of this discussion. Specifically, I am going to write about theories of knowledge, about epistemology and epistemological issues rather than disciplinary paradigms and paradigm components. In a very real sense, however, it is impossible to make a sharp distinction between disciplinary paradigms and epistemological issues. Already one of the background assumptions necessary for the very idea of a disciplinary paradigm to make sense is that a body of knowledge must be coherent; beliefs must be internally consistent and must support each other. To embrace the notion of a disciplinary paradigm is to embrace, broadly, some sort of *coherence* account of knowledge or 'truth'. It is to take up a specific epistemological stance and to reject a naive correspondence or naive realist account of 'truth'.[1] Even more importantly, within a disciplinary paradigm are a set of assumptions about human beings (described in Chapter 1 as anthropological presuppositions) and about the nature of physical reality (described as ontological presuppositions). These metaphysical assumptions correspond closely with, in epistemological terms, assumptions or statements about 'knowers' and 'the world to be known'. Theologically, these topics are discussed most often as 'humanity' and 'creation', respectively, and it is this close correspondence that makes an examination of a theologian's epistemological assumptions so important.

   1. See Michael DePaul, 'Coherentism', in Robert Audi (ed.), *The Cambridge Dictionary of Philosophy* (Cambridge: Cambridge University Press, 1995), pp. 133-35; Keith Lehrer, 'Coherentism', in Jonathan Dancy and Ernest Sosa (eds.), *A Companion to Epistemology* (Oxford: Blackwell, 1993), pp. 67-70.

When theologians engage in discussions about humanity and/or creation they are making epistemological statements; they are either describing or assuming one or more characteristics of *knowers* and/or *the world to be known*. In other words, they at least implicitly take up a specific epistemological perspective on humans as knowing agents and the world as an object (or a subject) to be known. Theologians also tend to make 'truth' claims. When they justify or substantiate these claims they engage with their statements on an epistemological level. Thus paradigmatic assumptions about human beings and the nature of physical reality (put theologically, assumptions about humanity and creation) turn out to be epistemological assumptions as well; they are assumptions about knowers and the world to be known. Thus, *the feminist Christian theological paradigm I identified in Chapter 3 is structured around a co-existent epistemological framework*. However, just as I needed to explore in detail the notion of a disciplinary paradigm before I could identify the paradigmatic elements of this feminist Christian theological paradigm, so too I shall now explore in greater detail certain developments in the field of feminist epistemology in order to identify the outlines of the epistemological framework co-existent with the feminist Christian theological paradigm.

This task, however, is made difficult by the fact that there is no single conception of 'feminist epistemology' to which to point or from which to begin. Since the 1980s a diverse body of work has been developed by various feminist epistemologists; some are in dialogue specifically with history or philosophy of science traditions, some locate their work at the furthest reaches of postmodern thought, some contribute to the development of feminist standpoint epistemology, and some take up and explore questions of epistemic-moral-political agency arising from (highly specific examples of) lived experiences or 'everyday' life.[2] But these distinctions, although useful as a heuristic device, are in fact anything but clear. At a minimum they must be understood to have permeable and overlapping boundaries; I suggest they are best understood as characterizing an author's emphasis rather than as sharply defining the extent of her epistemological endeavours.

---

2. See Alcoff and Potter (eds.), *Feminist Epistemologies*. This is a thorough and cogent representative sample of the diversity of approaches taken by feminist epistemologists. The contributors to the volume are, with only one Australian exception, working in the US or Canada.

4. *Feminist Epistemology*

Sandra Harding, for example, is the author of *The Science Question in Feminism* as well as *Whose Science? Whose Knowledge?*, *and* she has contributed greatly to developing a feminist standpoint theory, *and* her thought has been transformed as she has taken into account and then posited postmodern notions of subjectivity, *and* one of her driving concerns is to ascertain how to 'create research that is *for* women in the sense that it provides less partial and distorted answers to questions that *arise from women's lives*…'[3] Similarly, Donna Haraway's work fits under the rubric 'history of science', yet her 'Situated Knowledges' essay is a highly influential essay on feminist standpoint epistemology; meanwhile, her conceptions of a 'cyborg world' and 'cyborg identities' are deliberate attempts to name and simultaneously promote a postmodern sensibility concerning '*lived social and bodily realities* in which people are not afraid of their joint kinship with animals and machines…'[4] In short, both Harding's and Haraway's work can be approached from any of the perspectives mentioned above, and *needs* to be approached from at least two or more simultaneously in order for something of the intricate texture of their thought to be perceived. To paraphrase Linda Alcoff and Elizabeth Potter, 'the work of these feminist philosophers, among others, is in the process of producing a new configuration of the scope, contours, and problematics of epistemology *in its entirety*'.[5]

According to Alcoff and Potter, far from being concerned with defining the necessary conditions according to which *S* knows that *P* propositions can be said to be true, feminist epistemologists in North

---

3. Harding, 'Rethinking Standpoint Epistemology', pp. 49-50 (second italics added). As far as her debt to postmodernism goes, she describes 'the subjects/agents of knowledge for feminist standpoint theory [as] multiple, heterogeneous, and contradictory or incoherent, not unitary, homogeneous, and coherent…' (p. 65).

4. See Donna Haraway, 'A Cyborg Manifesto', in *idem*, *Simians, Cyborgs, and Women: The Reinvention of Nature* (New York: Routledge, 1991), p. 154 (italics added). See also *idem*, 'Situated Knowledges: The Science Question in Feminism and the Privilege of Partial Perspective', *Feminist Studies* 14.3 (Fall 1988), pp. 575-99, and *idem*, *Primate Visions: Gender, Race, and Nature in the World of Modern Science* (London and New York: Verso, 1989). 'Situated Knowledges' also appears in *Simians, Cyborgs and Women*).

5. Alcoff and Potter, 'Introduction: When Feminisms Intersect Epistemology', *Feminist Epistemologies*, p. 3 (italics in original).

America are concerned to show in any number of ways how it is the case that 'values, politics, and knowledge are intrinsically connected'.[6] This assumption signals, I suggest, the existence of a feminist epistemological paradigm as unlike preceding epistemological paradigms as the feminist Christian theological paradigm is unlike preceding theological paradigms. This suggestion is by no means original. In 1983, in their introduction to *Discovering Reality*, an oft-cited collection of feminist essays on epistemology and metaphysics, Sandra Harding and Merrill B. Hintikka quote a sentence from Louise Marcil-Lacoste's essay in the same volume and add their own pithy interpretation of it:

> 'In introducing historicity, materiality, and values as fundamental epistemological categories, feminist writings represent a forceful challenge to critical thought seen as formal or meta-discourse'. In the Kuhnian sense, feminists introduce a new paradigm for human understanding.[7]

Following their lead, I am taking it as a given that since the 1980s there has been, within the academic discipline of philosophy, a feminist epistemological paradigm for human understanding.

Paradoxically, as more metaphors and models are developed and the contours of this paradigm become more evident, one of the fundamental metaphysical presuppositions running through it prohibits the sufficiency of *any* single paradigm for human understanding. In other words, a basic tenet inherent in the feminist epistemological paradigm is that no single theory of knowledge can ever adequately express, convey or provide an avenue to the whole truth—if, indeed, there is such a thing as 'the whole truth'. Further, it is also accepted as a given that every theory of knowledge must inevitably exclude or deny other theories, others' approaches to knowledge and others' knowledge claims. Women have long been excluded from traditional Western, Euro-American knowledge-making practices on the basis of a set of metaphysical presuppositions inherent within all of the hegemonic epistemological frameworks associated with that tradition—the most fundamental presupposition being that women *qua* women are incapable of the highest levels of epistemic agency, however that is defined. Therefore, to purposefully create an epistemological paradigm that can-

---

6. Alcoff and Potter, 'Introduction', p. 3.
7. Sandra Harding and Merrill B. Hintikka (eds.), *Discovering Reality: Feminist Perspectives on Epistemology, Metaphysics, Methodology, and Philosophy of Science* (Dordrecht: D. Reidel, 1983), p. xiv.

4. *Feminist Epistemology* 99

not but hinder the expression of some others' epistemic agency seems to many to be a dubious exercise at best. Lorraine Code argues that:

> A feminist epistemology would seem to require a basis in assumptions about the essence of women and of knowledge. Hence it would risk replicating the exclusionary, hegemonic structures of the masculinist epistemology, in its various manifestations, that has claimed absolute sovereignty over the epistemic terrain.[8]

Recalling Mary Midgley's description of every statement, every proposition resting upon a 'mass of background truisms' and thus only being intelligible in the context of those background assumptions, Code is correct in naming the existence of a set of feminist epistemological assumptions about 'women' and 'knowledge'. However, these assumptions, I suggest, are deliberately inclusive rather than exclusive, flexible rather than rigid. To put it another way, the assumptions made by feminist epistemologists are quite different from the assumptions made by masculinist epistemologists. Moreover, there is no 'law' that says that any epistemology (or any epistemological paradigm) *must* pit itself against all others, must seek to obtain a position of hegemonic domination over every 'other' epistemological theory or paradigm.[9] And indeed, instead of trying to become the one dominant epistemological paradigm in North America at this time, feminist epistemologists are concerned primarily with transforming the entire notion of epistemology. Code is thus correct when she states that 'there can be no feminist epistemology in any of the traditional senses of the term'.[10] Again this points to the creation of an entirely new disciplinary paradigm. The question is, how do some (primarily White, economically

---

8. Code, *What Can She Know?*, p. 315 (italics in original).
9. See Janice Moulton, 'A Paradigm of Philosophy: The Adversary Method', in Harding and Hintikka (eds.), *Discovering Reality*, pp. 149-64.
10. Code, *What Can She Know?*, p. 314. Code is most reluctant to acknowledge the existence of a feminist epistemological paradigm, primarily, I believe, for reasons having to do with issues of power and privilege and race and class. The feminist epistemological paradigm that I have identified within North American philosophy is, like its theological counterpart, almost entirely the creation of White, middle- and upper-class, highly educated women. This does not mean, however, that it is or could ever be the only alternative to what she terms 'masculinist epistemology'. If one rejects the assumption that different paradigms must be not just incommensurable but incompatible with each other, then there is no reason why two, three, or half a dozen paradigms cannot co-exist.

and educationally privileged, North American) feminist epistemologists understand 'epistemology'? What assumptions and value judgments do they share? How do they characterize knowers, the world to be known, and the processes for making knowledge?

The feminist epistemology I have found most useful to my own project of identifying the epistemological framework accompanying one feminist Christian theological paradigm is that dealing explicitly with feminist standpoint theory, and/or with conceptions of knowers and the world to be known that fit together to convey an 'epistemology of everyday life' (Lorraine Code). Accordingly, I am not going to look extensively at issues arising in feminist contributions to history or philosophy of science discussions, nor am I going to venture too far down any feminist postmodern tracks. Nor, again, am I going to try to 'prove' the existence of a feminist epistemological paradigm in the same way that I established the existence of one feminist Christian theological paradigm. The reason I focus more on standpoint theory and an epistemology of everyday life than, for example, on exploring recent developments in feminist empiricism is that it has become almost axiomatic in feminist Christian thought that engaged, critical reflection on the various factors (political, economic, military, industrial, ideological, religious) that converge to shape to a significant degree the contours of one's social, communal and interpersonal life is an essential component of every theo-ethical endeavour. In other words, it is morally and theologically unconscionable to base the claims one makes as a theologian on a closed set of past revelations given to humankind by a transcendent God. Theologically, it has long been held that the truth will set you free, but, say certain feminist Christian theologians, first you must come to know the truth—not as it descends from above, but as it is lived out around you. Such liberating knowledge, it is tacitly accepted, comes primarily from critical engagement with one's lived-context. In epistemological terms, this perspective resonates most strongly with (some versions of) feminist standpoint theory.[11]

Therefore I shall limit the rest of this chapter to a detailed reading of three key essays contributing to feminist standpoint theory: Nancy

---

11. Consciousness-raising groups (of the sort central to the North American women's liberation movement) played an important role in the early development of feminist theology, and, together with the Marxist-inspired influence of the Latin American notion of *concientizacion*, help contribute to the epistemological affinity with standpoint theory shared by most feminist Christian theologians.

4. *Feminist Epistemology*

Hartsock's 1983 essay, 'The Feminist Standpoint: Developing The Ground For A Specifically Feminist Historical Materialism'; Donna Haraway's 1988 essay, 'Situated Knowledges: The Science Question in Feminism and the Privilege of Partial Perspective'; and Sandra Harding's 1993 essay, 'Rethinking Standpoint Epistemology: What is "Strong Objectivity"?'.[12] In the following chapter I shall take a broader approach to the issues of epistemic agency, epistemic community and everyday life, looking at some of the contributions to North American feminist epistemology made by Katherine Pyne Addelson, Lorraine Code, Evelyn Fox Keller, Helen Longino, Lynn Nelson and Elizabeth Potter. Taken together this chapter and the next will provide the conceptual tools I need to identify the epistemological elements in the work of Rosemary Radford Ruether, Carter Heyward and Sallie McFague.

'The Feminist Standpoint: Developing the Ground for a Specifically Feminist Historical Materialism'[13]

Nancy Hartsock's essay is widely cited as one of the ground-breaking works on feminist standpoint epistemology.[14] First published in *Discovering Reality*, it appears in a slightly revised form in Hartsock's book *Money, Sex, and Power*.[15] To contextualize the following discussion, it is important to note that in the Notes section in *Discovering*

---

12. Nancy Hartsock, 'The Feminist Standpoint: Developing the Ground for a Specifically Feminist Historical Materialism', in Harding and Hintikka (eds.), *Discovering Reality*, pp. 283-310; Haraway, 'Situated Knowledges'; Harding, 'Rethinking Standpoint Epistemology'.

13. In 1998, Hartsock published an essay in which she re-addressed the issue of a feminist standpoint (or standpoints) and in particular responded to others' interpretations of her initial standpoint essay. While I was unable to obtain her most recent text at the time of writing, it seems as though the points she still considers to be salient are the points that I focus on in the following reading. See Nancy Hartsock, *The Feminist Standpoint Revisited and Other Essays* (Boulder, CO: Westview Press, 1998), pp. 227-48.

14. See Sandra Harding, *The Science Question in Feminism* (Ithaca, NY, and London: Cornell University Press, 1986), p. 26. Harding also names Jane Flax, Hilary Rose and Dorothy Smith as contributing to the body of work known as feminist standpoint theory.

15. Nancy Hartsock, *Money, Sex, and Power: Toward a Feminist Historical Materialism* (New York and London: Longmans, 1983), pp. 231-51.

Reality Hartsock mentions that her 'discussions with Donna Haraway and Sandra Harding have been intense and ongoing over a period of years'.[16] To further connect these essays, Haraway's 'Situated Knowledges' essay was originally a response, delivered at the Western Division meetings of the American Philosophical Association in San Francisco, March 1987, to Sandra Harding's book *The Science Question in Feminism*, in which Harding took up (among other things) Hartsock's development of the notion of a feminist standpoint. Finally, Harding's 1993 essay is a reflection upon and refinement of her own attempts to develop more fully the notion of a specifically feminist standpoint while taking increasingly into account Haraway's comments on her own efforts. All of which is to say that in choosing to examine these three essays, each one individually recognized as a valuable contribution to feminist epistemology, I am also eavesdropping on an intricate and long-running conversation.

Nancy Hartsock's stated purpose in 'The Feminist Standpoint' is 'to show how...a feminist standpoint can allow us to understand patriarchal institutions and ideologies as perverse inversions of more humane social relations'.[17] The placement of this sentence in her essay is critical; even before explaining to her readers what a feminist standpoint is, Hartsock makes a value judgment. She judges that social relations *as they are* are in some fundamental way(s) inhumane, and it is the value of 'more humane social relations' that justifies her search for a feminist standpoint—a standpoint that 'exposes the real relations among human beings as inhumane, points beyond the present, and carries a historically liberatory role'.[18] To put it another way, the vision she *values* as a goal or end, more humane social relations, is held up as evidence to justify a specific means (the development of a feminist standpoint) to that end. I stress this point even before examining her construction of a feminist standpoint because it reveals the dependency of her entire project on an explicit, *a priori* value judgment. Importantly, this fact does not negate her epistemological project; on the contrary, the fact that she does not deem it necessary to describe in detail the values she embraces as both 'end' and 'justification of the means' seems to indicate that she is writing a feminist epistemology

16. Hartsock, 'The Feminist Standpoint', p. 306. Interestingly, this statement is nowhere to be found in the endnotes to *Money, Sex, and Power*.
17. Hartsock, 'The Feminist Standpoint', p. 284.
18. Hartsock, 'The Feminist Standpoint', p. 285.

from within at least the bare bones of a pre-existent conceptual paradigm. Her unstated expectation that others share her values and that she is writing to and/or for a like-minded community of knowers is revealed through her unproblematic (or unproblematized) use, in the concluding sentence of her introduction, of the words 'us' and 'more humane social relations'.

What then, according to Hartsock, is a standpoint? Firstly, a standpoint is an engaged position in social relations; it is not a distanced reflection upon those particular social relations most visible to a detached observer. Nor is a standpoint simply the perspective of an individual, engaged activist. A standpoint is a collective effort, a collective understanding requiring 'both science (analysis) and...political struggle on the basis of which this analysis can be conducted'.[19] A standpoint is a 'vantage point' formed by the efforts of a mass movement; it is the result of praxis, combining both political action on the part of an oppressed group (in Marx's case the proletariat and in Hartsock's case women) and critical reflection on that action.[20] It is not easy to create or achieve a standpoint; a standpoint is not a 'natural' perspective available to an individual simply because that individual is a member of an oppressed group. According to Hartsock it is not the case that the oppressed simply live 'true' lives and the oppressors' 'false'—the lives of the oppressors are real indeed, as are the oppressors' worldviews. They are real; the issue (revealing the need for an alternative standpoint/theoretical perspective) is that these worldviews are presented (by the oppressors) as whole when in fact they are dangerously incomplete, 'partial and perverse'.[21]

In a theoretical step deliberately analogous to 'Marx's proposal that a correct vision of class society is available from only one of the two major class positions in capitalist society',[22] the most important epistemological claim Hartsock advances in her feminist standpoint theory is that a correct vision of a gendered society is available from only one of the two major gender positions in Western capitalist society.[23] She

19. Hartsock, 'The Feminist Standpoint', pp. 285, 288.
20. Hartsock, 'The Feminist Standpoint', p. 284: '...women's lives make available a particular and privileged vantage point on male supremacy...'
21. Hartsock, 'The Feminist Standpoint', p. 285.
22. Hartsock, 'The Feminist Standpoint', p. 284.
23. Hartsock uses the term 'gender' three times in phrases paralleling 'the ruling class' and 'the ruling gender' ('The Feminist Standpoint', pp. 285, 302, 304). It is

names these two theoretical positions 'feminist standpoint' and 'abstract masculinity', and sets out to establish (1) what are the foundations for a feminist standpoint, and (2) how a feminist standpoint reveals the partiality and perverseness of the epistemological and metaphysical presuppositions and values inherent in the view from 'abstract masculinity'.[24] Again, just as the value of humane social relations (as opposed to social relations constituted by the oppression and domination of many by a few) implicitly grounds her project, so too an a priori metaphysical commitment determines her decision to base a feminist standpoint on the structural differences between women's lives and men's lives. In short, she appropriates from Marx his conception of *reality* as consisting of 'sensuous human activity, practice'.[25] The implication, she notes, is that persons are what they *do*, and that what they *do* structures how they will understand themselves and the world in which they act. The epistemological significance of this metaphysical stance is that males and females do, on a day-to-day basis, significantly different things, and therefore know themselves, others, and the world in which they act in significantly different ways. Accordingly, Hartsock bases her epistemological approach on 'a schematic and simplified account'[26] of the differences, in everyday lived practices (or 'material life'), between the actions of males and females. *It is the understanding of the world, and of humans in relation to the world, available from critical engagement with and reflection upon the activities of females as a group in Western capitalist societies that constitutes Hartsock's feminist standpoint.*

Specifically, the one aspect of material life that Hartsock considers to be structured in fundamentally opposing ways for men and women, regardless of class or society, is what she terms 'the sexual division of labor'.[27] How does she characterize the sexual division of labour, or the

because she uses the phrases 'ruling class' and 'ruling gender' that I write 'gendered society' rather than 'sexed society', although elsewhere in the essay she is insistent on acknowledging the sexual (biological) distinction dividing humankind.

24. Hartsock, 'The Feminist Standpoint', p. 296.
25. Hartsock, 'The Feminist Standpoint', p. 285, quoting from Karl Marx, 'Theses on Feuerbach', in *The German Ideology* (ed. C.J. Arthur; New York: International Publishers, 1970), p. 121.
26. Hartsock, 'The Feminist Standpoint', p. 289.
27. Hartsock, 'The Feminist Standpoint', p. 289. Hartsock does note that her strategy 'contains the danger of making invisible the experience of lesbians and women of color' (p. 290). But she assumes some minimum of what can be termed

4. Feminist Epistemology

differences between what men as a group and women as a group do in their daily lives? She begins by establishing a base-line reason for labour, for doing work: 'The real point of the production of goods and services is, after all, the continuation of the species, a possibility dependent on their use.'[28] Here she exposes the perversity of valuing the *exchange* of goods and services over their *use*, a perverse valuation mirrored in the social prestige accorded to the 'capitalist' but denied the 'worker'. Similarly, she notes that the work of those male workers engaged in the production of goods and services for exchange is accorded social value in comparison with the work females do that is for immediate use but not exchange, such as housework and childrearing. In other words, she implies that bringing home the bacon is, in Western capitalist societies, always a more prestigious activity than frying it up to be eaten.

Regarding men's labour she adheres to Marx's distinction between the 'capitalist' and the 'worker', asserting that the male capitalist, because he has no involvement with production whatsoever, that is, because he is not physically involved with the production of concrete goods, is 'at the furthest distance from contact with concrete material life'.[29] The male worker *is* immediately involved in the work of 'transforming natural substances into socially defined goods',[30] but the difference between the male worker and the female worker (or even the female capitalist) is that 'quittin' time' really is 'quittin' time' for the male, whereas it is not for the female. She goes home and keeps working, doing the repetitious work necessary to ensure ongoing, basic human survival, including the production/reproduction of children. 'Women's activity as institutionalized has a double aspect—their contribution to subsistence, and their contribution to childrearing'.[31]

On the basis of this schema (though described in far greater detail) and her prior value judgements and metaphysical presuppositions, Hartsock maintains that the institutionalized sexual division of labour, as manifest in Western capitalist societies through the removal of the

---

'an institutionalized commonality' among all women in Western societies, and proceeds to construct her standpoint on the basis of these 'institutionalized social practices' (p. 289).

28. Hartsock, 'The Feminist Standpoint', p. 287.
29. Hartsock, 'The Feminist Standpoint', p. 292.
30. Hartsock, 'The Feminist Standpoint', p. 292.
31. Hartsock, 'The Feminist Standpoint', p. 291.

male capitalist from the means of production, the imposition of time-limits on the male worker's participation in the 'sensuous' activity of production, and the demand that females do the vast majority of the day-to-day subsistence chores, including childbearing and child-rearing, in addition to any work they do to produce goods or services for exchange, does provide the foundation for a feminist standpoint. But again it is important to note that when interpreting the consequences of this sexual division of labour Hartsock relies on two presuppositions: (1) the real reason for, and hence the *value* of work or labour is to maintain human life, and (2) 'life itself consists of sensuous activity'.[32] By implication, women do the vast majority of work that matters, work that actually sustains life, and thus are far more involved than men in real life itself. Again Hartsock is quite explicit that this account is not to be understood as definitive of the lives of all individual females or males, but is an account of the lives of women and men as socially institutionalized groups at a particular historical time.[33]

According to Hartsock a feminist standpoint must be able to expose the perspective from 'abstract masculinity' as partial and perverse, that is, as a reversal of what is *really* the case, while incorporating and explaining the simultaneous reality of the perspective from and effects on the world of 'abstract masculinity'. In order to examine how she does this it is necessary first to provide a brief description of how Hartsock characterizes 'knowers' and 'the world to be known' from the perspective of abstract masculinity and then from the theoretical perspective of a feminist standpoint. The fundamental conception of 'knowers', or more precisely of individual human nature, advanced by those immersed in 'abstract masculinity' is that 'of the self in opposition to another who threatens one's very being'.[34] Importantly, 'one's very being' is itself sharply divided: 'the body is both irrelevant and in opposition to the (real) self, an impediment to be overcome by the mind'.[35] From this perspective, a 'real' human is understood to be utterly independent, as disembodied as possible, and continually engaged in attempts to dominate all isolated others with whom he comes into contact. One's existence (his existence) as a fully human being is in fact dependent on his dominating another.

32. Hartsock, 'The Feminist Standpoint', p. 292.
33. Hartsock, 'The Feminist Standpoint', p. 289.
34. Hartsock, 'The Feminist Standpoint', p. 296.
35. Hartsock, 'The Feminist Standpoint', p. 298.

4. *Feminist Epistemology*

What of the world according to abstract masculinity? To paraphrase Hartsock, it is a world in which the emphasis is on stasis and control, quantity not quality, and human (read male) separation from nature.[36] It is a world filled with sharp, hierarchically ordered dualisms: mind over body, culture over nature, abstract over concrete, ideal over real, male over female, masculine over feminine. The world is in fact two worlds, one 'abstract and deeply unattainable, the other useless and demeaning'.[37] Not surprisingly, in this account 'real' humans (masculine male capitalists) occupy the more valued of the two worlds.

From Hartsock's feminist standpoint, knowers and the world take quite a different shape. To begin with, knowers are thoroughly embodied; 'There is some biological, bodily component to human existence'.[38] In fact, one of the reasons Hartsock uses the phrase 'sexual division of labour' in this essay 'is to keep hold of the bodily aspect of existence—perhaps to grasp it over-firmly in an effort to keep it from evaporating altogether'.[39] Secondly, rather than being in a constant state of opposition to all others, all human existence is understood to take place within 'a complex relational nexus'.[40] More accurately, both girls and boys begin and live their lives within a complex relational nexus, but in Western capitalist societies this relationality is devalued and assigned to the feminine/female/concrete/bodily aspect of existence—or to 'the useless and demeaning world'. However, from the perspective of the inhabitants of this useless world, it looks very useful indeed. Necessary, in fact, for life itself. It is also a world of ongoing change, 'a world characterized by interaction with natural substances..., a world in which quality is more important than quantity, a world in which the unification of mind and body is inherent in the activities performed'.[41] It is a world in which life is known not to flourish when tightly controlled by another, yet in which the impetus is toward a profusion of interdependent life-forms.[42] It is a world of

---

36. Hartsock, 'The Feminist Standpoint', p. 290.
37. Hartsock, 'The Feminist Standpoint', p. 297.
38. Hartsock, 'The Feminist Standpoint', pp. 283, 289, 298.
39. Hartsock, 'The Feminist Standpoint', p. 289.
40. Hartsock, 'The Feminist Standpoint', p. 294.
41. Hartsock, 'The Feminist Standpoint', p. 290.
42. Hartsock, 'The Feminist Standpoint', p. 293. Strictly speaking, the second half of this sentence is my own extrapolation from Hartsock's text; she does not discuss 'life' apart from human life.

process, flux, change and growth, in which utterly independent, isolated beings do not exist. Initially and ultimately, all are dependent for life, not on the domination of the other, but on the flourishing of the others, be the others plants, animals or humans.

While this brief description of Hartsock's account does not do it justice, it is nonetheless sufficient, if her account is at all accurate, to serve as confirmation of the partiality of the perspective from abstract masculinity, a perspective that, in the name of impartiality, denies the fundamental life-sustaining importance of relational involvement with others and with physical creation.[43] How then does Hartsock express the perverseness of this perspective? That is, how does she understand the perspective from abstract masculinity to be a *reversal* of 'the proper order of things' and a *reversal* of 'the proper valuation of human activity'?[44] She exemplifies such a reversal by examining the tendency in abstract masculine thought (and action) to substitute death for life, for example by valorizing killing over giving birth.[45] And she expresses the reality, the lived truth of this false-but-socially-institutionalised reversal in the following words:

> Men's power to structure social relations in their own image means that women too must participate in social relations which manifest and express abstract masculinity. The most important life activities [the most abstract] have consistently been held by the powers that be to be unworthy of those who are fully human most centrally because of their close connections with necessity and life: motherwork (the rearing of children), housework, and until the rise of capitalism in the West, any work necessary to subsistence. In addition, these activities [the most concrete] in contemporary capitalism are all constructed in ways which systematically degrade and destroy the minds and bodies of those who perform them.[46]

---

43. Hartsock, 'The Feminist Standpoint', pp. 283-84. She emphasizes that humans are a part of physical creation, are 'inextricably both natural and social'.

44. Hartsock, 'The Feminist Standpoint', p. 299.

45. Hartsock, 'The Feminist Standpoint', p. 301. In this section of the essay Hartsock analyses Georges Bataille's writings to make her point, a point astonishingly similar to that made by Charlotte Perkins Gilman in her 1923 book, *His Religion and Hers: A Study of the Faith of the Fathers and the Work of Our Mothers*, in which Perkins notes how perverse it is that 'man's' religions are built on death, not birth. See Rosemary Radford Ruether, *Womanguides: Readings Toward a Feminist Theology* (Boston: Beacon Press, 1985), p. 265.

46. Hartsock, 'The Feminist Standpoint', p. 302.

4. Feminist Epistemology

Hartsock's point is that the devaluation and denigration of material life is a lived reality affecting both the devaluers and the devalued, albeit in drastically different ways. Furthermore, because activities closely associated with the maintenance of material life are so devalued, they have been institutionally structured in inhumane ways, leading to the hastening to death (emotional, spiritual, and physical) of those who perform such activities.

Which brings me back to where I started this reading, to the issue of values. For in the end Hartsock again justifies the development of a feminist standpoint because it reveals 'the inhumanity of human relations', and 'it embodies a distress which requires a solution'.[47] From a feminist standpoint as she defines it, the values of co-operation, connection and relatedness are defined as being fundamentally more important and more real than domination, isolation, radical independence and struggle unto death. Moreover, an epistemology based on such an understanding of reality, including human beings, as fundamentally composed of and maintained by and through 'continuity and relation' is able to expose patterns of domination and isolation, instances of radical independence and struggles unto death as both real and perverse—perverse precisely because the lived consequence of domination and isolation is death rather than life. But again Hartsock is making a value judgement. She is judging humane and ongoing social relations, or social relations not defined and controlled by the domination of many by a few, to be more valuable, more worthy than social relations of domination and oppression, and hence more expressive of what life truly ought to be about. In other words, her epistemological standpoint is simultaneously a moral standpoint. There is, in her work, no separating ethics from epistemology.

'Situated Knowledges'

As with the Hartsock essay, I shall begin by identifying Haraway's desired ends, or her reason for knowledge-seeking in general. This will make explicit what she values knowledge for, and by extension the value judgements underlying her work. Fortunately, regarding what she believes knowledge is for, or why knowledge matters, Haraway is quite explicit. She wants to speak of a world 'that can be partially shared and that is friendly to earthwide projects of finite freedom, adequate mate-

---

47. Hartsock, 'The Feminist Standpoint', p. 303.

rial abundance, modest meaning in suffering, and limited happiness'.[48] She writes of seeking 'knowledge potent for constructing worlds less organized by axes of domination', and of knowledge that provides 'a vision of the means of ongoing finite embodiment, of living within limits and contradictions'.[49] In short, she values knowledge for its potential in influencing the establishment and maintenance of humane, ongoing, earthwide relations. However, it is easier to see that this is what she does value by identifying more specifically what she does *not* value: domination, oppression, conspicuous consumption (gluttony), rampant suffering, and notions of transcendence, of disembodied infinitude and mastery that she characterizes as 'the god trick, the god's eye view'.[50] I want to emphasize that Haraway is explicit in naming what she values knowledge for and what she does not value, and to suggest that one reason she is so clear is because she asserts an integral relationship between ethics, politics and epistemology. Three times in the essay she states that 'politics and ethics ground struggles for and contests over what may count as rational knowledge'.[51] According to Haraway ethics, morals matter in epistemology because knowledge claims are claims on people's lives; politics matter because knowledge is often produced and used by those with political power to deny or constrain the lives of those who do not have access to such power. To put it another way, Haraway insists that knowledge is created and contested by 'power-differentiated communities' *whose agendas are not innocent*, and she refuses to separate discussions of knowledge from discussions of ethics and politics.[52] With this firmly in mind, what then is Haraway addressing in 'Situated Knowledges'?

48. Haraway, 'Situated Knowledges', p. 579.
49. Haraway, 'Situated Knowledges', pp. 585, 590.
50. Haraway, 'Situated Knowledges', see pp. 581, 582, 584, 586 ('only those occupying the positions of the dominators are self-identical, unmarked, disembodied, unmediated, transcendent, born again'), 587 and 589. Haraway's use, and even, I would argue, dependence upon theological metaphors (in this and other essays) is quite striking, and worthy of a more detailed study, perhaps one entitled, 'Why Can't a Cyborg be a Goddess?'
51. Haraway, 'Situated Knowledges', p. 587. See also pp. 579 and 593.
52. Haraway, 'Situated Knowledges', see pp. 577, 580, 589. In this regard she is in complete agreement with Sandra Harding, who, in *The Science Question in Feminism*, stated: 'The problematics, concepts, theories, methodologies, interpretations of experiments, and uses [of science] have been and should be selected with moral and political goals in mind, not merely cognitive ones' (p. 250).

4. Feminist Epistemology

Donna Haraway's essay was written in response to Sandra Harding's book, *The Science Question in Feminism*. However, Haraway does not so much respond directly to Harding's work as lift out what she considers to be the crux of the issue identified by Harding—the problem of 'objectivity' in feminist epistemology. To over-simplify, by 1986 Harding had identified a double trend among feminist epistemologists': first, the embrace of a 'social construction of *all* knowledge' perspective, in which traditional notions of supposedly value-neutral 'objectivity' are revealed to hide both the historical specificity and the subjective interests of all knowledge claims/claimants; and second, the insistence on the possibility and necessity of 'accurate' knowledge of the world. 'Situated Knowledges', therefore, is Haraway's answer to the vexing problem of 'how to have *simultaneously* an account of radical historical contingency for all knowledge claims and knowing subjects, a critical practice for recognizing our own "semiotic technologies" for making meanings, *and* a no-nonsense commitment to faithful accounts of a "real" world…'[53]

To answer this question or to solve this problem, Haraway not-so-simply redefines 'objectivity', but in order to redefine objectivity she must also redefine the nature of knowers and the world to be known. In other words, she presents a worldview to accompany her epistemological conception of objectivity, a conception in which objectivity turns out primarily to be about accountability (ethics), hence the reason her accompanying characterization of human beings (her anthropological presuppositions) is necessary; she cannot speak of 'what is' without also speaking of *who* is accountable to *what*. This indivisible relationship between accountability or responsibility (Haraway uses the words almost interchangeably) and objectivity is a critical aspect of her thought, and Haraway emphasizes it even before she begins her revision of 'objectivity'.

> Feminists don't need a doctrine of objectivity that promises transcendence, a story that loses track of its mediations just where someone might be held responsible for something… Immortality and omnipotence are not our goals. But we could use some enforceable, reliable accounts of things not reducible to power moves and agonistic, high-status games of rhetoric or to scientistic, positivist arrogance.[54]

---

53. Haraway, 'Situated Knowledges', p. 579 (italics in original).
54. Haraway, 'Situated Knowledges', pp. 579 and 580.

With, therefore, the understanding that the following explanation of Haraway's 'feminist objectivity' will not be complete until I have also examined her description of knowers (her accompanying anthropology) and the world to be known (her ontological presuppositions)—and these must always be held together with her identified ethical/political values—how does Haraway revise objectivity?

To begin with she defines objectivity as a particular *relationship* between the knower and that which the knower is trying to know. 'All Western cultural narratives about objectivity are allegories of the ideologies governing the relations of what we call mind and body, distance and responsibility'.[55] To borrow Nancy Hartsock's phrase (used by Haraway in 'Situated Knowledges'), objectivity according to 'abstract masculinity' separates mind from body and insists on 'distance' as a prerequisite for an objective view of an 'other'. From the perspective of 'abstract masculinity' responsibility is separated almost if not entirely out of the 'objective' equation, because responsibility implies an involved relationship, and therefore brings connective impurities into what 'ought' to be a purely uninvolved examination of, or look at, the other.[56] Haraway tells another story, that is, she posits a different relationship between knowers and the known: 'Feminist objectivity is about limited location and situated knowledge, not about transcendence and splitting of subject and object. It allows us to become more answerable for what we learn how to see'.[57] The term 'feminist objectivity' is thus not a reference to a *state* (of disembodied uninvolvement), but to a relationship, a relationship between knowers and the world to be known, including other knowers, that enables or fosters more adequate and responsible understandings of particular aspects of the world. It can never be a relation between one knower and the entire world, for one knower is never located in relation to the entire world. Indeed, one knower is only ever located in one specific place at a time, and what can be seen from that place at that time is precisely and only that which is within sight. The 'god's eye view from nowhere' is thus a dangerous illusion, neither objective (for one who is nowhere is in relation to nothing) nor ever possible. However, as Haraway redefines it, '…objectivity turns out to be about particular and

---

55. Haraway, 'Situated Knowledges', p. 583.
56. My reliance on visual metaphors in this discussion of Haraway's work will be explained below.
57. Haraway, 'Situated Knowledges', p. 583.

4. *Feminist Epistemology* 113

specific embodiment.... The moral is simple: only partial perspective promises objective vision'.[58]

But again, this understanding of objectivity (or an objective observer) as necessarily embodied, particular, specifically limited, as necessarily responsible for what is known, does not make sense if the world is understood to be composed of fixed, isolable, passive and inherently meaningless compounds, elements and entities. That world is a world in which ruthless manipulation and dissection lead to knowledge, lead to control, lead to power.[59] It is a world in which, theoretically, nothing can remain hidden from view forever. Absolute and perfect knowledge of everything is possible. It is not, however, the world according to Haraway.

In what she describes as 'a simple, perhaps simple-minded, maneuver', Haraway proposes to reconceptualize the world as an 'active entity'; she asserts the agency of the world.[60] Specifically, she states that 'situated knowledges require that the object of knowledge be pictured as an actor and agent, not as a screen or a ground or a resource, never finally as slave to the master that closes off the dialectic in his unique agency and his authorship of 'objective' knowledge'.[61] When the world and objects of knowledge within the world are understood to be active agents, Haraway's characterisation of objectivity as a faithful and responsible account of the relations between a specifically situated knower and an object/subject of knowledge begins to make sense. 'Accounts of a 'real' world do not...depend on a logic of 'discovery' but on a power-charged social relation of 'conversation'. The world neither speaks itself nor disappears in favor of a master decoder. The codes of the world are not still, waiting to be read'.[62] One fairly important consequence of this approach is that, while knowers may manage,

---

58. Haraway, 'Situated Knowledges', pp. 582-83.

59. 'Feminists, and others who have been most active as critics of the sciences and their claims or associated ideologies, have shied away from doctrines of scientific objectivity in part because of the suspicion that an 'object' of knowledge is a passive and inert thing. Accounts of such objects can seem to be either appropriations of a fixed and determined world reduced to resource for instrumentalist projects of destructive Western societies, or they can be seen as masks for interests, usually dominating interests' (Haraway, 'Situated Knowledges', p. 592).

60. Haraway, 'Situated Knowledges', p. 593.
61. Haraway, 'Situated Knowledges', p. 592.
62. Haraway, 'Situated Knowledges', p. 593.

and are morally and epistemically obligated to try to provide a faithful and responsible account of a 'conversation' that occurred with an object/subject of knowledge at a specific time and place, the chances of exactly the same conversation ever taking place again are non-existent; what's more, that object/subject could have been telling lies, perhaps on purpose:

> Feminist objectivity makes room for surprises and ironies at the heart of all knowledge production; we are not in charge of the world. We just live here and try to strike up noninnocent conversations... [W]e give up mastery but keep searching for fidelity, knowing all the while we will be hoodwinked.[63]

So objectivity refers to the embodied, situated and thus limited or partial relationship/conversation between the knower and the object/subject of knowledge, described as accurately as possible by the knower, and in as responsible a manner, and with as much awareness of the potential consequences of this description, as possible.

Haraway's notion of objectivity is thus fully compatible with feminist standpoint theory. She has written that 'there is good reason to believe that vision is better from below the brilliant space platforms of the powerful'.[64] Or, the vantage points or standpoints of the subjugated 'are least likely to allow denial of the critical and interpretive core of all knowledge'.[65] Haraway is saying that the subjugated have *less* reason to be dishonest when describing the shape and nature of the relations they see in the world around them. But, and this is an important 'but' in Haraway's thought, 'subjugation is not grounds for an ontology; it might be a visual clue. Vision requires instruments of vision... Instruments of vision mediate standpoints; there is no immediate vision from the standpoint of the subjugated'.[66] What there is is a potential for critically analysing and evaluating how 'visual systems work', analyses *less* inhibited by the 'dazzling illuminations of the god trick' and therefore *more likely* to be objective.[67] Unlike Hartsock, who understands praxis, or immersion in 'sensuous human activity' joined with critical reflection on that activity to provide the grounds for

---

63. Haraway, 'Situated Knowledges', p. 593 and p. 594.
64. Haraway, 'Situated Knowledges', p. 583.
65. Haraway, 'Situated Knowledges', pp. 583-84.
66. Haraway, 'Situated Knowledges', p. 586.
67. Haraway, 'Situated Knowledges', p. 583 and p. 584.

4. *Feminist Epistemology* 115

objective knowledge claims, Haraway turns to vision, seeing, as a metaphor for knowing. Her reason for doing so is two-fold: in order to keep conversing intelligently about modern sciences and technologies, and in order to emphasize the specific, partial and mediated character of all knowledge:

> I want a feminist writing of the body that metaphorically emphasizes vision again, because we need to reclaim that sense in order to find our way through all the visualizing tricks and powers of modern sciences and technologies that have transformed the objectivity debates… The 'eyes' made available in modern technological sciences shatter any idea of passive vision; these prosthetic devices show us that all eyes, including our own organic ones, are active perceptual systems, building on translations and specific *ways* of seeing, that is, ways of life… [T]here are only highly specific visual possibilities, each with a wonderfully active, partial way of organizing worlds.[68]

Again, *all* views are partial, in that *all* vision is mediated through devices designed and crafted to make visible some specific, limited aspect of the world, or object/subject of knowledge. Whether human lenses, electron microscopes or the Hubble telescope, each device is radically limited in what it is able to 'see'. What visions there are are inescapably partial. There is no all-seeing, all-knowing eye, either in or above the world.

In presenting her case for the partiality of all visions, Haraway insists both on knowers seeing (or relating to what they *can* see) responsibly, that is, objectively, *and* on knowers' *positioning* themselves to see responsibly: 'one cannot relocate in any possible vantage point without being accountable for that movement. Vision is *always* a question of the power to see—and perhaps of the violence implicit in our visualizing practices'[69] (italics in original). Haraway is addressing two distinct issues here, both related to her conception of knowers. First, she is reminding the reader of the locatedness, the situatedness of all embodied visual perspectives; it is quite possible, in relocating oneself to see some object/subject of knowledge responsibly, that one will relocate oneself into standing on another's neck.[70] Second, she is

---

68. Haraway, 'Situated Knowledges', p. 582 and p. 583.
69. Haraway, 'Situated Knowledges', p. 585.
70. I take her point to be that, even when every intention is made to be a responsible knower, the very fact of being in the world with others (human and non-human) complicates matters greatly, and there is no escape to a 'pure', 'innocent'

reaffirming the power-charged, relational nature of seeing. Whether it be an unobjective relation of imposed domination, or an objective, partial and situated attempt at engagement with the 'other', seeing is not an innocent activity.

Given the difficulties facing those who would be responsible epistemic agents in accordance with Haraway's account of objectivity and vision (including necessarily embodied positioning/locatedness), how *does* she characterize knowers in such a way as to render objective knowing a possibility? In her concisely expressed conception of human nature or subjectivity, Haraway rejects the term 'being' and replaces it with the metaphor 'splitting':

> The split and contradictory self is the one who can interrogate positionings and be accountable, the one who can construct and join rational conversations and fantastic imaginings that change history. Splitting, not being, is the privileged image for feminist epistemologies of scientific knowledge. 'Splitting' in this context should be about heterogeneous multiplicities that are simultaneously salient and incapable of being squashed into isomorphic slots or cumulative lists. This geometry pertains within and among subjects.[71]

According to Haraway then, it is the 'split', 'multiple' subject, one who possesses '(at least) double vision', who is able to fully 'investigate the varied apparatuses of visual production, including the prosthetic technologies interfaced with our biological eyes and brains'.[72] However, in a confusing if not utterly contradictory move (in that it seems to contradict her valuation and affirmation of limited, finite embodiment), Haraway then metaphorically disembodies this already split and multiple subject: 'Feminist embodiment...is not about fixed location in a reified body, female or otherwise, but about nodes in fields, inflections in orientations, and responsibility for difference in material-semiotic fields of meaning'.[73] Because, on the face of it, this statement does contradict her explicitly stated values as well as her metaphysical characterization of the agency of the world, I want to suggest that her intention is to emphasize (in Hartsock's words, 'perhaps to grasp overfirmly') (1) the impossibility of an essential, immutable, 'natural'

---

location in or from which to relate to others. Rather, being responsible to one 'other' may well result in unintentionally harming another.

71. Haraway, 'Situated Knowledges', p. 586.
72. Haraway, 'Situated Knowledges', p. 589.
73. Haraway, 'Situated Knowledges', p. 588.

4. Feminist Epistemology 117

bodily identity, (2) the shifting character of the ethical, political, and epistemic discourses about and/or inscriptions on bodies which are themselves not staying still, and (3) the fact that in advanced Western capitalist societies at this time in history bodies do have different meanings in different contexts, according to different visualizing technologies and practices. I believe she is trying to accommodate more differences among and between women than Hartsock did, and she does not want to privilege one difference above all others. Rather, she wants to acknowledge that split and multiple (I think of them as contradictory and cantankerous) selves exist together in overlapping as well as opposing communities, and she is trying to locate situated, hence objective, knowledges within communities composed of collections of partial visions and hesitant, stuttering conversations.[74] She is advocating a politics, an ethics, and an epistemology based on solidarities created out of fragments, bits and pieces, solidarities as flexible as they are fixed, solidarities always partial, always plural, always accountable to the project of making possible the means of ongoing finite embodiment.[75]

To conclude, Haraway's vision of feminist objectivity is a vision 'of elaborate specificity and difference and the loving care people might take to learn how to see faithfully from another's point of view, even when the other is our own machine'[76] Her world is a tricky sort of agent, with a stake (or perhaps just a delight) in throwing mud in our eyes from time to time.[77] Her knowers are political, technological,

---

74. Haraway, 'Situated Knowledges', pp. 589-90: 'Feminism loves another science: the sciences and politics of interpretation, translation, stuttering, and the partly understood' (p. 589). 'Situated knowledges are about communities, not about isolated individuals' (p. 590).

75. Haraway, 'Situated Knowledges', p. 584. 'The alternative to relativism is partial, locatable, critical knowledges sustaining the possibility of webs of connections called solidarity in politics and shared conversations in epistemology'.

76. Haraway, 'Situated Knowledges', p. 583.

77. Haraway uses the south-western Native American image of the Coyote, or Trickster figure, when describing the sort of agency she envisions the world having. I have deep reservations about White North Americans appropriating this image, however, particularly given that Haraway is using it as an image with which 'to save the world'. Looking for present-day salvation for an industrialized, capitalist, Western society in the form of a single aspect of a complex symbol system of an indigenous culture/people almost entirely destroyed by White colonizers is, well, problematic, to say the least.

'material-semiotic' critters, or, as she writes in another context, 'cyborgs'.[78] She is explicit in stating the ethical/political values underlying her work; she acknowledges the fact that a set of metaphysical presuppositions accompanies her epistemology; and she explicitly names those presuppositions with regard to both the world to be known and knowers.

'Rethinking Standpoint Epistemology'

In 'Rethinking Standpoint Epistemology' the issue of objectivity is, as it was for Donna Haraway, Sandra Harding's central concern. Valuing most highly 'liberatory knowledge projects'[79] (while she never elaborates on this expression it seems that she has in mind something similar to Hartsock's conception of 'emancipatory knowledge' and Haraway's depiction of 'knowledge for constructing worlds less organised by axes of domination'), Harding sets out to establish why feminist standpoint epistemology provides a necessary (but not sufficient) ground for starting to maximize objectivity.[80] In other words, Harding attempts to explain how it is that feminist standpoint theory as she describes it provides a strongly objective *starting point* for knowledge-seeking enquiries. Importantly, her repeated emphasis in this essay on 'start-[ing] thought from marginalized lives' marks a critical shift in the focus of feminist standpoint theory.[81] Whereas in 1983 Hartsock was clear that 'the' feminist standpoint provides the best resource for *answers* to questions arising from liberatory knowledge projects, Harding focuses almost exclusively on establishing the best ground(s) for formulating those *questions*. To this end she, like Haraway, looks to the concept of objectivity for assistance.

Unlike Haraway, however, Harding does not so much radically redefine the concept of objectivity as extend it, applying it to *both* the context of discovery and the context of justification. She locates observers (or knowers) in the same causal plane as the observed (the world

---

78. Haraway, *Simians, Cyborgs, and Women*, pp. 176-81.

79. Harding, 'Rethinking Standpoint Epistemology', pp. 62, 66, 71. (Harding uses the phrase 'liberatory knowledge projects' three times.)

80. Harding, 'Rethinking Standpoint Epistemology', p. 57.

81. Harding, 'Rethinking Standpoint Epistemology', p. 50. See pp. 54-60 for further examples of starting thought but not finding the answers in marginalized lives.

4. *Feminist Epistemology*

to be known) and insists that the factors affecting the observers are also affecting the observed; hence those factors (social, historical, political, economic, physical, material, etc.) must be made explicit in order to provide the possibility, if not the certainty, of the fullest understanding of the object/event/process under observation.[82] Rather than identify seemingly extraneous or anomalous influences on an object/event/process at the *end* of a study in order *then* to remove them, she wishes to identify, in order to take into account, as many influences as possible *from the outset* of any knowledge-seeking endeavour. Her point, as it is in Haraway's account, is that there is no view from nowhere; no knowers are able to transcend their particular location, nor is any object of knowledge able to be known apart from the location/context of those doing the knowing.[83]

This is the crux of the matter in Harding's account of feminist standpoint epistemology: whenever an object is being studied that object is always viewed through pre-existent historical perceptions and interpretations of the object, including accompanying historical valuations of the object. Once this fact is acknowledged, a study that does not include analyses of those historical perceptions, social influences and valuations cannot be considered to be maximally objective. Only those knowledge-seeking endeavours firmly and consciously located in a specific time and place and conducted by knowledge-seekers who are firmly and consciously self-reflexive can be considered to meet the criteria of strong objectivity.[84] Harding claims feminist standpoint theory provides 'systematic methods for locating knowledge in history'.[85] She starts from the premise that all thought is indelibly marked by its era, but rather than assert this as a constant but peripheral epistemological issue, she moves this premise to centre stage: 'Standpoint epistemology sets the relationship between knowledge and politics at the center of its account in the sense that it tries to provide causal accounts—to

---

82. Harding, 'Rethinking Standpoint Epistemology', pp. 64, 69, 71.
83. Harding, 'Rethinking Standpoint Epistemology', p. 63. 'The thought of an age is *of an age*, and the delusion that one's thought can escape historical locatedness is just one of the thoughts that is typical of dominant groups in these and other ages'.
84. Harding, 'Rethinking Standpoint Epistemology', pp. 63-65 and pp. 69-72.
85. Harding, 'Rethinking Standpoint Epistemology', p. 50.

explain—the effects that different kinds of politics have on the production of knowledge'.[86]

In other words, she is saying that standpoint epistemology incorporates a methodology in and through which knowledge claims are made concrete, not allowed to transcend the historical, political, economic and social (in which is included race, class, sex, religion, etc.) situations of the community or communities making those knowledge claims.[87] This emphasis on communities as the agents of knowledge production is of fundamental significance in her account of standpoint epistemology:

> Communities and not primarily individuals produce knowledge. For one thing, what I believe that I thought through all by myself (in my mind), which I know, only gets transformed from my personal belief to knowledge when it is socially legitimated. Just as importantly, my society ends up assuming all the claims I make that neither I nor my society critically interrogate.[88]

As with Hartsock's and Haraway's account of standpoint epistemology, there are strong and inseparable moral and political components running through Harding's thought.[89] By insisting on attending to the

---

86. Harding, 'Rethinking Standpoint Epistemology', pp. 55-56.
87. Harding, 'Rethinking Standpoint Epistemology', pp. 52, 57, 65 re: communities and n. 11 re methodology.
88. Harding, 'Rethinking Standpoint Epistemology', p. 65. Harding characterizes individual knowers in much the same way as Haraway: 'the subjects/agents of knowledge for feminist standpoint theory are multiple, heterogeneous, and contradictory or incoherent' (p. 65). Harding is explicit on this point: not only are there numerous heterogeneous communities of knowers, but each individual knower is herself or himself 'multiple', 'contradictory' and 'incoherent' at the same time as she or he is a member-participant in a number of (possibly conflicting) communities. However, unless one provides a nuanced account of individual knowers as also accountable for their knowledge claims (as Haraway does) the image of human nature or individual subjectivity expressed through such metaphors as 'contradictory', 'incoherent' and 'multiple' eventually works against the possibility of responsible epistemic agency, whether that agency is understood individually or communally. See Code, *Rhetorical Spaces*, p. 15.
89. It is not surprising that Harding's refusal to separate or make a sharp distinction between epistemology, morals and politics is evident in 'Rethinking Standpoint Epistemology'. In 1986 she wrote: 'It is within moral and political discourse that we should expect to find paradigms of rational discourse, not in scientific discourses claiming to have disavowed morals and politics. This assertion of the priority of moral and political over scientific and epistemological theory and activity makes

collective *activities* of members of marginalized communities as the methodological starting point for liberatory knowledge projects, it is possible to raise questions *whose answers matter to those communities*. In other words, via standpoint epistemology it is not only possible but mandatory to raise precisely those questions which members of dominant communities would not usually have cause to ask, either because they have no investment in or need to know the answers, or because those questions and concerns literally do not exist in the dominant communities.[90] According to Harding, because of its focus on asking the most pertinent questions possible, feminist standpoint epistemology potentially contributes to a democratic expansion of human knowledge-seeking projects.[91]

However, to use a spatial metaphor, there is a vast distance between a question and an answer, a distance Harding accentuates rather than bridges with her insistence that the answers are not to be found where the questions are asked.[92] In n. 19 Harding writes, 'We shall return later to the point that, for standpoint theorists, reports of marginalised experience or lives or phenomenologies of the 'lived world' of marginalised peoples are not the *answers* to questions arising either inside or outside those lives, though they are necessary to asking the best questions'. At issue, I suggest, is the fact that she does not return to this point, nor does she provide any sort of epistemological prescription for obtaining the 'best' answers to any questions. She describes how to ask good (in the sense of morally and politically and epistemically responsible) questions, but she does not suggest any way for communities to negotiate between conflicting answers to those questions. Thus the limitation of feminist standpoint epistemology as characterized by Harding lies in the fact that she never adequately explains where or how 'answers' come to be acknowledged as 'answers'. And if, as Harding proposes, maximally objective answers are *not* to be found in the epistemically privileged yet socially and politically marginalized

---

science and epistemology less important, less central, than they are within the Enlightenment world view'. See Harding, *The Science Question in Feminism*, p. 251.

90. Harding, 'Rethinking Standpoint Epistemology', pp. 54, 56.

91. Harding explains her use of the terms 'democracy' and 'democratic' in n. 52. She begins from John Dewey's proposal: 'those who will bear the consequence of a decision should have a proportionate share in making it' (p. 81).

92. Harding, 'Rethinking Standpoint Epistemology', pp. 56-63.

standpoints giving rise to the most pressing questions of our time, then it would seem that those answers can be formulated only (again, how?) in socially and politically dominant communities, the very communities with no communal investment in asking the questions, let alone answering them in accordance with Harding's conception of 'strong objectivity'.

In fact, Harding seems to be rather confused on the issue of *which* communities can be responsible epistemic agents and produce liberatory, maximally objective knowledge. She writes that 'it cannot be that women are the unique generators of feminist knowledge', asserting that men too can and must start their thought from women's lives, thus producing 'specifically feminist knowledge'. Then, however, she immediately and affirmingly quotes what Patricia Hill Collins has to say about Black feminist knowledge: 'Other groups cannot produce Black feminist thought without African-American women. Such groups can, however, develop self-defined knowledge reflecting their own standpoints'. Following soon after she writes that 'a maximally critical study of scientists and their communities can be done only from the perspective of those whose lives have been marginalized by such communities'. I suggest that Harding cannot have it all ways. Knowledge produced by, say, a White male community in the US that consciously took into account the privileges and opportunities afforded to White males *qua* white males but not White females *qua* White females in the US at the end of the twentieth century can be much more objective (in the sense of honestly situated) than 'knowledge' produced with no acknowledgement of the power of maleness and Whiteness combined. But, if Patricia Hill Collins is correct, without the active participation of White feminist women it cannot be White feminist thought, nor, according to Harding herself, can those White males be *maximally* critical, *maximally* aware of the consequences of their power and privilege on the lives of 'others'.[93]

Given the difficulties inherent in Harding's essay, I shall conclude this discussion of feminist standpoint epistemology by referring back to the contributions of Nancy Hartsock and Donna Haraway. Hartsock's specifically feminist historical material standpoint is a theoretical approach solidly embedded in an analysis of the forms and consequences of the sexual division of labour in Western capitalist societies.

---

93. Harding, 'Rethinking Standpoint Epistemology', pp. 67-69.

4. Feminist Epistemology 123

Her feminist standpoint theory is grounded on the fact that babies are 'produced' by and out of female bodies, and that this production, as well as all subsequent labour necessary to ensure the child's continuing existence, profoundly affects the ways in which females relate to and understand other people and the world. Hartsock maintains that the fullest and most accurate knowledge of the political, social and economic practices occurring in this historical moment is available only from an engaged feminist standpoint. In other words, the most ethically and epistemically accountable answers to the questions 'what is happening?', 'why?', and 'what ought we to do about it?' are not to be found in the world according to 'abstract masculinity', for that world is a world removed from the most pressing concerns of human existence.

Donna Haraway's visionary understanding of 'situated knowledges' is at once several worlds removed from Hartsock's analysis yet remarkably compatible with it. According to Haraway all knowledge claims are situated, all knowledge claims are partial, and all knowledge claims are simultaneously moral and political claims. There do exist, however, communities with less of a stake in seeing the world through the eyes of the dominant reality-definers. This does not mean that what is seen from the vantage points of the politically, morally and epistemically subjugated is a reflection of 'pure' reality. It simply means that these communities are less bound to pre-determined interpretations of the world that just happen to support or sanction the status quo. Just as Hartsock based her feminist standpoint epistemology on the inescapably mundane and extraordinary fact of childbirth and the care and feeding of messy, hungry bodies, so too Haraway deliberately turns her back (though never her attention) away from the 'dazzling space platforms' of the powerful. She denies neither their existence nor their power, but by asserting the active and unpredictable agency of the world she inserts an epistemological monkey wrench into all merely human knowledge endeavours. However, though the world-as-agent plays tricks upon humans, still Haraway acknowledges the importance of human attempts to come to know the world. But the sort of 'objective' knowledge she strives for is utterly removed from the 'objective mastery' that accompanies so many 'White Capitalist Patriarchal' knowledge claims.[94] According to Haraway 'objectivity' means being accountable to the non-innocent, power-charged conversations one

---

94. Haraway, 'Situated Knowledges', p. 592.

enters into with aspects of the world (including other humans) around one. 'Objectivity' is about living responsibly, with an active awareness of the always complex and never static relationships between humans and the Mars probe no less than between humans and panda bears.

In this chapter I have examined three distinct approaches to standpoint epistemology, a worthwhile place to begin an investigation into feminist conceptions of epistemology because, as Helen Longino concisely puts it, 'standpoint epistemologies notice systematic distortions in description and analysis produced by those occupying social positions of power'.[95] In other words, standpoint theories provide the means to describe broadly the fact that knowledge is *made*—not merely 'found'—by specific epistemic agents in specific social, political and economic locations. Further, who is doing the making affects what sort of knowledge gets made. To use Donna Haraway's expression, there is a 'non-innocent' relationship between knowledge, knowledge-makers (or epistemic agents), and power. Standpoint epistemologies, however they are formulated, foreground this critical point. Feminist standpoint theorists argue that women in particular often have not been accorded knowledge-making status but have been, as a category, profoundly affected by the putative knowledge claims of elite men.

Keeping in mind this non-innocent relationship between knowledge, knowledge-makers and power (for it is a theme that resonates strongly in most if not all work in feminist epistemology), it is time now to explore how other feminist epistemologists have characterized knowers, the world to be known, and the production of knowledge.

---

95. Longino, 'Subjects, Power, and Knowledge', p. 106.

Chapter 5

EPISTEMOLOGICAL COMMUNITIES AND THEIR CONSEQUENCES

At the end of the previous chapter I noted that according to feminist standpoint theories, women as a category have been systematically disadvantaged by traditional Western Euro-American epistemologies. While on one level this is a straightforward assessment of the social, political and moral effects of various hegemonic masculinist theories of knowledge (and their accompanying presuppositions concerning the nature of 'women'), on another level this statement covers up a more complex situation. Simply, for some time the notion of 'women' as a *monolithic* category has been untenable.[1] The situations, locations and lived experiences of different women cannot be spoken of in universal terms—to do so is to cover up the significant differences that exist among women. Accordingly, one way out of this dilemma is to resist the temptation to categorise 'women' or 'women's experience' in sweeping terms. To quote Judith Plaskow's and Carol Christ's words from over a decade ago, 'the notion of women's experience must be taken as an invitation to explore particularity rather than to homogenize significant differences'.[2]

However, feminist standpoint theory seems to require both the possibility of referring to some sort of category of 'women' (albeit not

---

1. There are those who support the use of 'an operational essentialism, a false ontology of women as a universal in order to advance a feminist political program'. According to Judith Butler, Gayatri Spivak and Julia Kristeva are among them. While I perceive this to be an important political strategy in some instances, it is, for reasons which will become clear throughout this chapter, not usually a viable *epistemological* option. See Judith Butler, 'Gender Trouble, Feminist Theory, and Psychoanalytic Discourse', in Linda J. Nicholson (ed.), *Feminism/Postmodernism* (New York and London: Routledge, 1990), p. 325.
2. Judith Plaskow and Carol Christ (eds.), *Weaving the Visions: New Patterns in Feminist Spirituality* (San Francisco: Harper & Row, 1989), p. 3.

necessarily a monolithic one) and the possibility of identifying epistemically 'better' and 'worse' standpoints for making knowledge in any given society. The problem, according to Helen Longino, is as follows:

> Women occupy many social locations in a racially and economically stratified society. If genuine or better knowledge depends on the correct or a more correct standpoint, social theory is needed to ascertain which of these locations is the epistemologically privileged one. But in a standpoint epistemology, a standpoint is needed to justify such a theory. What is that standpoint and how do we identify *it*? If no single standpoint is privileged, then either the standpoint theorist must embrace multiple and incompatible knowledge positions or offer some means of transforming or integrating multiple perspectives into one. Both of these moves require either the abandonment or the supplementation of standpoint as an epistemic criterion.[3]

Accepting the issues facing standpoint theory (and feminist epistemology broadly) as stated above by Longino, i.e., that women do participate in numerous different social locations and live in societies organized along many different axes, not simply in a single society divided simply along sex (or sex/gender) lines, and that a terribly stark conception of standpoint theory potentially could be used to support the silencing of all knowledge claims made by epistemic agents in any way tinged with social, economic, or political privilege, in this chapter I am going to examine how feminist standpoint epistemology has been supplemented by various feminists' reconceptualizations of knowers, the world to be known, and processes for knowledge making. In keeping with one of the fundamental premises of standpoint epistemology, however, I am examining only the work of those feminist epistemologists who take it as a given that all knowledge is *situated*, or *positional*, is located relative to a particular time or era *and* place *and* group of knowledge makers, or epistemic agents.[4] Precedent for this approach has been set by Lynn Hankinson Nelson, who suggests that

> the notion of 'situation' or 'location' is increasingly complex and fertile in feminist theory (and certainly more complex than prefeminist empiricist and Marxist epistemologies were capable of conceptualizing), and I

---

3. Longino, 'Subjects, Knowledge and Power', p. 107 (italics in original).
4. Lorraine Code suggests that the concept of positionality 'responds more adequately to the historical/political exigencies of the 1990s' than does the concept of a standpoint. See Code, *What Can She Know?*, p. 317.

5. *Epistemological Communities and their Consequences* 127

view it as bridging recent feminist empiricist epistemologies, standpoint epistemologies, and some postmodern arguments.[5]

I shall begin by re-examining a point raised only briefly by Hartsock, Haraway and Harding, yet one which is a critical component in many North American feminist epistemological works.

As stated in the previous chapter, according to Nancy Hartsock a standpoint is an engaged position in social relations. It is not the perspective of an individual, whether a 'detached observer' or an involved activist. Instead, a standpoint is achieved through both *collective* effort and *collective* analysis.[6] In other words, an individual, by herself or himself, can neither establish nor speak from a standpoint known only to herself or himself. Similarly, Donna Haraway, in an almost throwaway comment, notes that 'situated knowledges are about communities, not about isolated individuals'.[7] And lastly Sandra Harding, when discussing feminist standpoint theory, states the following:

> the fact that feminist knowledge claims are socially situated does not in practice distinguish them from any other knowledge claims that have been made inside or outside the history of Western thought and the disciplines today; all bear the fingerprints *of the communities that produce them*.[8]

The issue I want to highlight is the fact that all three theorists share the assumption that knowledge is made, not by isolated individuals, but through a process of communal engagement and reflection. *Thus in feminist standpoint theories it is communities, not individuals, who are the agents of knowledge production.*

This notion that epistemic agency is primarily communal and only in some secondary, limited way a characteristic or property of individuals is, I believe, fundamental to standpoint epistemologies, yet functions as a deep background assumption and is mentioned directly only rarely. However, I suggest that it is of such significance in standpoint theories (feminist or otherwise) that they make no sense apart from it.[9] Further,

---

5. Lynn Hankinson Nelson, 'Epistemological Communities', in Alcoff and Potter (eds.), *Feminist Epistemologies* (New York and London: Routledge, 1993), p. 152 n. 1.
6. See above, Chapter 4.
7. Haraway, 'Situated Knowledges', p. 590.
8. Harding, 'Rethinking Standpoint Epistemology', p. 57 (italics added).
9. In this regard I respectfully disagree with Helen Longino, who asserts that feminist empiricism and feminist standpoint theories 'have in common a focus on

there is a vital corollary to this assumption of communal rather than individual epistemic agency. If it is necessarily communities which produce knowledge rather than individuals, then knowledge (or 'the truth') is not something that is entirely pre-existent and complete, just waiting to be discovered by any individual who stumbles upon it. Instead, knowledge is constructed, is made by those communities *acknowledged by the wider society* to possess the expertise to make knowledge claims about specific subjects. Knowledge of humankind and the world is therefore made not by just any random communities, but specifically by those communities widely accorded (1) epistemic credibility (Code) and (2) cognitive authority (Addelson).[10]

This rich notion of 'epistemological communities' receives explicit attention and development in the thought of Lynn Hankinson Nelson and Elizabeth Potter, among others. In the following pages I shall examine how this notion of epistemological communities has been developed, beginning with a discussion of the underlying conceptions of human nature or subjectivity that support such a notion of epistemological communities. This will lead in turn to an examination of the issues of cognitive authority and epistemic credibility, issues that cannot be discussed without also discussing questions of power and epistemic privilege. Lastly, I shall conclude this chapter by discussing the impossibility, within the North American feminist epistemological paradigm as I understand it, of there being one eternal truth—a stance that is, arguably, the most charged and potent consequence following on from the idea that knowledge is made and made again, not simply 'found'. The world becomes a very different sort of place when perceived from this perspective; ultimate answers about the nature of creation disappear. Obviously the theological ramifications of this account of 'truth' are rather important; it is thus vital to be able to identify this approach to knowledge and truth if it is present (whether as a developed idea in its own right or tagging along as a consequence of some other presupposition) in the epistemological framework of feminist Christian theologians. I need to be clear from the outset,

---

the individual epistemic agent, on the autonomous subject' (Longino, 'Subjects, Knowledge and Power', p. 109). I would argue that within feminist standpoint theories there is at least implicitly no such thing as an autonomous subject, or an epistemic agent who can know something all by herself.

10. See Code, *What Can She Know?*, pp. 222-64; and Addelson, 'Knower/Doers', pp. 265-73.

5. *Epistemological Communities and their Consequences*   129

however, that the following description of epistemological communities and their epistemic consequences is representative of no one feminist philosopher's work. Rather, I draw together certain themes and issues present to varying degrees in the work of a number of philosophers. My representation of these themes is not necessarily indicative of the way they have been developed by individual authors.

    Because I shall refer again to rhetorical spaces in this chapter, before I sketch an account of epistemological communities I ought to clarify a distinction alluded to but not dwelt upon in the first chapter, that is, the difference between rhetorical spaces and epistemological communities. There I adapted and extended somewhat Lorraine Code's notion of rhetorical spaces to my own use when I wrote that a rhetorical space surrounds an epistemological community, and that it is within this 'space' that statements made by members within that community make sense, are intelligible. The difference between an epistemological community and the rhetorical space that envelops that community is critical, and can best be described by example. I, as a White woman, can never be a member of the epistemological community that produces feminist African-American, or womanist, theological texts. However, if I enter the rhetorical space surrounding the womanist theological community I can learn the theories, or the metaphysical assumptions, the models, metaphors and value judgments used and held by that particular epistemological community, and in doing so I then simultaneously affirm its existence and am able to comprehend more fully the knowledge claims produced by that community. Further, I *must* enter that rhetorical space in order to converse intelligibly or meaningfully with members of that epistemological community about their knowledge claims, just as they must be willing to enter the rhetorical space in which I speak if they wish to converse meaningfully with me or any other member of the feminist Christian theological community in which I work about the knowledge claims made by that community. *It is within the rhetorical spaces surrounding epistemological communities that knowledge claims are shared with other epistemological communities.* One does not have to be a member of a specific epistemological community in order to comprehend knowledge claims made by that community, but one does need to be an acknowledged member of an epistemological community to contribute to the process of making the knowledge claims produced by that community. To put it simply, a rhetorical space is the 'location' in which knowledge claims are intelligible; an epistemological community is the 'location' of the *production* of those knowledge claims. With that distinction in place, it is time now to examine more closely the notion of epistemological communities.

Epistemological Communities

I begin with a brief examination of the understanding of human subjectivity (or subjectivities) underlying and making possible the feminist philosophical notion of epistemological communities. Regarding their philosophical conceptions of subjectivity, or, more broadly, human nature, all the feminist epistemologists whose work I have been drawing upon reject 'ideals [that] presuppose a universal, homogeneous, and essential "human nature", [one] that allows knowers to be substitutable for one another'.[11] Beginning with the assumption that there is no such thing as human nature in general, feminist epistemologists justify this assertion by noting the fact and constraints of human embodiment, includeing the fact that no two bodies are exactly alike. As Lorraine Code notes, 'the facts of having a certain kind of sensory apparatus, and bodies that fall within certain ranges of size and agility, structure possibilities of experience, shaping and limiting possible ways of knowing'.[12] Further, drawing on Annette Baier's conception of persons as essentially 'second persons', Code stresses the physical and cognitive dependence of children upon adults.[13] The formation (never entirely completed) of an individual's subjectivity is literally dependent on her or his relations with others, others who feed and care for him (or not), who teach her how to live (well or poorly) in a world inhabited by others.[14] As 'second persons' humans' very being (at an ontological level) is dependent upon and interrelated with other beings. I (for any I) *am* only because you (many of you) *are*. Such an interdependency, according to Code, 'is continuous, if variously located and elaborated,

---

11. Lorraine Code, 'Taking Subjectivity into Account', in Alcoff and Potter (eds.), *Feminist Epistemologies* (New York and London: Routledge, 1993), p. 16.
12. Code, *What Can She Know?*, p. 42.
13. Code refers to Annette Baier's essay, 'Cartesian Persons', in *Postures of the Mind: Essays on Mind and Morals* (Minneapolis: University of Minnesota Press, 1985), pp. 74-92.
14. Code, *What Can She Know?*, pp. 82-84.

5. Epistemological Communities and their Consequences

throughout people's histories, manifesting itself in patterns of reciprocal influence'.[15]

But again, humans are never in a relationship with everyone, everywhere. We are only in relations with specific others in specific times and places. Thus, as Helen Longino puts it, 'subjectivity is conditioned by social and historical location'.[16] It follows from this that as humans move in and out of different places, are affected by different social and historical movements and events, and engage in different relations with others, then their subjectivities will be changed, or rather are always in process. This process often produces contradictions and incoherencies (or multiplicities) within a 'single' subject, as well as highlighting multiple differences between subjects.[17] However, the fact of embodiment within a physical world—constant and relatively enduring even as our bodies themselves are always subtly or drastically changing—does seem to ground most feminist epistemologists' conceptions of human subjectivity.[18] Broadly, then, subjectivities are embodied, interdependent, multiple affairs, never wholly unitary, fixed or static. They are formed and transformed through interrelations with close-by others, historical and social locations (within which are included received worldviews and value judgments), physical settings, and peculiarly individual physical characteristics: height, weight, eye colour, hair colour, physical abilities or lack thereof, reproductive capability, etc. Maria Lugones' description of the individuals who comprise communities, although not explicitly addressing the concept of subjectivity, does, I believe, convey beautifully the current conception of human nature/subjectivity within much feminist epistemology. Lugones locates her own thoughts on community 'in the midst of concrete, complex, nonreducible, cantankerous, fleshy, interrelated, positioned

---

15. Code, *What Can She Know?*, p. 84.
16. Longino, 'Subjects, Power and Knowledge', p. 108.
17. See Harding, 'Rethinking Standpoint Epistemology', p. 65.
18. See Code, *Rhetorical Spaces*, p. 71. Code notes that 'despite their persuasiveness, postmodern critiques of the uniform and coherent conceptions of subjectivity, which they attribute to humanism or to the Enlightenment tradition, bypass a vital feature of the very possibility of human survival to chronological maturity. I am referring to the fact that it is not possible to lead a minimally coherent human life unless one's environment, both material and human, sustains a core of realist-empiricist assumptions'.

subjects, noncontainable within any easy, abstract, hard-edged, simple classification'.[19]

I suggest that this understanding of human nature is a necessary corollary to feminist conceptions of epistemological communities. According to Lynn Hankinson Nelson,

> epistemological communities are multiple, historically contingent, and dynamic: they have fuzzy, often overlapping boundaries; they evolve, dissolve, and recombine; and they have a variety of 'purposes' and projects which may include (as in the case of science communities) but frequently do not include (as a priority) the production of knowledge.[20]

In other words, epistemological communities resemble, in many respects, the individuals who comprise them. Kathryn Pyne Addelson defines epistemological communities as 'communities of knowers/doers', as 'people who, over a period of time, perform some sort of collective activity together'.[21] Further, and of critical importance, she asserts that *the relations among members of [an epistemological community] are founded in communication*'.[22] Given the significance of communication within this understanding of epistemological communities, it does not seem to be a coincidence that both Lynn Hankinson Nelson and Elizabeth Potter begin their explanations of epistemological communities by first positing the *epistemic* dependency of an individual upon a pre-existent socio-linguistic community.

For example, Nelson asserts that without interpersonal relationships with others in a socio-linguistic community the 'development [of that section of an individual's brain] necessary to language use will never occur'.[23] According to Nelson,

> [o]ur current understandings of neurobiological development, for example, indicate that interpersonal experience is a necessary causal factor in the fetal and postnatal neurobiological development that permits

---

19. Maria Lugones, 'Community', in Alison M. Jagger and Iris Marion Young (eds.), *A Companion to Feminist Philosophy* (Oxford: Blackwell Publishers, 1998), p. 466.
20. Nelson, 'Epistemological Communities', p. 125.
21. Addelson, 'Knower/Doers', p. 280.
22. Addelson, 'Knower/Doers', p. 280. She uses the term 'social world' rather than 'epistemological community', but defines social worlds as 'communities of knowers/doers'. Accordingly, I take her statements about social worlds to apply to epistemological communities as well.
23. Nelson, *Who Knows*, p. 286.

5. *Epistemological Communities and their Consequences*

language acquisition, conceptualization, and many perceptual experiences.[24]

Thus individuals are, in addition to being physically dependent on a pre-existent community of others for survival (and for the development of their 'second personhood'), *epistemologically* dependent on interactions with others in order to develop physiologically into an individual who shares the capacities necessary *to know* with others, including the capacity for language use.

Rather than delve into the world of neurobiology, Elizabeth Potter follows Wittgenstein's 'attack on the very possibility of a private language'.[25] According to Potter there is no way to justify the belief that a private language (created in isolation by a single individual) would necessarily contain all the distinctions and concepts contained in 'our' language: *distinctions and concepts upon which knowledge and truth claims depend*. In her words,

> Wittgenstein argued that there is no way for the isolated individual—who doesn't yet have any concepts including especially concepts of 'same' and 'different', the concept of pointing to something and naming it, or the concept of reference—to make this distinction between statements that are true and those that seem to him to be true.[26]

In other words, individuals are *epistemologically* dependent upon a shared, communal or public language which contains these concepts and distinctions and which is used by two or more people to express, apply and debate the application of these concepts. It is necessarily through shared language that knowledge claims are made and debated, not through private languages. Potter's point is that the public language necessary for making knowledge exists prior to the individual who learns to use this language. She then describes the epistemological consequences of this claim:

> If the individual is not linguistically prior to the community, then the individual cannot be epistemically prior either. And it follows that the epistemic community cannot be comprised of a set of epistemically independent individuals; we must, therefore, begin to view the community as comprised of epistemically interdependent individuals.[27]

---

24. Nelson, *Who Knows*, p. 285.
25. Potter, 'Gender and Epistemic Negotiation', p. 163.
26. Potter, 'Gender and Epistemic Negotiation', pp. 163-64.
27. Potter, 'Gender and Epistemic Negotiation', p. 165.

And again, this community either exists *prior* to any individual who might one day become a member of it, or is the simultaneous co-creation of a number of interdependent individuals. Accepting the assumption that at least some sort of shared language is necessary in order both to structure interpretations of experience (i.e., linguistic concepts such as 'same' and 'different') and to discuss those interpretations (or those potential knowledge claims), there are at least two ways, then, in which an individual is dependent on pre-existent epistemological communities. On the one hand an individual is dependent on linguistic interactions with others in order to be able *to develop physiologically* into someone with the capacity to know, and on the other hand an individual is dependent on linguistic interactions with others in order *to gain a set of concepts* according to which aspects of the world, including other human beings, are identified, organized and distinguished from one another.[28] In the English language these concepts include such epistemologically loaded notions as 'true' and 'false', 'right' and 'wrong', 'fact' and 'error'.

But such shared terms/concepts are themselves used within a variety of much larger discursive or theoretical frameworks—theoretical frameworks around which specific knowledge making endeavours are organized. Different epistemological communities embrace different theoretical frameworks (or conceptual paradigms). When used in a feminist Christian theological text, for example, 'sin' and 'salvation' have rather different meanings than when they are used by a male Southern Baptist preacher in the context of a tent revival. Their meanings are tied to, or are contextually dependent upon, the theory or set of theories and practices embraced by the epistemological communities that make use of those terms/concepts.[29] This issue highlights again the necessarily communal, rather than individual, nature of knowledge-making: shared theoretical frameworks are indispensable to knowledge making endeavours.

According to Nelson, one consequence of 'our' epistemological dependence on shared language and shared theoretical frameworks means that an individual can genuinely know something only when it is possible that others do or *could* know it as well:

28. See Nelson, *Who Knows*, p. 288.
29. To put it in the language of the first section of this book, the meanings of individual terms or metaphors are paradigm-dependent, and each epistemological community is structured around a slightly or very different conceptual paradigm.

5. *Epistemological Communities and their Consequences* 135

> If an individual claimed to know something that was not in keeping with the knowledge and standards of her community (or any other), it would require a change in such standards and knowledge [or practices and theories] for the individual to know—and, then, of course, some community would know.[30]

In order for Nelson's assertions to make sense she must make a critical distinction between knowledge and belief: an individual can believe anything she or he likes, but her or his beliefs are not and cannot be knowledge claims unless others can affirm them, and the possibility of such affirmation depends on the prior existence of a communally shared set of theories and practices within which that individual's knowledge claim makes sense. I take Nelson's point to be an elaboration of a claim made by Lorraine Code: 'for something to *count* as an item of knowledge, it must be possible for at least some members of an epistemic community to locate it within the context of what one might call a "communication system".'[31] Therefore an individual's beliefs can only be acknowledged to be knowledge by the community that uses specific practices and theories and evaluates putative knowledge claims that are intelligible within the framework of those theories and practices, a framework inclusive of specific models and metaphors, or, in Code's words, of a communication system. By the time an individual *knows* something, so too do other members of the epistemological community responsible for the network of theories and practices within which that knowledge claim is expressed, again through specific metaphors and models. And that knowledge claim could not have been expressed, let alone evaluated and acknowledged, without the existence of the theories, practices, metaphors and models *of the community* that evaluates, promotes and sometimes denies putative knowledge claims.

Lorraine Code, quoting from Wittgenstein's *On Certainty*, states simply that 'knowledge is in the end based on acknowledgement'.[32] As Nelson's and Potter's work demonstrates, such acknowledgment is possible only within epistemological communities—communities structured around a shared language and a shared theoretical framework

---

30. Nelson, 'Epistemological Communities', p. 140.
31. Lorraine Code, *Epistemic Responsibility* (Hanover and London: University Press of New England, 1987), p. 171 (italics in original).
32. Code, *What Can She Know?*, p. 215, quoting Wittgenstein, *On Certainty*, no. 378.

(conceptual paradigm) or worldview.³³ These communities exist *prior to* any individual potential member, and are comprised of epistemically *interdependent* members. Within such communities individuals can achieve *both* meaningful agreement *and* meaningful disagreement with one another on many issues, and when at least some number of them comprehend a potential knowledge claim and agree that it is credible, then *that community* makes that knowledge claim. Importantly, knowledge claims made by a specific community are almost always of epistemological significance to other knowledge-making communities; in other words, no epistemological community is an island unto itself. The rhetorical space surrounding one epistemological community necessarily overlaps with the rhetorical spaces of other epistemological communities. If rhetorical spaces did not overlap, communication with other epistemological communities would be impossible. Further, fundamental theoretical assumptions about the nature of humans and the world are shared by many epistemological communities.³⁴ So, for example, a knowledge claim about evidence of life forms on one of Jupiter's moons, if made by a community of astronomers, would have epistemological significance to communities of biologists, chemists, physicists, theologians and ethicists, as well as to communities of believers in extra-terrestrials and alien-worshippers. However, if the same knowledge claim was initially made by a community of alien worshippers then the epistemological significance of that claim would be accorded much less value by the other epistemological communities named above.

Cognitive Authority

The issue of the relative value assigned by the wider society to knowledge claims made by different epistemological communities is of fundamental significance in the work of many North American feminist

---

33. Not all epistemological communities technically share a conceptual paradigm or theoretical framework; some of them may share simply a general worldview. These sorts of epistemological communities, however, typically do not have the production of knowledge as one of their primary or explicit goals.

34. For example, at this time metaphysical presuppositions shared by most epistemological communities include the assumption that the earth is round, not flat, and the assumption that female babies are the product of two X chromosomes, rather than the result of the moist south wind, as Thomas Aquinas and others of his era assumed.

5. *Epistemological Communities and their Consequences* 137

philosophers. As Kathryn Pyne Addelson succinctly puts it, '*who* makes knowledge makes a difference. Making knowledge is a political act'.[35] Importantly, this statement applies both to individual (potential) members of epistemological communities and to epistemological communities as knowledge-making bodies. According to Addelson, knowledge-making communities acknowledged by the wider society to be epistemological communities have had conferred upon them at least some degree of 'cognitive authority'. She explains this phrase by stating: 'We take their understanding of factual matters [about] the nature of the world within their sphere of expertise as knowledge, or as the definitive understanding'.[36]

Elsewhere she writes of knowledge-makers as those groups of people upon whom 'institutional warrant for making and dispersing knowledge' has been conveyed.[37] Within the context of her work it is clear that she does not mean that those epistemological communities granted 'institutional warrant' or a high degree of cognitive authority are the *only* epistemological communities worthy of the name.[38] Rather, her concern is with making explicit the fact that knowledge production is a value-laden, political process. Within a single society, knowledge made by certain epistemological communities is more highly valued than knowledge made by other communities. Epistemological communities engaged in highly valued knowledge-making endeavours are considered to be prestigious,[39] and the weight of the cognitive authority

---

35. Addelson, 'Knower/Doers', p. 267 (italics in original).

36. Kathryn Pyne Addelson, *Impure Thoughts: Essays on Philosophy, Feminism, and Ethics* (Philadelphia: Temple University Press, 1991), p. 62.

37. Addelson, *Impure Thoughts*, p. 110.

38. See Addelson, 'Knower/Doers', p. 265: 'In this article, I will give some reasons that a feminist epistemology is (and should be) an epistemology for knowledge makers. I don't mean by this that "all women" are included as knowledge makers in the epistemology I sketch here—although I believe that all women are knowledge makers and should be respected as such. Who makes knowledge varies with the politics of a situation. In this academic anthology, it makes sense to speak of (and to) academic knowledge makers'.

39. See Addelson, *Impure Thoughts*, pp. 74-75: 'The sciences differ in prestige, physics having more than economics, and both having more than educational psychology. Specialities in a science, too, differ in prestige, experimental having more than clinical psychology, for example. Prestige differences affect researchers' judgments on which metaphysical and methodological commitments are to be preferred'.

granted to these communities (and by extension to some individual members of these communities) has more immediate political impact than knowledge made by non-prestigious epistemological communities. This is evident, for example, in terms of what is taught as knowledge in classrooms or what is the focus of popular media coverage or what research receives government funding. Simply put, some epistemological communities are more epistemically powerful than others. The knowledge claims made by those communities tend to have a much greater impact on how the world is understood and defined than knowledge claims made by less prestigious, less powerful epistemological communities. To quote from an essay written by Addelson and Elizabeth Potter,

> [b]ehind the feminist critiques [of traditional, 'objective' approaches to the production of knowledge] lies our recognition that traditional selections are not independent of the values of those who make them. The selections that feminists criticize are made by people who have the authority to make them and thus to produce the knowledge their selections shape. *Feminist critiques ultimately point to the hierarchical structure of cognitive authority that allows the perspective of some to determine the shape of knowledge for all.*[40]

This quotation, while emphasizing the hierarchical structure of cognitive authority (and implicitly disavowing direct correspondence notions of knowledge and truth), should be read from the perspective of a rich conception of epistemological communities and sub-communities as overlapping with and jostling against one another. The granting of cognitive authority to epistemological communities is not a once-and-for-all occurrence, but an ongoing process with some epistemological communities gaining in prominence at one time but at other times receding in distinction (although not always disappearing entirely). For example, in the aftermath of World War II the study of genetics was not accorded a high degree of value; now, however, work in genetics is a highly prestigious epistemological endeavour. Evelyn Fox Keller, writing specifically of scientific communities, describes the process in this way:

> One of the characteristics of scientific development that most plagues historians is the enormous diversity of viewpoints that can continue to

---

40. Addelson, *Impure Thoughts*, p. 222. (The words appearing in brackets are taken from p. 221. Italics added.)

5. *Epistemological Communities and their Consequences* 139

persist long after it appears that consensus has been reached. The difficulty arises not only because consensus is never total, but also because of the fact that consensus always means the consensus of a particular community. *Scientists make up many communities, and these communities vary by subject, by methodology, by place, and by degree of influence.* Science by itself is a polyphonic chorus. The voices in that chorus are never equal, but what one hears as a dominant motif depends very much on where one stands. At times, some motifs appear dominant from any standpoint. But there are always corners from which one can hear minor motifs continuing to sound [italics added].[41]

Keller's insight is critical—hegemonic knowledge claims, or those knowledge claims made by dominant epistemological communities, are never the *only* knowledge claims of an era.

At this point an examination of Lorraine Code's treatment of the relationship between power, knowledge and knowers will serve as a bridge between the previous discussion of epistemological communities *as communities* and a closer examination of the issues facing individuals who attempt to become acknowledged members of 'institutionally warranted' epistemological communities.

Code's analysis of the relationship between power and knowledge, and the affect this relationship has on knowers in the world, is heavily influenced by Michel Foucault.[42] In a footnote in *What Can She Know?* she summarizes her interpretation of his 'power/knowledge complex':

> The power Foucault locates in the power/knowledge complex is not the hegemonic, sovereign power of a political tyrant. It manifests itself, rather, in the 'totalizing' effects of established discourse, which suppresses other ways of thinking, rendering them invisible. There is neither a single locus nor an identifiable agent of power, yet power is at once constitutive of subjectivity and of possibilities of action and critique.[43]

In keeping with Addelson's conception of certain epistemological communities having institutional warrant to make knowledge claims, Code's understanding of 'established discourse' is that it is neither the

---

41. Evelyn Fox Keller, *A Feeling For The Organism: The Life and Work of Barbara McClintock* (New York: W.H. Freeman and Company, 1983), p. 174.

42. I use the word 'affect' rather than 'effect' in this sentence intentionally, for Code chooses to take a 'generous' approach to Foucault's work. Being most concerned with promoting individual and communal epistemic responsibility/accountability, her 'knowers', though also awash in seas of discourse, are arguably better swimmers than Foucault's.

43. Code, *What Can She Know?*, p. 177.

'voice' nor the creation of any lone individual; it is an *institutional* phenomenon. 'The totalising, controlling power of discourse that gains institutional hegemony—in medicine, psychiatry, criminology, psychology, or sociology—is sanctioned by social regimes and deployed to control and discipline populations'.[44] These institutional discourses matter, then, because they shape social reality by determining the invisible ideology or ideologies of any given society.

Code defines 'ideology' as 'an embedded, uncritical, mainly unconscious set of perceptions and understandings of the world which constitute a "common" framework in a given era, culture, or social space'.[45] The power of institutional discourse is in the influence it has on informing a given sociocultural ideology. Importantly, institutional discourses define not only how the physical world is conceived, but also the 'essential' characteristics and abilities of entire *categories* of people. In Code's words, '[p]ower-knowledge structures constitute people as categories—as homosexuals, women, blacks, mad people— defined and publicly understood according to rigid, stereotyped designations'.[46] Code is aware that individuals are never simply or only members of just one 'category' or 'class' of people, and that often the 'allowed' characteristics of one category of which they are a member are denied by another category of which they are also a member. However, by identifying stereotypical ideological designations and *not* confusing those designations with the actual people to whom they purportedly refer, Code provides a theoretical tool with which it is possible to discuss the ideological figure of 'woman' or 'women' *and* the effect this ideology has on real women's concrete, particular lives.

Difficulties abound, however, because *ideologies shaped by institutional discourses seem natural.* Ideologies, again, are those 'set[s] of meanings in terms of which people live their sociocultural situation'.[47] When 'the meanings' that structure daily life appear to be 'natural' and thus inevitable, the influence of the institutional discourse(s) on the shape of social reality becomes invisible. Yet these 'meanings', these 'facts' control the behaviours and thoughts (in that they determine the limits of what is thinkable) of the majority of any given populace the

---

44. Code, *What Can She Know?*, p. 201 and pp. 201-202.
45. Code, *What Can She Know?*, p. 196.
46. Code, *Epistemic Responsibility*, p. 244. See also *idem, What Can She Know?*, p. 196.
47. Code, *What Can She Know?*, p. 196.

majority of the time. For example, if 'women' as a category are, according to institutional discourse, incapable of the highest level of rational thought, it follows that most women will never be given the opportunity to participate in endeavours considered in that society to be 'intellectual', simply because it would be illogical to afford women such opportunities. The epistemological communities that made this knowledge claim concerning 'women's' inferior mental status may not be directly responsible for establishing the sociopolitical structures that make it difficult for women to gain entry into intellectual professions, but they are responsible for creating the conception of 'women' upon which those sociopolitical structures have been built.

Code emphasizes the mutually reinforcing relationship between knowledge and power at this point. Hegemonic institutional discourses incorporate those discursive contributions made by epistemological communities whose knowledge claims are *acknowledged to be knowledge* by 'people in positions of power'. These people in positions of power are members of epistemological communities possessing institutional warrant (Addelson) to acknowledge and act upon the knowledge claims of other epistemological communities.[48] Importantly, epistemological communities acknowledged to have a high degree of cognitive authority are composed of individuals who are most likely members of their society's dominant social and political categories. For example, in North America individual 'knowers' participating in dominant epistemological communities—those that contribute to hegemonic, institutional discourses—are most likely male, White, economically privileged, and well educated in the tradition of their White, economically and educationally privileged forefathers. That is, because of their location within socially privileged categories they are already people with access to positions of power.[49] In simplest terms, the powerful create the putative knowledge/facts that in turn confirm the power and privilege of the powerful, as well as the 'natural' inferiority of all members of non-dominant social categories. Individual exceptions are able to be tolerated/accommodated/subsumed within dominant epistemological communities because, as Code notes, so long as they are 'merely' isolated exceptions to the rule, the rule remains intact.[50] However, when

48. Code, *What Can She Know?*, p. 249.
49. Code, *Rhetorical Spaces*, p. 213. See also *idem, What Can She Know?*, p. 249.
50. Code, *What Can She Know?*, p. 57.

two or more 'exceptions' come together, there the possibility of disrupting hegemonic discourse exists.

Again relying on Foucault, Code emphasizes the promise of collective, localized strategies for disrupting dominant power-knowledge structures. She characterizes such collective efforts as 'microrevolutions' that produce 'rippling spheres of influence'.[51] Her point is that 'knowledge about' whole categories of people can be changed when the people so categorized collectively 'work at repudiating the confinement of the categorization and at deconstructing its implications'.[52] However, equally importantly, this collective effort is *located* in specific contexts and communities; it manifests itself through the efforts of specific groups working together within unique sociopolitical as well as physical (urban, suburban or rural) environments. The actions of each local group 'ripple' out and influence the wider sociopolitical context, eventually (potentially) altering the hegemonic institutional discourse.[53] In order for collective 'resistance' or 'subversion' (Code uses the former term in 1987, and both in 1991) to come into being, however, there must exist the possibility of an individual refusing 'to speak from within hegemonic discourse'.[54] In the context in which she writes of this 'discursive refusal' Code is alluding to the possibility of an individual choosing to reject ideological 'complicity', 'self-surveillance' and 'self-discipline'. She is fully aware that an individual is never located outside of any 'power relations'; nonetheless, if conscious of the existence and power of hegemonic discourses *a subject can choose to participate with others* in the creation of more 'ambiguous positions' from which imaginative and transformative discourse(s) can be spoken.[55]

Code's point, one which further supports the understanding of epistemological communities held by Nelson and Potter, is that hegemonic discourses cannot be disrupted by a lone, epistemically autonomous voice. One voice, disputing received and theretofore accepted 'general knowledge', is never acknowledged by the wider community or society to be a knowledgeable or epistemically credible voice. The speaker is

51. Code, *Epistemic Responsibility*, pp. 244-45 and *idem, What Can She Know?*, p. 289.
52. Code, *Epistemic Responsibility*, p. 245.
53. Code, *What Can She Know?*, p. 289.
54. Code, *What Can She Know?*, p. 297.
55. Code, *What Can She Know?*, pp. 297-98.

5. *Epistemological Communities and their Consequences* 143

'speaking nonsense'; he or she must be confused, angry, or insane and thus *not*, by definition, an epistemically credible speaker. Nor, at that moment, is the speaker perceived to be a personally/morally/politically autonomous agent. Paradoxically, in those instances when an individual seems to exercise 'epistemic autonomy' and comes to a cognitive conclusion that differs from or flatly contradicts 'received knowledge', she or he is denied *both* the status of a knowing agent *and* the status of an 'autonomous' moral-political agent.

Code thus demonstrates that epistemic credibility, and also an individual's moral and political agency, depends on the acknowledgment and affirmation of others.[56] Membership in an epistemological community (even a non-dominant one) conveys such epistemic credibility and agency to individuals who utter communal knowledge claims that conflict with hegemonic discourse(s). In other words, non-dominant epistemological communities are the 'places' where speakers who are often 'categorically' denied the possibility of being 'knowers' (because of sex, race, class, physical or mental ability, age, sexual orientation, etc.) *are* communally acknowledged to possess epistemic credibility. The fact that they live in real, complex social, economic and political circumstances about which they know a great deal, if only because sheer physical survival requires such knowledge, is acknowledged. An individual must, then, seek out 'like-enough' others in order collectively to bear witness to the truths of their (personal-social-moral-political) lives. Such 'testimony' can be, and quite often is, denied by the dominant epistemological communities, *yet the denial itself acknowledges the existence of the epistemological community making the denied knowledge claim.* Having claimed the attention of other epistemological communities, the knowledge claims of the non-dominant epistemological community are acknowledged by the wider society to be 'real', even as the 'truth' of those claims is debated. The hegemonic discourse has been interrupted, disrupted, and forced to acknowledge a 'new reality'.

Creating new epistemological communities is not, however, the only way to disrupt and potentially transform institutional discourse. Helen Longino, writing of knowledge production in scientific communities, begins (like Addelson, Code, Haraway, Harding, Hartsock, Nelson and Potter) with the assumption that knowledge-making is a communal

---

56. Code, *What Can She Know?*, pp. 222-32.

rather than individual endeavour. She asserts 'that scientific knowledge is constructed not by individuals applying a method to the material to be known but by individuals in interaction with one another in ways that modify their observations, theories and hypotheses, and patterns of reasoning'[57] (Elizabeth Potter describes this interactive process as 'epistemic negotiation'[58]). Longino's concern is that very often members of a scientific community (or, I would suggest, any epistemological community) share a set of background assumptions, and that 'unreflective acceptance of such assumptions can come to define what it is to be a member of such a community (thus making criticism impossible)'.[59] These assumptions include 'social values and interests' that influence the choice of research as well as the observation or collection and interpretation of data. One way to make these background assumptions visible (and thus to limit the influence they have on shaping knowledge claims) is to include in already established epistemological communities 'representatives of alternative points of view' who hold different interests and social values.[60] Longino is aware, however, that it is by no means an easy task to alter the composition of an established epistemological community, particularly when embracing certain background assumptions and value judgments is a factor influencing (or determining) one's potential membership in such a community. This raises again the issue of the difficulties faced by an individual attempting to become an acknowledged member of an epistemological community bestowed with institutional warrant for making knowledge claims.

To begin with, an individual must have access to the rhetorical space surrounding a given epistemological community, for it is within this 'space' that knowledge claims made by that community are spoken. It is within this 'space' that an individual is taught, or is able to immerse herself or himself in and thus learn the language, theories, practices and value judgments embraced by that particular epistemological community. Very often initial access to such rhetorical spaces is provided via educational institutions. Entry into such institutions, however, is most often limited to those who are economically privileged enough to afford entry, at least in the United States. Unless blessed with unusual

---

57. Longino, 'Subjects, Power, and Knowledge', p. 111.
58. See Potter, 'Gender and Epistemic Negotiation', pp. 161-86.
59. Longino, 'Subjects, Knowledge and Power', p. 112.
60. Longino, 'Subjects, Knowledge and Power', p. 112.

5. *Epistemological Communities and their Consequences* 145

opportunity, then, a working-class or poor individual, regardless of sex or race or any other socially 'marked' characteristic, will never have the chance to attempt to become a member of an epistemological community granted a high degree of cognitive authority. In the case of White, economically privileged females, potential access to educational institutions is now more widely available; nonetheless, the influence of social ideology concerning the 'appropriate' areas of study for women (i.e., the humanities rather than the sciences, the 'soft' sciences rather than the 'hard' sciences, the arts rather than mathematics) is discernible—if not directly, then indirectly, when one counts the number of women actually practising certain professions. As Lorraine Code puts it, 'the sex of the knower is one of a cluster of *subjective* factors (i.e., factors that pertain to the circumstances of cognitive agents) constitutive of received conceptions of knowledge and of what it means to be a knower'[61] (italics in original). In the past 'women' as a category have been denied the status of knowing agents in many streams of traditional Western Euro-American discourse; accordingly, in a society still structured upon this conception of 'women' (as not-knowers) and 'men' (as knowers) one's sex has profound epistemological consequences.[62]

When an individual is a member of more than one non-dominant social category, i.e., is not male and/or not White and/or not heterosexual and/or not (in the United States) Christian and/or not physically able-bodied, etc., then the obstacles to entry into an epistemological community with institutional warrant for making knowledge claims become even more difficult to surmount. The insidious effects of social ideologies concerning the 'proper' roles and occupations of entire categories of people again make themselves felt. As Longino notes, 'each individual occupies a location in a multidimensional grid marked by numerous interacting structures of power asymmetry'.[63] Her point, like

---

61. Code, *What Can She Know?*, p. 4.
62. Code, *What Can She Know?*, p. 231. She notes, 'biologically reinforced stereotypes are peculiarly tenacious determinants of women's positions in epistemic communities. When so many disciplines and institutions to which women seek entry have persistent, constantly revived histories of producing (allegedly objective) "knowledge" that demonstrates their natural incapacity to do so, it is a monumental project just to establish the credibility needed to challenge the knowledge. Indeed, merely posing the challenge can be read as further evidence of feminine irrationality'.
63. Longino, 'Subjects, Power and Knowledge', p. 109.

Code's, is that an individual's membership in various social categories, which are themselves defined and evaluated *both* in hegemonic discourse *and* by the members of those categories (and those definitions and evaluations are never the same), is of epistemological significance.

Individuals' access to epistemically powerful communities is impeded (to varying degrees) by sociopolitical structures built upon stereotypic theoretical designations of whole categories of people. Should an individual be able to overcome the structural impediments in her or his way, she or he is next faced with the challenge of assenting to at least some of the underlying assumptions and value judgments held by members of the epistemological community she or he wishes to enter. These assumptions and value judgments often contradict the assumptions and value judgments held by other (less powerful) epistemological communities of which she or he is already a member. To paraphrase Audre Lorde's famous statement, an individual must become adept at using the master's tools. However, proficiency with those tools is only acknowledged after one has proven oneself capable of using them to build the master's house. Unfortunately, to extend the metaphor, the master's house is filled with walls, and those walls serve to separate members of privileged epistemological communities from the so-called 'non-objective', 'value-laden' perspectives of all those living outside those walls. When an individual member of one or more non-dominant social/epistemological/political categories somehow achieves the opportunity to use the master's tools, that individual can easily become ostracized from the very epistemological communities whose knowledge claims and value judgments she or he is trying to incorporate into more dominant discourse.

To summarize, the issues confronting an individual member of one or more non-dominant social categories who wishes to become an acknowledged member of an epistemological community with institutional warrant for making knowledge claims are multiple yet inseparable. That individual must overcome sociopolitical structural impediments, impediments such as lack of money (due to their relationship to the economic structure of society) and lack of educational opportunity (one aspect of which is the tendency for 'better' schools with 'better' teachers to be located in wealthy White neighbourhoods). Simultaneously, an individual member of non-dominant social categories must overcome the stereotypic theoretical understandings (or anthropological assumptions) concerning 'those' sorts of people (of which the

5. *Epistemological Communities and their Consequences* 147

individual is a representative member)—assumptions such as that 'they' are all stupid or lazy or simply incapable of high levels of rational thought. Then the individual must enter the rhetorical space, learn the theoretical assumptions and be acknowledged to be adept at the practices of a given epistemological community. At some point along the way an individual member of non-dominant social categories/ epistemological communities will almost inevitably become caught in an epistemological 'crunch'—a clash of conflicting assumptions and value judgments associated with different epistemological communities of which that individual is, and/or wishes to be acknowledged as, a member. All of which is to say that it is extremely difficult for people with 'different' social values and interests to become members of epistemological communities widely acknowledged to have cognitive authority. Barriers to entry are embedded in sociopolitical structures and institutions; they are embedded in theoretical underpinnings of society; and lastly they are inextricably tangled up in that individual's personal (yet understood to be dependent upon communal acknowledgment) sense of identity.[64] Fortunately, while it is extremely difficult, it is not (quite) impossible for members of non-dominant social categories to become members of epistemological communities with institutional warrant for making knowledge. And when sufficient numbers of these interdependent epistemic agents question, challenge and negotiate with each other and with socially privileged members of the epistemological community, then the knowledge claims made by that community can change. There is always a danger, however, that those individuals will be changed (in the sense of coming to accept as their 'own' the values, theories, and practices of an existing discipline) long before the knowledge claims of those epistemological communities change.

64. I will never forget hearing someone described, in a most derogatory way, as 'an apple'. The individual in question was a Native American who, it was asserted by other members of his tribe, was 'red on the outside but white on the inside'. In the course of conversation it became apparent that his values and approach to the study of Native American issues were not in accord with the values and 'way' of his tribe—an epistemological community of much lesser power and prestige than 'the academy' of which this man was also a member.

Enacting Truth

Throughout this discussion of epistemological communities (a discussion which has not done justice to the depth and rich complexity of the philosophers' work upon which it has been based), two points have been either argued or assumed: first, that knowledge is made, by more *and* by less powerful, epistemically privileged communities, and not simply 'found' by isolated individuals; and secondly, that the knowledge made by these communities (in particular the epistemically privileged ones) actually shapes the world. This point is expressed most clearly by Kathryn Pyne Addelson: 'Truth is not discovered, it is enacted'.[65] 'Enacting truth means living together so that our worlds, our lives, and our characters are made in certain ways'.[66] As I interpret her words, the 'truth' of (or our knowledge about) any given aspect of the world is created/constructed by 'our' relationship(s) to that aspect of the world *at least as much* as that truth or knowledge is constrained by any 'recalcitrant' features of that aspect of the world.[67] This insight, arguably one of the core presuppositions of the feminist epistemological paradigm I have been examining, is strongly reminiscent of Donna Haraway's reconceptualization of objectivity (as always shifting and never completely transparent yet *accountable* relationships between knowers and known) and her assertion of the active agency of the world.[68]

To put it in more concrete terms, when truth is conceived as enacted by communities the truthful answer to the question, 'is the mountain just a mountain, or is it a sacred site, or is it a uranium mine?' is not one single answer at all, but the answers of all those who are in a relationship with that mountain. For those who worship there, it is indeed a sacred site. For those who extract uranium from it, it is a uranium mine, and for those who pass by it unaware of either its

---

65. Addelson, *Impure Thoughts*, p. 111.
66. *Impure Thoughts*, p. 124.
67. Addelson, Evelyn Fox Keller writes of the 'recalcitrance' of nature and sex, reminding her readers that 'despite its unrepresentability, nature does exist'. Likewise, there are constraints 'imposed by the recalcitrance of sex'. She writes, 'both persist, beyond theory, as humbling reminders of our mortality' ('The Gender/Science System', in Nancy Tuana (ed.), *Feminism & Science* [Bloomington, IN: Indiana University Press, 1989], p. 43).
68. As discussed in Chapter 4.

5. *Epistemological Communities and their Consequences* 149

history as a sacred site or its history as a uranium deposit, it is just another mountain. As for the mountain's self-understanding, some things remain unknown. This example is stark, yet it highlights the point that truths about the 'same' aspects of world, even incompatible truths, can and do co-exist—though not always peacefully. Further, these truths are always relative to, or enacted within and by, the communities making those knowledge claims. However, the truths of some communities have a greater effect on how the world is shaped than the truths of other communities. This hypothetical example highlights again the relationship between making knowledge and power. In this scenario the mining company had the power to enact its truth, a power far greater than the power of the community for whom the mountain is sacred. Additionally, within the wider society within which both communities and the mountain are located the knowledge claims of the community for whom the mountain is a sacred site are valued less highly than the knowledge claims of the mining company. If they were accorded equal or higher value than the knowledge claims of the mining company it is probable that no mine would ever have been allowed to have been constructed there, and the truth of the mountain as a uranium mine would never have been enacted.

Approaching the subject of knowledge about the world (or, in Addelson's words, truth as enacted), Lynn Hankinson Nelson writes,

> That there is a world that constrains what it is reasonable to believe makes the most sense of what we experience—predictions misfire, theories fail, we can and do get things wrong... *What we are not warranted in assuming is that only one system could organize the world or that the world is of a determinate nature*, specifiable in categories our sense organs will lead us to discover.[69]

I include this quotation here to emphasize the deeply practical, pragmatic aspects present in all the feminist epistemologists' work I have examined. Rather than agonize over the certainty or uncertainty of the existence of the world, most feminist epistemologists simply accept that there is a physical reality that structures and limits existence.[70] Further, feminist epistemologists tend to emphasize those *limits* to

---

69. Nelson, 'Epistemological Communities', p. 134 (italics added).
70. See also Code, 'Taking Subjectivity into Account', p. 21: 'The fact of the world's intractability to intervention and wishful thinking is the strongest evidence of its independence from human knowers'.

existence, and, by extension, limits to human knowledge. By emphasizing as well the multiplicity and varieties of human existence (within individuals as well as within and between communities and cultures) and hence the varieties of possible human relationships to each other and the world, feminist epistemologists deny the possibility of any singular, eternal, monolithic knowledge claims.

To conclude, then, communities of interdependent, more and less epistemically powerfully people working and living together create *various* systems according to which different aspects of the world are known. For example, according to one system, as enacted by one epistemological community, human beings are known as collections of genetic sequences. According to another, humans are known as collections of recycled star dust, simply new incarnations of the same elements that have comprised the universe since it came into being. According to yet another, humans are known as split and multiple, fragmented and opaque subjectivities. These truths are all enacted, and they matter; moral, ethical, and political decisions are made on the basis of them. Depending on the power and prestige of the epistemological communities enacting them, they shape our relationship to the world around us, they determine how we treat one another.

The existence of *multiple* enacted 'truths' about the world, or multiple systems according to which the world is known, is made evident when communities are taken to be the agents of knowledge production. Simultaneously, it also becomes evident that knowledge-making is about world-making; the sort of knowledge 'we' make determines what sort of world 'we' live in. 'Objectivity' as traditionally defined by privileged Euro-American epistemologists, as the value-neutral, detached observation and record of a single external reality, simply has no place, no meaning within this approach to epistemology. Instead, the most pressing epistemological issue becomes that of 'epistemic responsibility'.[71] Drawing again on the concise words of Kathryn Pyne Addelson, '*The measure of any epistemology lies in how well it allows knowledge makers to be responsible. It does not lie in how well it gives us certified knowledge or the route to the truth of the one reality*'.[72] 'It is not our business to be omniscient', agrees Mary Midgley.[73]

---

71. *Epistemic Responsibility* is the title of a book, already cited, by Lorraine Code.
72. Addelson, 'Knower/Doers', p. 288 (italics in original).
73. Midgley, *Wisdom, Information and Wonder*, p. 232.

5. *Epistemological Communities and their Consequences* 151

It would seem, however, to be the business of epistemically responsible communities to realize that knowledge-making is as much a political and ethical as it is a cognitive process; to realize that knowledge claims made with cognitive authority shape the structure of society and of the world, thereby enabling some communities (human and non-human) and harming others; and to realize that no knowledge claim made by an epistemological community is ever the only or final word on the subject. Such an approach to knowledge making is not easy.

> [I]t requires courage to become reconciled to dealing in areas where certainty is not possible, where the subject matter is amorphous and, to a great extent, unmanageable, and where the kind of understanding [or knowledge] that can be reached will fall far short of perfect understanding. On all sides one is faced with the fact of one's own fallibility, of human fallibility in general, and of the need to acknowledge this fallibility if better understanding is to be achieved. These are the demands of epistemic responsibility.[74]

It is the hope and affirmation of many feminist epistemologists that such communal, consciously situated, responsible and fallible knowledge-making practices can lead to knowledge with emancipatory rather than damning effects: to knowledge (neither absolute, eternal, nor universal) conducive to, in Donna Haraway's words, 'earth-wide projects of finite freedom, adequate material abundance, modest meaning in suffering, and limited happiness'.[75]

In the following chapters I shall use the epistemological assumptions found within the feminist epistemological paradigm (as I have characterized it in this and the previous chapter) as a 'lens' through which to examine the epistemological assumptions inherent within the work of three feminist Christian theologians: Rosemary Radford Ruether, Carter Heyward and Sallie McFague.

---

74. Code, *Epistemic Responsibility*, p. 254.
75. Haraway, 'Situated Knowledges', p. 579.

Chapter 6

PARADIGMATIC AND EPISTEMOLOGICAL ELEMENTS IN THE
THEOLOGY OF ROSEMARY RADFORD RUETHER

In Chapter 3 I based an analysis of one feminist Christian theological paradigm on a close reading of three early feminist theological essays, including Rosemary Radford Ruether's 'Motherearth and the Megamachine'. There I concluded the following:

> underlying this feminist Christian theological paradigm are three primary metaphysical presuppositions: that of the full, unqualified and embodied humanity of all women, men, and children without exception; that of the inherent integrity of all non-human creation; and that of the finite character of all human and all earthly existence. Associated with this last supposition is the rejection of the notion of eternal life, a heaven above, and the idea of a new creation brought into being by an omnipotent, transcendent, wholly-other deity. Above all else, in this paradigm the finite matrix of existence is valued for its own sake.

In this chapter I return to Ruether's theology, seeking to find further evidence of these metaphysical presuppositions (and accompanying value judgments) in her work, but also to draw out the epistemological assumptions she makes, either implicitly or explicitly, regarding humans as knowers, the world to be known, and processes for making knowledge. As I noted in Chapter 4, paradigmatic assumptions about humankind and non-human physical reality correspond to epistemological assumptions about knowers and the world to be known, which in turn correspond theologically to assumptions about humanity (the subject of theological anthropology) and creation (or, more broadly, cosmology). Additionally, epistemological propositions concerning the acquisition of knowledge correspond (albeit somewhat loosely) to theological discussions of revelation. Accordingly, in my discussion of Ruether's characterizations of humankind, her statements concerning creation/the world/the cosmos, and her discussions of revelation (including any references she makes to acquiring or creating knowledge apart from the notion of 'revelation'), I shall note both the paradigmatic presuppositions she is making and the epistemological assumptions that accompany these metaphysical presuppositions.

Before I begin, however, I need to acknowledge both the extraordinary breadth of her scholarship and my own debt to Ruether as a feminist Christian theologian and historian. It is not too much of an exaggeration to say that a veritable 'cottage industry' has sprung up around her work as a historian and theologian. Numbers of articles, dissertations and books have been devoted, exclusively or in part, to analyses of various aspects of her thought; it is impossible to study feminist Christian theology without reference to her contributions. However, it is vital to note that Ruether's efforts toward constructing a systematic feminist theology represent only a portion of her intellectual endeavours. She is a leading authority on Christian anti-Semitism, with her book *Faith and Fratricide*[1] having received international acclaim. Likewise her (1972) book *Liberation Theology* was one of the earliest books written by a White North American about theological developments in Latin America as well as about Black theology as influenced by the Black Power movement in the United States. (She taught at the School of Religion of Howard University, a Black school, in Washington, DC, from 1966–76.)[2] To get a sense of how attuned she was to the importance of Latin American liberation theology, it must be kept in mind that Gustavo Gutiérrez's *A Theology of Liberation*, the foundational work in this area, was published in Spanish in 1971 and in English in 1973. Additionally, from the early 1970s she has been insistent on the relationship between ecological destruction and other forms of social domination. Most importantly, all of her work is rooted in and cannot be fully appreciated apart from her extensive study of Christian history, in particular early church history in the patristic period (the subject of her doctoral dissertation), as well as her encyclopaedic knowledge of non-dominant trends and heretical (and/or revolutionary)[3] movements throughout Christian history in Western culture.

---

1. Rosemary Radford Ruether, *Faith and Fratricide: The Theological Roots of Anti-Semitism* (New York: The Seabury Press, 1974).
2. Rosemary Radford Ruether, *Disputed Questions: On Being a Christian* (Nashville, TN: Abingdon Press, 1982), p. 81.
3. See Rosemary Radford Ruether, *The Radical Kingdom: The Western Experience of Messianic Hope* (New York and London: Harper & Row, 1970); *idem*,

Lastly, with Rosemary Keller she has edited and contributed to the three volume series, *Women and Religion in America*.[4] On the same topic her most recent contribution, again with Keller, is the highly praised *In Our Own Voices*.[5] Quite literally she has researched and written her way from Babylon and Canaan to the present. All of which is to say that it is an open question as to whether Ruether will be remembered most for her theological work or her historical research. In this chapter, however, I am limiting my study to those of her earlier works which I believe are in some way foundational to or precursors of her feminist theological development, and to her later works concerned explicitly with feminist Christian theology.

As for my personal debt to Ruether, or my own intellectual 'location' in relation to her work, I must admit from the outset that she has had a formative influence upon my own thought, an influence more apparent to me now than when I was her student at Garrett-Evangelical Theological Seminary. It was from Ruether that I learned to appreciate Christianity as nothing more and nothing less than one (complex) faith tradition among others—Christianity as an often contradictory collection of historical developments that neither 'completed' Judaism nor made (or makes) incarnate the last or necessarily 'best' word on the subject of religion. It was from Ruether that I learned to look for patterns of domination and subjugation as these course through history, taking on different forms, supported by varying justifications, but leading to the same end: the oppression of the less powerful by the more powerful. It was from Ruether that I learned to perceive no single oppression in isolation from any others, but to trace connections and, even more importantly, to acknowledge complicities, ambiguities, the absence of any 'pure' or innocent location from which to speak. It was from Ruether that I learned to seek out and listen to dissenting, minority voices within the Christian tradition, and it was Ruether who brought Jewish scripture (the Old Testament) to life for me. Her passion for the Jubilee tradition as expressed in Lev. 25.8-55, her appreciation of those trouble-making prophets and her insistence that

---

Women and Redemption: A Theological History (London: SCM Press, 1998).

4. Rosemary Radford Ruether and Rosemary Skinner Keller (eds.), *Women and Religion in America* (3 vols.; San Francisco: Harper & Row, 1981–86).

5. Rosemary Radford Ruether and Rosemary Skinner Keller (eds.), *In Our Own Voices: Four Centuries of American Women's Religious Writing* (San Francisco: HarperSanFrancisco, 1995).

the work of the prophets must ever be done anew, these elements of her thought became for me simply background assumptions that I welcomed and took up as my own.

Lastly, I will never forget hearing, second or third hand, I don't remember now, her off-the-cuff response to the question, 'Why do you stay in the church?' Legend has it that she replied, 'Because the church has photocopiers'. This story is vintage Ruether: pithy, pragmatic and profoundly aware of the power of the word *and* of the institution as creator and conveyor of the word. In addition, beneath the five words she spoke aloud runs her awareness of the all-pervasive presence of cultural ideologies and superstructures which sanction and support domination by the elite. From Ruether I learned that there is no retreat, no paradisial escape from the 'powers and principalities' of this world. There is simply the struggle to make this world a more just and loving place. One would be foolish not to take advantage of existing photocopying machines to assist one in this effort.

I have already mentioned how important the study of history is for Ruether; accordingly, in order to discern the paradigmatic and epistemological elements in her work as a feminist Christian theologian, I need to contextualize her theology, to locate it in relation to the efforts and conclusions of Ruether the historian.[6] As she herself notes,

> The effort to express contemporary experience in a cultural and historical vacuum is both self-deluding and unsatisfactory. It is self-deluding because to communicate at all to oneself and others, one makes use of patterns of thought, however transformed by new experiences, that have a history.[7]

Broadly, Ruether perceives the history of Western Christian culture (and all patterns of thought within this culture) to be the history (and product) of patriarchy, by which she means 'not only the subordination of females to males, but the whole structure of Father-ruled society: aristocracy over serfs, masters over slaves, king over subjects, racial

---

6. Writing of Ruether the historian and Ruether the theologian, while useful when trying to sift through her work in one short chapter, is, in fact, too simplistic a distinction to make. Ruether is always a theological historian and historical theologian. This is exemplified by the title of her latest major work, *Women and Redemption: A Theological History*.

7. Rosemary Radford Ruether, *Sexism and God-Talk: Toward a Feminist Theology* (Boston: Beacon Press, 1983), p. 18.

156   *Knowledge That Matters*

overlords over colonized people'.⁸ On a deeper level, she perceives this dichotomous cultural structure to have been sanctioned and supported by the symbolic representations of humanity, divinity and creation provided by the dominant strains of Christian thought. *Over and over again* she refers to the unfortunate convergence, in the earliest days of the Christian movement, of two formative strands of dualistic thought: one from apocalyptic Judaism (not, ironically, a dominant or long-lasting trend in Jewish history)⁹ and the other from Hellenistic philosophy, based on a Platonic interpretation of the nature of the cosmos.¹⁰ *To comprehend Ruether's interpretation of the last two thousand years of the history of Western Christian culture, as well as her understanding of the task facing feminist Christian theologians today, it is vital to understand her analysis of the Christian synthesis of these two strands of thought: the one religious/mythological and the other philosophical, both highly symbolic.*

On the one hand, from the apocalyptic tradition Christianity inherited an understanding of this world, perceived as originally a blessed creation, as having been taken over by the power of evil. What is expected (and required) is the intervention of God in order to defeat the forces of evil, establish a thousand year reign of justice, and then re-establish a perfect, *everlasting* creation (the importance of immortality

---

    8. Ruether, *Sexism and God-Talk*, p. 61. She understands the history of patriarchy to include histories of resistance to and rejection of patriarchal structures and ideologies, but she insists on locating these revolutionary moments within the overarching history of patriarchy.
    9. Ruether, *Liberation Theology*, p. 56: 'Rabbinic Judaism after the fall of Jerusalem repudiated this apocalyptic literature'.
    10. See Ruether, *The Radical Kingdom*, pp. 4-11, 148; *Liberation Theology*, pp. 16-17, 55-59, 115, 120-22, 125; *Faith and Fratricide*, pp. 41-47 and 95-96; *New Woman/New Earth: Sexist Ideologies and Human Liberation* (San Francisco: Harper & Row, 1975), pp. 16-17, 190; *Disputed Questions*, pp. 68-69; *Sexism and God-Talk*, pp. 237-40, 244; *To Change the World: Christology and Cultural Criticism* (New York: Crossroad, 1989), pp. 39-40, 48; *Gaia and God: An Ecofeminist Theology of Earth Healing* (San Francisco: HarperCollins Publishers, 1992), pp. 22-29 (on the influence of Platonic thought), pp. 69-73 (on Jewish and Christian apocalyptic thought) and pp. 230-34 (on the combination and adaptation of both the Jewish apocalyptic and Platonic strands of thought); *Women and Redemption*, pp. 14-15, 20, 27, 29. This list of citations is not exhaustive, but it is representative of the extent to which Ruether grounds *all* her work upon her understanding of the effect of the convergence, in Christianity, of these two strands of thought. I cannot over-emphasize its importance in her thought.

and eternal incorruptibility is stressed primarily in the later apocalyptic accounts—those contemporary with the early Christian movement).[11] The notion of an original paradise serves as a point of reference against which the present, unjust era is compared and found wanting, and in terms of which the future 'new creation' is described.[12] On the other hand, from Hellenistic philosophy, in particular from Plato, Christianity inherited an understanding of physical reality or matter, including human bodies, as being of lesser value than 'the invisible, eternal realm of thought'.[13] According to Ruether, within this symbolic system 'mind or consciousness is primal, eternal, and good. Body or visible corporeality is secondary, derivative, and the source of evil, in the form of physical sensations to be mastered by the mind'.[14] Referring to Plato's *Timaeus*, Ruether notes that 'this hierarchy of mind over body is duplicated in the hierarchy of male over female, human over animals'; further, in his *Republic* this symbolic representation is extended to include 'the class hierarchy of rulers over workers'.[15] In other words, within this symbolic worldview the dualistic, hierarchical order of things (social and political) on this material earth is reflective of an eternal form or ideal, even if all matter, all materiality is tainted with corruptibility.

Following the apocalyptic line of thought, within the Christian tradition there arose a strong tendency to posit and value a future, new creation (one unattainable by humankind and thus brought about entirely by God's efforts) as infinitely superior to this world, this perverted creation. When combined with Plato's depiction of human bodies (in particular female bodies) as the rather unsatisfactory hosts of immortal souls, as well as his notion of mutability (change) and sensation (feeling) as *evidence* of the corruption pervading all material things, the result was the denigration of 'the flesh' (or material reality in any form) and positive expectation of a God-effected, other-worldly rescue from bondage to this material reality. Unlike earlier Jewish thought, in which it was believed that if the people of Israel simply obeyed God's commandments and kept their covenant with God then

---

11. See Ruether, *Sexism and God-Talk*, p. 239.
12. Ruether, *The Radical Kingdom*, pp. 6-7.
13. Ruether, *Gaia and God*, p. 22.
14. Ruether, *Gaia and God*, p. 24.
15. Ruether, *Gaia and God*, p. 24.

their communities would flourish *and* the earth would yield up an abundant harvest, in Christian thought humans came to be understood as relatively powerless, as being at the beck and call of the forces of evil (in particular in the form of bodily sensations).[16] An intimate relation between humans, the rest of creation and God was denied. Instead, the spirit was seen to be at war with the flesh. And, in Christian thought, 'woman' was quickly identified as having been responsible 'for the advent of evil in the world'.[17] Female responsibility for evil was joined with the metaphysical presupposition concerning the inferiority of women (and all those who are 'like' women, e.g. slaves, serfs, peasants, animals.) According to Ruether, 'the female [came] to represent the qualities of materiality, irrationality, carnality, and finitude, which debase the 'manly' spirit and drag it down into sin and death'.[18]

Ruether identifies the hierarchical dualisms (God over man, transcendent over immanent, heaven over earth, mind over body, spirit over matter, male over female, master over slave, etc.) inherent within this symbolic understanding of the cosmos, whether presented as salvation myth or metaphysical fact, as the ideological ground and justification for social structures and systems that perpetuate patriarchy and oppression. Of critical importance is the fact that 'these ideologies try to make that social structure look "natural", inevitable and divinely given'.[19] Accordingly, Ruether stresses the epistemological as well as the world-shaping consequences of this hierarchical, dualistic theological and philosophical inheritance:

---

16. Augustine in particular agonized over his inability to control his own body, one 'member' of which seemed to have a tendency to rise to the occasion when Augustine wished it wouldn't. See Rosemary Radford Ruether, 'Misogynism and Virginal Feminism in the Fathers of the Church', in *idem* (ed.), *Religion and Sexism*, p. 162.

17. Ruether, *Sexism and God-Talk*, p. 168.

18. Ruether, *Sexism and God-Talk*, pp. 168-69; see also *Women and Redemption*, p. 273: 'The classical Christian paradigm defines women as created to be dominated and blames women as deserving redoubled domination for resisting it…'

19. Ruether, *New Woman/New Earth*, p. xiv. This quotation from Ruether could just as easily have come from Lorraine Code. In the previous chapter, referring to Code's understanding of 'institutional discourses' and quoting her definition of ideology, I wrote, '*ideologies shaped by institutional discourses seem natural.* Ideologies, again, are those "set[s] of meanings in terms of which people live their sociocultural situation".'

6. *The Theology of Rosemary Radford Ruether*

> Apocalyptic dualism, interpreted as gnostic body-soul dualism, gave to classical Christianity a dualistic mode of moral, epistemological and ontological perception. Such a dualistic mode of perception of reality not only impedes a holistic theology of liberation, but it is also substantially responsible for constructing the very world of alienation from which we seek liberation. We can analyze this alienation as operating on three levels: (1) alienation from oneself; one's own body; (2) alienation from one's fellow person in the 'alien' community; (3) alienation from the 'world'; from the visible earth and sky.[20]

Alert to the almost all-pervasive presence in Western culture of this hierarchical, dualistic perception of humankind, divinity and physical creation, Ruether identifies sexism, racism, classism, colonization/ imperialism, and environmental degradation as the 'logical' (and closely related) historical consequences of a social and spiritual mentality trapped within this mode of perception.[21] Further, this mode of perception is the historical legacy of (the dominant strains of) Western Christian theology.

Regarding the *current* historical context in and out of which she writes her own theology, in the following quotation from *New Woman/ New Earth* Ruether summarizes her conclusions regarding the historical (and symbolically related) patterns of domination which she has traced through several millennia.

> All the crises of history are converging: racism, sexism, colonialism, the technological depletion of the earth. The scientific knowledge for an ecological technology, based on renewable energy resources, the reintegration of farm and town, home and work in a pattern of diversity and balance modeled after ecological systems—this theoretically is not beyond our grasp. But the social structures and psychology of historical oppressive power; the legacy of class, racist, imperialist, and sexist structures of domination raise obstacles against a humanistic implementation

---

20. Ruether, *Liberation Theology*, pp. 16-17.
21. Ruether, *Liberation Theology*, pp. 17-22. She perceives 'Cartesian epistemology [to have] carried on much the same presuppositions of Platonism and [to have] couched its view of knowledge in terms of subject-object dualism. Thinking and knowing were a process whereby a non-material thinking subject reduced all around him, including his own body, to the status of an object to be mastered' (p. 17). Thus Descartes both preserved and reinforced, in terminology suitable for his day, a sharp hierarchical split between mind and body, spirit and matter, self and other.

of such possibilities, which we do not yet know how to begin to overcome.[22]

Given her awareness of the historically oppressive consequences of the dominant symbolic/mythological/metaphysical perceptions of humankind, God, and physical creation in Western culture, the task facing Ruether the theologian is simple, and simply enormous: to re-conceptualize humanity, divinity and the cosmos, to create an alternative perception (non-dualistic and non-hierarchical) of the relations among humans, between humans and that which is holy, and between humans and the earth. According to Ruether, what is required is 'a revolution in theology that totally overcomes the traditional antinomies of dualistic ontology and epistemology; that dualism of the spiritual and the temporal…'[23]

Ruether's Understanding of Theology

Before examining her theological conceptions of humankind, divinity, creation/the world and revelation, I need first of all to describe what Ruether perceives theology to be about. In *Liberation Theology* she characterizes theology as that 'mode of reflection that mediates between the existence and the transcendent horizon of human life'.[24] She continues by asserting, 'If theology is really to speak meaningfully about the mediating point between the "is" and the "ought" of human life, then it takes as its base the entire human project…the whole range of human sciences and the whole history of human cultures of self-symbolization'.[25] The points she makes here, but, typically, does not emphasize, are critical if one is to comprehend her theological judgments about humans and the world 'we' have constructed out of this physical creation (a distinction which I shall explore in detail later). On the one hand she perceives the scope of theology to include *all* aspects of human existence, including scientific and technological developments. She rejects the post-Enlightenment separation of theology or religion from life's practical concerns (the separation of theology and ethics of which I wrote in Chapter 2); she refuses to relegate 'theology'

---

22. Ruether, *New Woman/New Earth*, p. 183.
23. Ruether, *Liberation Theology*, p. 182.
24. Ruether, *Liberation Theology*, p. 2.
25. Ruether, *Liberation Theology*, pp. 2-3.

6. The Theology of Rosemary Radford Ruether

to the contemplation of 'other-worldly' concerns. Instead, her approach to theology is profoundly this-worldly.

On the other hand, for Ruether theology, perhaps more than any other human knowledge-seeking or knowledge-making endeavour, is an ongoing process of *self-symbolization*. Theology is a human attempt to name what is important, what is considered to be of ultimate meaning and value in life within specific human cultures and societies. It is reflective of both human *experiences* and *queries* concerning the nature of existence now and in the past (what 'is' and what has been), and simultaneously it is a judgment upon human existence. It is a judgment based on imagined (and imaginatively symbolized, or mythed) possibilities for the future, what 'ought' to be, or 'the transcendent horizon of human life'. Importantly, Ruether uses the metaphor 'transcendent' often, but almost always accompanied by the word 'horizon'. By relating 'transcendent' to 'horizon' in this way she pulls the 'transcendent' down from above and places it on the human plane, either in front of or before humanity. This spatial shift resonates with Schleiermacher's depiction of God as the source of life and Tillich's description of God as ground of being. Imagined and hoped for horizons of human life well up from the ground, from the concrete situations in which people find themselves in need of salvation; they do not burst in from above. In locating the transcendent on the temporal horizon *before* humanity rather than in a heaven *above* humanity Ruether is deliberately uniting the temporal (or historical) and the 'spiritual'. She is rejecting a sacred/secular split.

From her approach to theology as a thoroughly human project (and to a great extent 'projection') stem two interrelated epistemological consequences, of both of which Ruether is profoundly aware: (1) that *who* has been formulating these symbolic questions (based on their particular experiences of the divine, themselves, their communities and the world, all in an interacting, dialectical relationship)[26] not only shapes the queries posed but also the responses given; and (2) that definitive answers are not to be found 'in once and for all events of a particular sacred history',[27] but must be reformulated continually in order 'to illuminate and interpret' new experiences.[28] As she informed Thomas Merton in 1967, 'only theology bred in the crucible of experience is

---

26. Ruether, *Sexism and God-Talk*, p. 12.
27. Ruether, *Liberation Theology*, p. 3.
28. Ruether, *Sexism and God-Talk*, p. 12.

any good'.[29] Because Ruether understands 'human experience [as] the starting point and the ending point of the hermeneutical circle',[30] it follows that she allows no single theological proclamation to stand as the final word or the ultimate truth; different experiences require different symbolizations. Thus her approach to theology as an *ongoing*, continually incomplete epistemological or knowledge-making endeavour is remarkably compatible with the assumptions, within the feminist epistemological paradigm, of the situatedness of all knowledge claims, and of multiple enacted 'truths', or of the impossibility of 'one' truth ever being adequate.[31]

Given that she understands all theological reflection to be grounded in experience ('what have been called the objective sources of theology; Scripture and tradition, are themselves codified collective human experience'),[32] Ruether downplays any suggestion that feminist or any other sort of liberation theology is unique in stressing the epistemological importance of 'experience'. Rather, what is unique to feminist Christian theology is that, for the first time in history, women's experiences are being considered as worthy and vital resources for theological reflection. Moreover, this action

> explodes as a critical force, exposing classical theology, including its codified traditions, as based on male experience rather than on universal human experience. Feminist theology makes the sociology of theological knowledge visible, no longer hidden behind mystifications of objectified divine and universal authority.[33]

Implicit in this quotation is the assumption that all attempts at theological reflection are and cannot help but be *particular* and incomplete rather than universal. Ruether would agree with the words of Kathryn Pyne Addelson: '*who* makes knowledge [or theology] makes a difference'. What is also implicit in her insistence that all theological reflection is a product and reflection of experience, or the shape and

---

29. Thomas Merton and Rosemary Radford Ruether, *At Home in the World: The Letters of Thomas Merton and Rosemary Radford Ruether* (ed. Mary Tardiff, OP; Maryknoll, NY: Orbis Books, 1995), p. 25.

30. Ruether, *Sexism and God-Talk*, p. 12.

31. Ruether, *Women and Redemption*, p. 280: 'We need to own *as ongoing revelation* the process of continuous reinterpretation that lies behind our restatements of redemptive gender equality in new, more socially embodied terms' (italics added).

32. Ruether, *Sexism and God-Talk*, p. 12.

33. Ruether, *Sexism and God-Talk*, p. 13.

nature of existence as lived (differently) by various people at various times, is the influence of existentialist thought on her theology. (In Chapter 2 I noted Bultmann's injunction that theology must begin with 'an analysis of that understanding of human existence which is given with existence'.) Ruether's analysis of 'human existence' reveals that it is and has always been diverse, shaped in different ways by the social structures and systems into which people are born. Importantly, she has never written of 'women's experience' as though it were a homogeneous source for theological reflection; instead she has paid close attention to the way different women's lives are affected differently by the social structures that, to a large extent, determine the shape of their lives. In 1972, with reference to the power of these social structures, she wrote, 'Women's liberation is therefore *impossible* within the present social system except for an elite few'.[34] Like Code she is profoundly concerned with the effects of the ideologies that support oppressive social, political and economic systems. In 1975 she noted that 'a monolithic analysis of sexism as the ultimate oppression obscures the way in which sexism is structurally integrated with class and race'. She continued by calling for the women's movement to 'reach out and include in its struggle the interstructuring of sexism with all other kinds of oppression...'[35]

Thus it is axiomatic in Ruether's thought that theological reflection drawn from similar experiences of human existence by a relatively small, professionally and politically privileged group of elite males (or females) cannot possibly be universally authoritative. Rather, it reflects the perspectives, concerns and judgments of a privileged few as they have responded to the personal and historical crises arising within their particular socioeconomic, political and cultural locations. It is from this perspective that Ruether, discussing the development of Crisis or Neo-orthodox theology, writes of Karl Barth's theological response to the First World War, a response written, as I noted in Chapter 2, out of a sense of the inadequacies of the then dominant liberal theological paradigm: 'For Karl Barth...the defects of this liberal theology came as a personal, existential problem. He found that this theological and cultural currency left him without a prophetic word to preach in a time of profound crisis and reversal of that optimistic faith'.[36]

34. Ruether, *Liberation Theology*, p. 116 (italics in original).
35. Ruether, *New Woman/New Earth*, p. 125.
36. Ruether, *The Radical Kingdom*, p. 114.

Not only does this quotation reveal both the existential and contextual nature of Ruether's understanding of all theology,[37] it also illumines one of the sources of her deeply held conviction that theology *must be prophetic*; it must seek continually to provide an 'ought' that stands in judgment over against what 'is'.[38] The point is that all her characterizations of humanity, divinity and creation/the world, as well as of 'revelation', are consciously and deliberately limited, made relative to the fabric and crises of her time and place, *and* imbued throughout with value judgments. The title of one of her more recent works, *Gaia and God: An Ecofeminist Theology of Earth Healing*, conveys her value-laden understanding of the crisis most relevant to this time: the ongoing, humanly caused destruction of the earth, sanctioned in part by received conceptions of 'God' and 'his' relation to this creation (Gaia). Over and against what is, i.e., environmental degradation (related to manifold social oppressions) and increasing earth-wide impoverishment, she posits a vision of redemption, a vision of a healed earth, healed relations among all earth creatures and between humans and the physical environment upon which we depend for life. Again, this vision is consonant with the metaphysical presuppositions inherent within the feminist Christian theological paradigm concerning the value and integrity of non-human creation.

With this extended introduction to Ruether's thought (as historian and theologian) in place, it is time now to examine her conceptions of humankind and creation. In the course of this examination I shall be seeking to identify the metaphysical presuppositions she embraces regarding humans and creation, or physical reality (in Chapter 1 I termed these 'anthropological' and 'ontological' presuppositions, respectively). Because these metaphysical presuppositions are also epistemological,

---

37. See Ruether, *Gaia and God*, p. 273. In the penultimate paragraph she affirms again the dialectical relationship between particularly located 'existence' and the 'transcendent horizon' against which what 'is' is evaluated: 'we remain committed to a vision and to concrete communities of life no matter what the "trends" may be. Whether we are immediately "winning" or "losing" cannot shake our root understandings of what biophilic life is and should be, although we need to adapt our strategies to the changing fortunes of the struggle'.

38. See Merton and Ruether, *At Home in the World*, p. 21: 'when I want prophetic insight I look to Barth, Bonhoeffer, Bultmann, etc.'. While in her work she expresses many assumptions about humankind and creation that are in direct opposition to Barth's, it does seem as though she has been deeply influenced by the prophetic edge to his work.

6. *The Theology of Rosemary Radford Ruether*   165

that is, because they also shape her understandings of humans as knowers and the world to be known, I shall sometimes use paradigmatic language and sometimes epistemological language when discussing her assumptions. In the section on theological anthropology I shall weave into the discussion Ruether's statements concerning making or acquiring knowledge. To do this I shall use, as she sometimes does, the theological language of 'revelation'. Lastly, in the section on creation I shall include a brief discussion of Ruether's conception of 'God/ess', for without an understanding of her sense of the divine, her conception of creation and her prophetic judgments upon human actions in this world cannot be fully appreciated.[39]

Ruether's Theological Anthropology

In order to comprehend Ruether's theological conception of humankind as diversely embodied (to misquote Paul, as female *and* male, slave *and* free, Jew *and* Greek), it is vital to acknowledge the tension in her thought between what she perceives as the past and current historical reality of different human lives, and what she honours or values as a deeper metaphysical reality—a sacred truth that has been perverted in and through history. Fundamentally Ruether perceives every individual to be fully human, and uniquely so. Historically, however, it has been the narrow image of an elite, ruling-class male that has been taken to be normative of what it is to be fully human. It is on the basis of the deeper truth of the full and unique humanity of every person that Ruether criticizes any system of thought, any sociopolitical structure that hinders the full developmental potential of any class or category of people. In *Sexism and God-Talk* she relates both this metaphysical stance and the historical reality of the oppression of women's lives to the task of feminist Christian theology:

> The critical principle of feminist theology is the promotion of the full humanity of women. Whatever denies, diminishes, or distorts the full humanity of women is, therefore, appraised as not redemptive... This negative principle also implies the positive principle: what does promote the full humanity of women is of the Holy, it does reflect true relation to the divine, it is the true nature of things, the authentic message of redemption and the mission of redemptive community. *But the meaning of this positive principle—namely, the full humanity of women—is not*

---

39. See Ruether, *Sexism and God-Talk*, p. 46.

fully known. It has not existed in history... Still, the humanity of women, although diminished, has not been destroyed. It has constantly affirmed itself, often in only limited and subversive ways, and it has been touchstone against which we test and criticize all that diminishes us.[40]

In this quotation it is perhaps not evident that Ruether, while embracing a deeper metaphysical reality (that of the full humanity of women) and using it to judge history, does not perceive such a metaphysical presupposition to be an abstract, immutable form or to reveal an unchanging essence of 'woman'. I believe it is accurate to say that Ruether would correlate the notion of 'full humanity' to the notion of 'authentic existence'. Writing of 'authentic existence', Ruether states: 'Authentic and inauthentic existence are universal human possibilities. They exist where they actually exist, and this dialectic changes its boundaries constantly and ultimately runs across each of our hearts'.[41] It is always within history, within and often in opposition to received social structures which impose unjust constrictions on human lives, that the meaning of 'full humanity' is made and remade in particular contexts. Ruether clearly stresses the open-ended character of her presupposition of the 'full humanity' of women:

> How women continue to experience themselves autonomously and struggle against...male subjugation of their experience is hardly known. What women might be like, how we would symbolize the polarities of self and other, thinking and feeling, activity and receptivity outside these traditions of male domination is something that we cannot know until a nonsexist society is created where women are recognized as full human persons...[42]

Nonetheless, while we do not live in a non-sexist (or non-racist or non-classist) society (and therefore all our patterns of thought are shaped by sexist, racist and classist propositions, including those metaphysical presuppositions that reject such oppressive assumptions), there are histories of 'subversive' resistance to the metaphysical characterization of 'woman' as inferior to 'man', of 'slave' as inferior to 'master'. Within these histories are found proleptic moments, glimpses both realized and anticipatory, of authentic, fully human existence. And Ruether locates her own knowledge claims in line with these past

---

40. Ruether, *Sexism and God-Talk*, pp. 18-19 (italics added).
41. Ruether, *Liberation Theology*, p. 136.
42. Ruether, *New Woman/New Earth*, pp. 158-59.

histories. The epistemological importance of this move on her part cannot be overemphasized. Keenly aware that humans are historical, social creatures who cannot know themselves apart from historical, communal patterns of thought, patterns often corrupted in Western culture by the hierarchical dualities discussed earlier, she asserts the relation of her own knowledge claims to other, non-dominant historical developments. She locates a sacred 'truth' in these alternative traditions that is deeper, more fundamental than the 'truth' of hierarchical oppressions:

> To find glimmers of this truth in submerged and alternative traditions through history is to assure oneself that one is not mad or duped. Only by finding an alternative historical community and tradition more deeply rooted than those that have become corrupted can one feel sure that in criticizing the dominant tradition one is not just subjectively criticizing the dominant tradition but is, rather, touching a deeper bedrock of authentic Being upon which to ground the self. One cannot wield the lever of criticism without a place to stand.[43]

There are two elements in this quotation that need to be highlighted. First, for Ruether, no individual exists apart from 'community and tradition'. Secondly, one can challenge the dominant tradition (or prevailing knowledge claims) only from the standpoint of an *alternative* community and tradition. Within her theological anthropology she continually asserts the communal nature of existence and experience; for Ruether, humans are thoroughly social creatures, and this is as true for humans as knowers as it is for humans as people in need of redemption. Writing of the increasing awareness of the evil of sexism in the United States in the twentieth century, and referring to this knowledge as 'consciousness', Ruether notes: 'Consciousness is much more of a collective social product than modern individualism realizes. No one can affirm an idea against the dominant culture unless there is at least a subcultural group that gives people both the ideas and the social support for an alternative position'.[44] This understanding of the collective nature of knowledge-making resonates strongly with the notion of epistemological communities expressed in Chapter 5. The following quotation from Ruether is also strikingly consonant with Code's depiction of the illusion of epistemic autonomy and the power of institutional ideology:

43. Ruether, *Sexism and God-Talk*, p. 18.
44. Ruether, *Sexism and God-Talk*, p. 184.

> The woman who experiences dissenting thoughts alone, without any network of communication to support her, can hardly bring her own dissent to articulation. Without a social matrix, she will simply be terrorized into submission by the authorities that surround her or acquiesce in their judgment that she is a 'witch' or a 'madwoman'.[45]

The 'social matrix' of which Ruether writes is an epistemological community that acknowledges the epistemic participation of individual members of that community at the same time as it affirms *the identity* of those making the knowledge claims. '*Psychologically, one cannot affirm a feminist identity against the historical weight of patriarchal oppression by oneself*'.[46] Ruether's awareness of the communal nature of an individual's personhood or 'being' is a key component in her theological anthropology. She affirms that '"human being" is precisely that form of being constituted by mutual recognition'.[47] Importantly, within her affirmation of the full humanity of all persons is the implicit assumption that women as well as men, slave as well as free, Jew as well as Greek all have the capacity to be epistemic agents-in-community; moreover, this capacity is an integral aspect of one's self, one's self-identity as a human being or 'thinking animal'.[48] It is critically important to note again that Ruether's positive evaluation of her metaphysical assertion of the full humanity of women is an ontologically open-ended assertion. She does not posit an 'essential' understanding

---

45. Ruether, *Sexism and God-Talk*, p. 184.
46. Ruether, *Sexism and God-Talk*, p. 193 (italics added).
47. Ruether, *The Radical Kingdom*, p. 134.
48. Merton and Ruether, *At Home in the World*, p. 49. In response to Merton's characterization of her as 'a very academic, cerebral, abstract type' (p. 43), Ruether responded in the postscript of her next letter to him, 'If I weren't a woman would it have occurred to you to accuse me of being cerebral?... I am just as fleshy as you, baby, and I am also just as much a "thinking animal" as you'. This is one of the few times she explicitly writes of human embodiment; it is striking in that her response to Merton's words indicates the extent to which an understanding of human existence as necessarily embodied is implicit throughout all her work. I suspect that because she spends so much time demolishing the idea that minds/spirits/souls are distinct from and more valuable than bodies she feels it is unnecessary to affirm, from a different angle, the same point: that humans are necessarily embodied creatures, 'fleshy, thinking animals'. Ruether tends not to use ten words when one will do.

of 'women' or 'men'. Rather, in her thought human subjectivity is always in process. 'Identity' is not and can never be a fixed or static given.

However, one's self-identity is (and cannot help but be) shaped by the beliefs of the communities in which one lives, and especially by one's relations with others, relationships shaped by those beliefs. She writes, therefore, of the full humanity of all persons, male and female, in order that this knowledge claim will inform social/communal beliefs and thus help to free women and men from the bonds of theological, philosophical, psychological and biological assertions of 'woman's' inherent inferiority and irrationality.[49] Here are found echoes of Nelson's and Potter's insistence that the epistemological community is prior to the individual. Here also Ruether stresses the liberatory, emancipatory aim of feminist Christian theological formulations. Metaphysical presuppositions concerning human beings, as these are communally embraced and, in Addelson's words, enacted, can either hinder or encourage the becoming of fully human people. Her theological anthropology is deliberately constructed to encourage such communal becoming. She writes to redeem humanity from oppressive conceptions of entire categories of people.

Importantly, for Ruether theological (and also epistemological) communities are comprised of past historical voices and knowledge claims as well as living epistemic agents. The affirmation and encouragement of Mary Magdalene and Olympe de Gouges is just as real, just as present and valuable (and potentially redemptive) to her as the acknowledgment of her contemporaries. She stands in their company (and in the company of Ann Lee and Lucretia Mott and the Marquis de Condorcet)[50] when she affirms the full humanity of women. Thus in Ruether's thought epistemological communities—as standpoints in and from which knowledge claims are made—are *not* to be confused with sociological communities, or communities comprised only of people who share the same combinations of sex, race, class, religion, etc. The

---

49. Re the psychological, see Ruether, *New Woman/New Earth*, p. 137. 'Psychoanalysis has become the chief tool, replacing patriarchal religion, for rationalizing and sanctifying the inferiority of women'. Re the biological, see *New Woman/New Earth*, pp. 15, 71-72.

50. See Rosemary Radford Ruether, *Mary: The Feminine Face of the Church* (Philadelphia: Westminster Press, 1977), p. 87; *Sexism and God-Talk*, p. 184, 199; *To Change the World*, p. 51; *The Radical Kingdom*, p. 45.

connective bonds between members of an epistemological community are instead *paradigmatic*; they are the shared metaphysical presuppositions upon which shared value judgments, shared visions of what 'ought' to be are grounded. Thus Ruether, in the postscript of a letter to Thomas Merton, cheerfully locates herself in a theological/epistemological community with the third century theologian Origen: 'I am one of those mad Origenists who believe that when God is all in all, even the last enemy of Satan will be redeemed.'[51]

Nonetheless, while her conception of epistemological communities implicitly stresses the fundamental importance of shared paradigmatic elements, she also explicitly acknowledges the importance of shared or similar lived experiences in shaping the knowledge that supports such paradigmatic assumptions. Emancipatory knowledge, or 'revelation', tends more often than not to arise from the lived experiences of oppressed communities. 'Revelation', writes Ruether, 'is *concientizacion*' (italics in original). 'Revelation is that redeeming and liberating insight which makes people aware of the social contradictions that define their lives, and thrusts them toward a process of liberation from dependency and oppression'.[52] That 'revelation' is as epistemological in Ruether's thought as it is theological is evident in the following quotation, taken from Chapter 9, 'Is There a Black Theology?', of her book *Liberation Theology*:

> He [the black man] knows the white man well, the way a servant knows the secrets of a master's household, from the backstairs view. From this vantage point, he knows the faults of the white man better than the white man knows himself. This is true of all oppressive relationships. The oppressed must know the one he serves, but the oppressor, by disregarding him, knows nothing really about the oppressed.[53]

In this regard Ruether is in complete agreement with Donna Haraway's (qualified) affirmation of feminist standpoint theory, quoted in Chapter 4: 'there is good reason to believe vision is better from below the brilliant space platforms of the powerful'.[54] Such knowledge is necessary for survival; among other things, it is knowledge of power: who

---

51. Merton and Ruether, *At Home in the World*, p. 86.
52. Ruether, *Liberation Theology*, p. 183. See also p. 179, 'It would be called "Black Power" and "Black Pride" in the Black movement in the USA; or "consciousness raising" in the women's movement'.
53. Ruether, *Liberation Theology*, p. 142.
54. Haraway, 'Situated Knowledges', p. 583.

6. *The Theology of Rosemary Radford Ruether* 171

has it, how they can use it, and what its effects are.[55] Like Harding, Ruether does not consider this sort of knowledge to be unattainable by people in positions of privilege and power over others, but she is aware that there is not a sense of urgency, of life-or-death need for this knowledge on the part of the oppressor. For Ruether, revelatory knowledge is made incarnate as one discerns (always with others) one's participation in the sociopolitical and economic structures that divide the people of the world into 'haves' and 'have nots', on both metaphysical and physical levels: those who have the capacity for reason and those who are not; those who are deemed to have enough to eat and those who have not. In her own words,

> I...see the perspective from the 'bottom' as key to my feminist liberation methodology. From my summer in Mississippi [in 1965] until today I find that the crucial way to see the dominant system of patriarchy, including its racism, classism, and colonialism, in critical perspective is to put myself constantly in those places where, in solidarity with its victims, I can see it from the underside.[56]

Ruether characterizes the knowledge gained and shared by 'oppressed groups committed to the struggle for justice for their community' as 'crucially revelatory', yet she is well aware that such knowledge does not have hegemonic status in the world; rather, it is the knowledge of a 'cognitive minority'.[57] Such situated, value-laden knowledge cannot be value-neutral, but then, for Ruether, no knowledge is or can ever be value-neutral; it is not possible to abstract fact from value.[58] The following quotation conveys most of her epistemological assumptions, and reveals why it is that she rejects as untenable a notion of value-neutral knowledge claims:

---

55. See Rosemary Radford Ruether, 'Introduction', in *idem* (ed.), *Women Healing Earth: Third World Women on Ecology, Feminism, and Religion* (Maryknoll, NY: Orbis Books, 1996), p. 1: 'I have for thirty years been deeply concerned with the oppressive use of power by my own country against subjugated people in the "Third World". My own experience of "crossing worlds" between affluent and poor, white and people of "color", and between "first"and "third" world has been revelatory and transformative for my understanding and my life. By viewing the ruling classes of my country from the underside, its evils and lies are revealed and put in the context of a larger reality and call for justice'.
56. Ruether, *Women and Redemption*, p. 222.
57. Ruether, *Women and Redemption*, pp. 222-23.
58. Ruether, *Gaia and God*, p. 39.

> Rather than assuming a standpoint outside of and unrelated to reality, from which 'objective' knowledge is possible, the observer is an integral part of the reality observed... What is constituted as the web of relationship will also be shaped by how we relate to it. The knower must take responsibility for shaping the reality that is known in ways that can be benign or destructive... [T]he knower cannot avoid ethical responsibility, not only in terms of how the knowledge may be subsequently used, but also in terms of what kind of relationship is implied by the stance of knowing itself.[59]

This pithy account of Ruether's presuppositions concerning humans as knowers in the world combines Hartsock's insistence that reality be conceived (on an ontological level) as inclusive of the sensuous interaction between humans and their physical environment—of which they are inescapably a part—with Haraway's insistence that 'objectivity' be conceived as an awareness of the relational (and world-shaping) character of all knowledge. With Haraway, Code and Addelson, Ruether also emphasizes *responsibility* as an important (if not the most important) element in any epistemological framework. But for Ruether, epistemic responsibility is not simply a philosophical or ethical or even political goal, although it is all of those things. To deny any epistemic responsibility for the knowledge claims one affirms, to pretend to abstract oneself from any relationship with one's surroundings (both human and non-human), is to commit a grave sin. It is to contribute to the 'distortion and corruption of human relationality'.[60] For Ruether 'sin exists precisely in the distortion of relationality',[61] *which is the consequence of 'false naming'*, false naming that supports the exploitation of 'others' (both human and non-human) as 'its' instead of 'Thous'.[62] Such false naming has shaped the 'entire symbolic universe' in the image of which Western Christian culture has been constructed.[63]

---

59. Ruether, *Gaia and God*, p. 39. This quotation comes from near the end of Ruether's discussion of recent developments in quantum and astrophysics.

60. Ruether, *Sexism and God-Talk*, p. 163. That humans are inescapably relational, interdependent creatures is one of Ruether's core anthropological presuppositions.

61. Ruether, *Sexism and God-Talk*, p. 181.

62. Ruether, *Sexism and God-Talk*, p. 163 and pp. 161 and 174 (on her use of Buber's I and Thou). See also her *New Woman/New Earth*, p. 211.

63. Ruether, *Sexism and God-Talk*, p. 173.

6. The Theology of Rosemary Radford Ruether

In relating her conception of sin (as distorted relationship) to human societies structured around distorted or false metaphysical presuppositions, Ruether incorporates within her theological anthropology the traditional theological understanding that the sins of the fathers have been visited upon the children; or, to put it another way, that humanity exists in a 'fallen' state.[64] For Ruether, this fallen state is 'a reality that perpetuates itself, both through socioeconomic and political structures and through ideology that shapes education and socialization at every level'.[65] Most importantly, this fallen state is rooted in and sustained by false epistemological assumptions concerning humans as knowers, e.g., the false assumption that women are less capable of rational thought than men; the false assumption that knowers are not in an interdependent relationship with each other as well as with the rest of creation, or the world that is known; and the false assumption that knowledge itself, to be worthy of the name, must be eternal and immutable: ideal forms abstracted from the messy, complicated, and interdependent character of physical reality, a reality that is both historical (and therefore ever-changing) and finite.[66]

For Ruether there is a profound connection between the traditional Christian rejection of the finite character of existence (a rejection she repudiates almost as often as she locates the origin of this belief in the Christian synthesis of apocalyptic and Hellenistic thought) and knowledge claims that seek to transcend any relationship to time, place and human authorship. This flight from finitude is simultaneously theologically and epistemologically irresponsible; according to Ruether it is a projection of human desires to deny the inescapable limits of creaturely existence:

---

64. Ruether, *Sexism and God-Talk*, p. 161.
65. Ruether, *Sexism and God-Talk*, p. 164. She is particularly critical of the socializing of males and females into so-called complementary 'masculine' and 'feminine' roles: 'What is called "masculine" is the egoistic attitudes of the powerful, and what is derogated as "feminine" is the defeated traits of the powerless, both of which have little to do with the full potential of men and women as they might exist in an equalitarian society' (Ruether, *New Woman/New Earth*, p. 142). See also *Sexism and God-Talk*, p. 111, and *Women and Redemption*, p. 166, where she writes that 'both masculinity and femininity are false distortions of humanness'.
66. See Ruether, *New Woman/New Earth*, p. 211; *Sexism and God-Talk*, pp. 264-65; *Gaia and God*, pp. 251-53.

> We should not pretend to know what we do not know or to have 'revealed' to us what is the projection of our wishes. Moreover, whatever we wish is not thereby proved to be probably true or something upon which we should 'wager' our lives. There needs to be a compatibility between our wishes and what we know of our finite nature and primary responsibilities.[67]

And for Ruether, our primary responsibilities are to this earth and all the creatures of this earth, born and yet unborn. 'It is not our calling to be concerned about the eternal meaning of our lives, and religion should not make this the focus of its message. Our responsibility is to use our temporal life span to create a just and good community for our generation and for our children'.[68] Theologically, humans are called to revere life, to attend to life out of a sense of committed love.[69] We are not called, nor are we able, to escape its ambiguities and tragedies. This is the 'ought' that Ruether lays upon Western Christian culture at this time, from her place as a privileged White woman living in the US at the end of the twentieth century: humans ought to stop denying our own finitude and acknowledge the finite nature of this earth; humans must begin to live responsibly, within the limits of existence given with existence.[70] Because all people are fully, blessedly human, the resources necessary for life must be shared equitably among all, not hoarded by the privileged, powerful few. But humans are not the only earth creatures whose survival matters. Humans must acknowledge the relational truths revealed by the earth sciences: that we are dependent for life on the flourishing of plants and animals whose habitats are daily being destroyed.[71]

Dependency is a fundamental character of human existence. Most often this dependency has either been denied or, conversely, utterly

---

67. Ruether, *Sexism and God-Talk*, p. 257.
68. Ruether, *Sexism and God-Talk*, p. 258. See also her *New Woman/New Earth*, p. 211. She writes of 'using the human capacity for consciousness, not to alienate ourselves from nature, but rather, to nurture, perfect, and renew her natural harmonies, so that earth might be fair, not only for us and our children, but for all generations of living things still to come'.
69. See Ruether, *Gaia and God*, p. 273 and p. 57.
70. See Ruether, *To Change the World*, p. 66: 'The Western dream of infinitely expanding power and wealth defies the actual finitude of ourselves and the world and conceals the exploitative use of other people's resources. It must be replaced with a new culture of acceptance of finitude and limits'.
71. See Ruether, *Gaia and God*, pp. 47-58.

embraced, used as an excuse for not acting responsibly where and when it is possible to do so. When combined with an image of an omnipotent Father God, who, it is supposed, eventually will make everything anew anyway, the result has been the callous domination of 'mere matter' (a word which comes from the Latin *mater*, or mother) and the domination as well of all those humans categorically identified with matter rather than with 'spirit'. The knowledge concerning humankind that Ruether seeks to make incarnate, the revelation made incarnate in her theology, is the awareness that humans are not only dependent upon the rest of creation for life, but are also responsible for tending to creation that it might continue to sustain life for the full measure of the earth's days. The problem, according to Ruether, is that a world of powers and principalities has been constructed within this blessed creation, and may yet destroy the earth.[72]

Creation and the World

For over thirty years Ruether has consistently maintained a distinction in her thought between 'creation' and 'the world'. She draws this distinction (although she transforms it somewhat in her thought) from Christian scripture (in particular Pauline texts in the New Testament), and often writes about it with the metaphors 'powers' and 'principalities', also drawn from Paul. Simply put, according to Ruether,

> In the New Testament 'the world' does not stand for the nature of the original Creation; it refers to Creation as fallen, existing under the servitude to man's idols and given over to an oppressive relationship between man and man. This is the theological identity of 'the world'... 'This world' is creation considered from the point of view of the Fall... 'This world' is the sphere governed under the law of alienation and oppression, under the dominion of the powers and principalities.[73]

According to Ruether, 'the world', constructed by humans in the (hierarchical) image of a symbolic universe projected by the ruling class elite, is a real but fundamentally distorted edifice. It is a place of 'alienation and oppression'; inclusive of all those social and political systems constructed around 'a false system of alienated dualisms'.[74] 'The

---

72. Ruether, *Gaia and God*, pp. 85-111.
73. Ruether, *The Radical Kingdom*, pp. 164-65. See also Merton and Ruether, *At Home in the World*, p. 28: ' "The world" is not creation, but is the sphere of the powers and principalities.'
74. Ruether, *Sexism and God-Talk*, p. 71.

world' is thus an expression of human attempts to deny the creaturely fact of interdependent, finite existence. However, and this is a critical point, Ruether's distinction between 'creation' and 'the world' is *not* to be understood as a facile separation of non-human 'nature' and human 'culture', with an accompanying positive evaluation of 'nature' and negative evaluation of 'culture'. Nor is her use of the metaphors of 'powers' and 'principalities' to be understood in the traditional sense of 'fallen angels', evil forces exerting their influences on powerless, helpless humans. Rather, for Ruether the powers and principalities of the world are human powers, human principles that systematically discriminate against and oppress entire categories of people, as well as non-human creatures and nature. These powers and principles are inhumane and unjust, and they have been repeatedly enacted to create an inhumane and unjust world.

In contrast to 'the world' of alienation and oppression, there is 'creation', which Ruether affirms as 'good'. However, her use of the word 'good' must be understood in the sense of 'holy' (a metaphor for which there is no epistemological equivalent), *not* in the sense of funda-mentally benign or benevolent.[75] Creation is as terrifying, as awe-full as it is wonderful; it is the incarnation of a fearsome, holy mystery, but it never existed in the form of an original paradise.[76] Nor is 'creation', in Ruether's thought, to be understood in a completed or static sense.[77] Creation is in process; the universe is still growing, constantly changing. Creation has a history, and this history is unfinished. Old stars die, and new stars and planets (and thus, potentially, new life forms) come into existence. They do not, however, arrive *ex nihilo*. Ruether affirms that whenever any aspect of creation perishes, the material stuff of that creature or plant or object is gathered into the divine (alternatively, 'cosmic') matrix of all being, where it becomes

---

75. Ruether is critical of 'the romantic project of return to nature', especially when this includes the elevation of all that is 'feminine' and the rejection of all that is 'masculine' or 'rational', including human technology. See Ruether, *Sexism and God-Talk*, pp. 41-42 and 84-85.

76. See Ruether, *Gaia and God*, p. 270: 'to know we stand on holy ground'. See also *idem, Sexism and God-Talk*, p. 168. Ruether considers various versions of the 'original paradise' myth 'to be a mythologizing of early infancy, in which the mother provides the time of ease and plenty from her own body…'

77. Ruether, *Sexism and God-Talk*, p. 70; see also Ruether, *Gaia and God*, pp. 251-53.

6. *The Theology of Rosemary Radford Ruether*   177

the substance that enables and sustains new life, new aspects of creation.[78]

Here I need to clarify and elaborate upon Ruether's conception of the relationship between creation and the divine. For Ruether there is an inseparable relation between creation (or 'being') and God/ess—'an unpronounceable and inadequate' term that Ruether uses when trying to write of the divine in an inclusive yet singular manner:[79]

> Feminist theology needs to affirm the God of Exodus, of liberation and new being, but *as rooted in the foundations of being rather than as its antithesis*. The God/ess who is the foundation (at one and the same time) of our being and our new being embraces both the roots of the material substratum of our existence (matter) and also the endlessly new creative potential (spirit).[80]

Ruether's conception of God/ess as 'the empowering matrix, She, in whom we live and move and have our being', is also inclusive of 'the total community of being', past, present, and unknown future.[81] 'It is this matrix...that is "everlasting", that subsists underneath the coming to be and passing away of individuated beings and even planetary worlds'.[82] Again, the divine matrix is not identified solely with the immanent stuff of 'being'. The divine matrix of all creation includes all that has been but is no longer, as well as a transcendent horizon of creative possibilities for creation, not all of which will ever be made incarnate.[83] In short, Ruether's conception of God/ess is as 'the source of being that underlies creation and grounds its nature and future potential for continual transformative renewal in biophilic mutuality'.[84]

---

78. See Ruether, *Sexism and God-Talk*, pp. 70-71, 258; idem, *Gaia and God*, p. 252.

79. Ruether, *Sexism and God-Talk*, p. 46.

80. Ruether, *Sexism and God-Talk*, pp. 70-71 (italics added). The influence of Paul Tillich's depiction of 'being' and 'new being' is clearly present in this quote.

81. Ruether, *Sexism and God-Talk*, pp. 266 and 257, respectively.

82. Ruether, *Sexism and God-Talk*, p. 257. The quote continues, 'Acceptance of death, then, is acceptance of the finitude of our individuated centers of being, but also our identification with the larger matrix as our total self that contains us all'. Here again she stresses the finite character of human lives.

83. Ruether, *Sexism and God-Talk*, p. 85. In many respects Ruether's conception of the divine matrix or Holy *Shekinah* (Hebrew word for presence of God) is similar to the characterization of the consequent nature of God in process theology. It is panentheistic, mutable, and *not* omnipotent.

84. Ruether, *Women and Redemption*, p. 223.

This last point is critical. The divine matrix, while in no way resembling a personal deity, is in Ruether's thought a positive, purposeful force or power, although not an omnipotent one. In addition, Ruether's conception of this 'empowering matrix' includes a yearning or a desire for relational mutuality among and between all aspects of creation. Such mutuality is never without ambiguity and tragedy; nonetheless Ruether seems to be suggesting that creation is a holy 'place' and 'process' in which life, although constrained and subject to the limits of existence given with existence, *seems to flourish in moderation*—when the 'powers' and 'principalities' of the human world do not prevent or prohibit such flourishing.[85]

Flourishing in moderation can also occur when transformative, justice-enhancing possibilities are made incarnate (or enacted) by human beings, who therefore must be regarded as co-creators of creation, as well as the creators of 'the world'. It is in this regard that Ruether's conception of 'creation' and 'the world' does not lend itself to a neat nature/culture split. Some cultural artefacts do belong, theologically, with creation and not with the world.[86] Among these transformative cultural artefacts Ruether identifies the Jubilee tradition of Lev. 25.8-12 as providing a baseline model of just relations among humans and between humans and the rest of creation, while at the same time acknowledging and seeking to minimize the harmful effects of 'the world' upon creation (both human and non-human).[87] Time is set aside every week for people and animals to rest and every seven years for the land itself to rest. Every fifty years debts are forgiven and slaves set free. In this way, periodically both 'humanity and nature recover their just balance'.[88] However, such a balance is never, in Ruether's thought, able to be maintained, unchanging, forever. At an ontological level change is the nature of creation and all existence.

---

85. In Chapter 4 I noted that Nelson, Keller and Code all wrote of reality's 'intractable' constraints; this notion is implicitly present throughout Ruether's work.

86. Ruether, *To Change the World*, p. 69: 'We must seek the life intended by God for us within these limits [of change and death]. The return to harmony in the covenant of creation is not a matter of cyclical return to the same, for each new achievement of workable balances is different, based on new environments and technologies. It is a historical project that has to be undertaken again and again in changing circumstances. Each great social movement, such as the labour movement, leaves some needed changes undone and generates new contradictions'.

87. Ruether, *Sexism and God-Talk*, pp. 254-55.

88. Ruether, *Sexism and God-Talk*, p. 255.

6. *The Theology of Rosemary Radford Ruether*

To conclude then, for Ruether this material earth, this creation of which humans are inextricably a part, is our home, but not ours alone. Upon (and often by misusing the material of) this life-sustaining earth humans have erected social, political, economic, technological and military structures and institutions that are used by an elite few to oppress the majority of people on earth, and to destroy and damage entire species of plants and animals and their habitat, thereby also threatening human survival. While she affirms that humans have the capacity to use our knowledge and power to co-create a more just, more equitable creation, she also affirms the tragic possibility that the powers and principalities of 'the world' will not be converted to the service of creation.[89] Again, creation is that of which humans, as 'thinking animals', are inextricably a part. Physical, material reality, including the interconnections and interdependencies which make up this never static material reality, is, in Ruether's thought, the foundation of the only life we can ever know. However, as theological and epistemological and ethical and political agents, we have yet to acknowledge the depth of our dependency upon creation; even now we are enacting the destruction of creation and of ourselves.

While the divine matrix will remain no matter what humans do, what has been destroyed will never be made anew. Thus the theo-ethical and epistemological demand Ruether lays upon humankind: to tend responsibly to an irreplaceable creation. With our attention thus focused,

> We can then recognize that the fragile fruit of the tree of life is indeed lovely and good for discernment, and eat the fruit with relish, making it a part of our bodies. This is the possible redemption of life on earth. But it is possible only when we put aside the impossible redemptions of final conquest of limits in a realm of immortal life untouched by sorrow, vulnerability, and finitude.[90]

Conclusion

I suggest that Rosemary Ruether's feminist Christian theology represents a thirty-year elaboration upon and refinement of the metaphysical presuppositions named at the beginning of this chapter. Profoundly

---

89. Ruether, *Women and Redemption*, p. 224: 'God cannot force this conversion upon us (I agree with process theology here.)... I believe failure is possible, though not fated'.

90. Ruether, *Women and Redemption*, p. 254.

aware of the interrelated nature of all theological assertions concerning humanity, God and creation, she has systematically transformed all of these concepts in order that her whole theology might consistently affirm, simultaneously, the full, unqualified humanity of every person without exception, the finite and blessed character of all life and all aspects of creation, and a sense of God as that non-omnipotent matrix of being which allows for the possibility but not the certainty of limited, finite life and lives. Her theological anthropology, while utterly senseless apart from her value judgment concerning the full humanity of every person, conveys no fixed essence of 'woman' or 'man', but rather reveals an understanding of human beings as differently embodied, thoroughly social creatures—as dependent upon our relations with non-human reality for our lives (and thus our identities) as we are upon our relations with other humans for our lives, identities and knowledge(s).[91] Finally, in close affinity with process thought, Ruether insists upon the constantly changing, never fixed or static nature of the entire cosmos, including the divine matrix of all that is. Neither theologically nor epistemologically does she affirm a final, unchanging truth.

Rather, she accepts the existence of multiple truths, each relative to a particular time and place and community of knowledge-makers, each inseparable from the value judgments and ethical/political requirements of those particular knowledge-makers. With the feminist standpoint theorists, Ruether perceives the knowledge of oppressed communities to be rather less distorted, more aware of the life-and-death dynamics of power than the knowledge of dominant/dominating communities. Ruether also identifies, within present-day epistemic communities, the voices, values and insights of past epistemic agents. From Mary Magdalene to Mary Wollstonecraft, Margaret Fell to Margaret Mead, Ruether's understanding of the social matrix in which both self(in relation)-identity and communal knowledge are developed is inclusive of those historical agents whose presuppositions and value judgments can be interpreted to support and enable 'us' (for some 'us') in 'our' struggles now. Lastly, Ruether is exceedingly clear about what she

91. I suggest that Ruether's anthropological and ontological assumptions are, in this respect, quite similar to Catherine Keller's recent description of 'a social ontology of the self'. See Catherine Keller, 'Seeking and Sucking: On Relation and Essence in Feminist Theology', in Rebecca S. Chopp and Sheila Greeve Davaney (eds.), *Horizons in Feminist Theology: Identity, Tradition, and Norms* (Minneapolis, MN: Augsburg Fortress, 1997), p. 77.

6. *The Theology of Rosemary Radford Ruether*

perceives to be the integral relationship between theology, epistemology and responsible action. The following quotation, cited earlier, sums up her understanding of both the purpose of theology and the purpose of knowledge: 'It is not our calling to be concerned about the eternal meaning of our lives, and religion should not make this the focus of its message. Our responsibility is to use our temporal life span to create a just and good community for our generation and for our children'.[92]

With this analysis of Ruether's metaphysical and epistemological presuppositions in place, it is now possible to discern those presuppositions that Carter Heyward and Sallie McFague share with Ruether. Accordingly, in the following chapters I shall refer again to Ruether's core assertions whenever they are shared by Heyward or McFague.

---

92. Ruether, *Sexism and God-Talk*, p. 258. See also *idem*, *New Woman/New Earth*, p. 211. She writes of 'using the human capacity for consciousness, not to alienate ourselves from nature, but rather, to nurture, perfect, and renew her natural harmonies, so that earth might be fair, not only for us and our children, but for all generations of living things still to come'.

Chapter 7

PARADIGMATIC AND EPISTEMOLOGICAL ELEMENTS IN THE
THEOLOGY OF CARTER HEYWARD

At the start of the previous chapter I named the significant influence Rosemary Ruether has had on my own academic and intellectual development. I begin this chapter in a similar manner, by elaborating briefly on the impact Carter Heyward's work has had on my theological understanding and imagination. If, through her theology, Rosemary Ruether taught and continues to teach me to locate my own work in relation to deep-rooted historical trends and patterns of thought, to ground my work historically, then, through her theology, Carter Heyward teaches me to ground and imagine my work in and through the particularities of my own life. She is a theologian who insists that theology cannot and must not be abstracted or removed from this life, here and now, wherever and however it is being lived. As she says, 'particularity is the window of all joy, sorrow, and knowledge for all of us'.[1]

In Heyward's case this means that her own imaginative, constructive efforts are rooted in the soil of North Carolina, where she was born and raised in a White Southern Protestant family.[2] It means that she grounds her work as an Episcopal priest, teacher and theologian in the specificities of her own Christian, feminist, lesbian life, even as she

---

1. Carter Heyward, *Touching Our Strength: The Erotic as Power and the Love of God* (San Francisco: Harper & Row, 1989), p. 10. This quotation comes at the end of a paragraph which she begins by stating, 'knowing our particular social locations and our limits is not only intellectually honest. It is intellectually empowering as a lens through which we may catch a glimpse of what is, paradoxically, universally true—that all people are limited by the particularities of their life experiences' (pp. 9-10).

2. See Carter Heyward, *Staying Power: Reflections on Gender, Justice, and Compassion* (Cleveland, OH: Pilgrim Press, 1995), pp. 66-76.

acknowledges that these aspects of her identity are constantly evolving, changing.³ Already it should be evident that elements in Heyward's thought resonate strongly with the concern for situated knowledges expressed by the feminist epistemologists discussed in Chapters 4 and 5. However, I want to acknowledge that it was primarily through Heyward's writings that I began to comprehend the epistemological necessity of acknowledging the particular, always tangled elements of my own life as these, inevitably, seep through whatever I write.

Perhaps the most profound influence Heyward has had on my theological development, however, comes from her unwavering insistence that 'we who currently constitute the Christian church are the temporary authors and guardians of "Christian truth". *It is ours to determine and ours to teach*'.⁴ Until I read Carter Heyward's theology, until I immersed myself in it for weeks and months on end, I never understood the extent to which I, as a student of theology, had unconsciously accepted the notion that it was appropriate to criticize elements of 'the tradition' but somehow not my place to claim it as my own and reconceptualize every element of it. In all fairness to Rosemary Ruether, it should have been possible for me to 'hear' this from her work, but I did not. It was not until I read Heyward that I realized that I too could be a constructive theologian. This may have had something to do with their different writing styles. Ruether writes in measured sentences meant to be read and studied, while Heyward often writes with a cadence and a rhythm that reminds me of rocking chairs and scorching summer days, of the kind of heat that soothes and sears you both at once. Her words are words for the ears to hear and the tongue to taste, not merely for the eyes to see.⁵ To put it another way, Heyward most often speaks and writes in one of my first languages, a language to which I respond with my heart as much as my mind.

Or it might be the case that I first read Heyward rather more closely, held onto her words a bit more tightly, simply because she writes *as* a White Protestant feminist lesbian. It is no doubt significant that I read

---

3. On identity, see Heyward, *The Redemption of God*, p. 217. Heyward is professor of theology at the Howard Chandler Robbins professor of theology at the Episcopal Divinity School in Cambridge, Massachusetts.

4. Carter Heyward, *Speaking of Christ: A Lesbian Feminist Voice* (ed. Ellen C. Davis; New York: The Pilgrim Press, 1989), p. 34 (italics added).

5. Much of Heyward's published work consists of sermons and talks written to be heard, not simply read.

most of Heyward's work for the first time in 1988–89, while an openly lesbian MTS student at Garrett-Evangelical Theological Seminary (a United Methodist institution);[6] unfortunately, lesbian and gay students in the MDiv programme at this school must remain closeted or face the probability that they will be asked to leave the programme, and hence not become ordained ministers, solely on the basis of their 'unacceptable' sexual orientation/preference. Accordingly, into this culture of fear and silence (and lesbian MDiv students literally walking away from me when they saw me coming, only to double back and speak to me when no one else was looking), Heyward's self-avowedly lesbian feminist words came as water to a drought-stricken land.[7] Like most good rainstorms, all this water was accompanied by a fair bit of thunder and lightning. 'That which does not bear directly upon human life and move toward the creation of justice in society is not worth our bother'.[8] Lightning. 'If we do not take seriously [the] sacred vocation of Christian interpretation it will be taken from us, as it is in every generation, by false prophets'.[9] Thunder, sounding right in my ear. For the first time I knew myself to be included in an author's 'we', and simultaneously felt enabled and empowered to participate in such interpretive and constructive work. It is therefore with a great deal of respect and gratitude for her (and its) existence that I now turn to an examination of the paradigmatic and epistemological elements in Heyward's theology.

As in the previous chapter, I shall begin by presenting Heyward's understanding of theology broadly considered, and shall then identify what I consider to be the central focus of her theological system, or, better, pattern. Without an understanding of this constant, driving focus it is impossible to comprehend how each of the paradigmatic elements in her theological pattern fit together. Following this brief overview I shall then identify and discuss her understanding of human beings (her theological anthropology) as knowing agents (including, inseparably, her epistemological assumptions concerning the production of know-

---

6. The MTS, or Master of Theological Studies degree, is directed primarily toward the academic study of theology, rather than to preparing students for ordination as ministers.

7. Importantly, two of her books were published and appeared at G-ETS in 1989, just when I most needed to read them, was most unsure of my own 'right' to be studying and beginning to write constructive theology.

8. Heyward, *The Redemption of God*, p. 20.

9. Heyward, *Speaking of Christ*, p. 34.

7. The Theology of Carter Heyward

ledge) and her understanding of the world (theologically, creation) as it is known. Throughout all these discussions I shall identify the discernible influences of past theological and philosophical developments on her work.

The Nature and Purpose of 'Theology' in Heyward's Thought

For Heyward, feminist Christian theology is not and must not become an individual, passive, 'cerebral exercise'.[10] It is instead a communal, active and ever-changing *process*: the process of enabling wherever and whenever possible the flourishing of love and justice among humans and between humans and other 'earth creatures' in the world.[11] In Heyward's thought, to do theology is neither to engage in individual spiritual navel-gazing nor is it to engage in individual intellectual self-stimulation. Rather, it is to attempt, always with others, to help bring justice and love to those places and lives from which they are absent or denied. Importantly, this is my conception of Heyward's understanding of the nature and purpose of her theology, drawn from statements made by her, such as the one quoted above: 'That which does not bear directly upon human life and move toward the creation of justice in society is not worth our bother'.

Her own *definition* of theology, if taken out of the context of her work as a whole, can appear to support only implicitly her communal, justice-centred understanding of the nature and purpose of theological reflection, or, better, theological praxis. For instance, she has defined theology as 'a capacity to discern God's presence here and now and to reflect on what this means',[12] and as 'critical, creative reflection on the patterns, shape, and movement of the Sacred in our life together'.[13] (Here the influence of existentialist thought is evident in the this-

---

10. Heyward, *The Redemption of God*, p. 20.

11. See Carter Heyward, *Our Passion for Justice: Images of Power, Sexuality, and Liberation* (New York: Pilgrim Press, 1984), p. 12 for a discussion of the communal nature of feminist theology. The phrase 'earth creatures', which Heyward uses particularly in her later work, originates (at least in feminist Christian theological discourse) with Phyllis Trible. It is Trible's translation of the Hebrew word *'adam*. See Phyllis Trible, *God and the Rhetoric of Sexuality* (Philadelphia: Fortress Press, 1978), pp. 72-143.

12. Heyward, *Our Passion for Justice*, p. 7.

13. Heyward, *Touching Our Strength*, p. 22, and n. 9 on p. 61. She takes her account of Bultmann's thought from his *Jesus Christ and Mythology*.

worldly focus of her theological attention. And indeed Heyward has named her own work to be in continuity with Bultmann's belief 'that the motivation for all theology is to be better able to comprehend our own existence'.[14]) Again, however, when taken out of context the definitions of theology offered by Heyward can be somewhat misleading unless they are read as referring to a *communal* or *collective* struggle to 'comprehend ourselves in a world *in which relation is broken violently*'.[15] This is a critical point, and one that I shall discuss in much greater detail when I examine her presuppositions concerning human beings and the world: the context in which she grounds all her theological praxis is that of a society, culture and world in which abusive relationships, whether between groups of people or between individuals, whether economically or symbolically structured and maintained, *are rampant*. The issue, for Heyward, is that once such knowledge or comprehension of the 'brokenness' of existence is achieved (albeit always partially, imperfectly, or, as she sometimes writes, 'through a glass darkly'[16]) it is a theo-ethical imperative that such knowledge be acted upon. It is for this reason that I describe the nature and purpose of theology in Heyward's thought as *the communal effort to co-create love and justice in the world*.

'A Theology of Mutual Relation': An Overview of Heyward's Theological Pattern

In Appendix A ('Roots of Relation in Liberal Protestantism: Schleiermacher') of her doctoral dissertation, later published as *The Redemption of God: A Theology of Mutual Relation*, Heyward names the theological and philosophical developments most influential in her thought:

> I see my work in continuity with [the] liberal relational theological tradition as informed (1) by the Barthian critique of its failure to acknowledge the depths of human sin; (2) by a Marxian critique of its bourgeois individualism; and (3) by a feminist critique of its indifference to structures of male dominance…[17]

---

14. See Heyward, *The Redemption of God*, p. 28.
15. Heyward, *The Redemption of God*, p. 35 (italics added). See also *idem*, *Our Passion for Justice*, p. 68: 'To immerse ourselves in theology and ministry of *radical participation* may be to survive' (italics in original).
16. See Heyward, *Our Passion for Justice*, pp. 33, 46, 126.
17. Heyward, *The Redemption of God*, p. 187.

While Heyward thus locates her work squarely in the liberal stream of post-Enlightenment thought, it is necessary to stress her rejection of any single theological paradigm (or any single theologian's work) as the only way to approach theology. According to Heyward, 'there is no universally correct theological system that can be applied to all people, everywhere, at all times'.[18] She is insistent on this point: theology ought not to consist of a single set of a priori presuppositions that are then applied, as from above, in the same way to every different situation or context.[19] Rather, and this is a value judgment closely aligned with the value judgments found in Latin American liberation theology and Black theology, as well as in Ruether's work, she affirms that theological praxis ought to (indeed cannot help but) grow out of the lived experiences and felt needs of different communities.[20] Importantly, this theological affirmation is simultaneously an epistemological affirmation. She writes: 'epistemologically, feminist theology moves from action to ideology, rather than vice-versa'.[21] I shall elaborate on this point in the discussion of her theological anthropology, but because Heyward begins all of her work by acknowledging not just the theological and philosophical traditions in which she participates but also the communities in which she lives and acts, and to whom she holds her work accountable, it is vital that I identify these communities as well, thereby contextualizing her theology. As mentioned above, Heyward writes as a White, North American, 'middle-strata', Christian feminist lesbian; she acknowledges that she writes primarily 'to serve

---

18. Heyward, *Touching Our Strength*, p. 223.
19. See Heyward, *The Redemption of God*, p. 12: 'The theologian's on-going constructive task is to discern common assumptions which are emerging in the praxis out of which and to which she speaks. Her task is *not* to determine which assumptions "have always been" Christian. No common understanding of such words as "God", "humanity", and "Jesus Christ" can be assumed as *a priori* to the theological task' (emphasis in original).
20. See Mud Flower Collective, *God's Fierce Whimsy: Christian Feminism and Theological Education* (New York: Pilgrim Press, 1985), pp. 17-21, for a discussion of the points of similarity and dissimilarity between feminist Christian and liberation and Black theological understandings of praxis. While this book is the result of a collective process, Heyward did much of the writing up and editing of the collective's insights. For this reason, where there appears to be collective agreement on an issue, I consider the opinions so stated to be representative of Heyward's thought.
21. Heyward, *Our Passion for Justice*, p. 228.

the interests of lesbians and gaymen', 'in the service of feminists and womanists—women and men of different colors', and 'on behalf of the interests of progressive and radical religious folk—especially, though not exclusively, christians and former christians'.[22] With the understanding that it is out of her experiences in these various, sometimes overlapping and sometimes conflicting communities that she crafts her theology, and to these communities that she holds her work accountable, it is time now to identify the distinctive elements of her theological pattern.

On the one hand, to attempt to sketch an outline of Heyward's theology *as* theology, that is, apart from a discussion of the epistemological elements running through it, is to risk thoroughly distorting her words. She herself has described the focus of much of her work as a concern with 'calling especially, though not exclusively, white liberal and radical christian women beyond our attachments to the individualistic 'self' concept of a liberal religious and political *epistemology*...'[23] On the other hand, before I can discuss the epistemological implications of her own characterization of her work as 'a theology of mutual relation, of knowing and being known', it is imperative that I wrestle with the meaning of 'a theology of mutual relation', or the distinctive shape of her theology as a whole.[24] To begin to make sense of what is unique to Heyward's theological pattern it is necessary first of all to identify the hermeneutical norm at the heart of all her writings. The interpretive norm central to her work, based, according to Heyward, on a value judgment, 'is right-relation or *the love of one's neighbor as oneself*'.[25]

---

22. See Carter Heyward, *When Boundaries Betray Us: Beyond Illusions of What is Ethical in Therapy and Life* (New York: HarperCollins, 1994), p. 248, for Heyward's discussion of the term 'middle-strata'. She does not use the term 'middle class' because it does not reflect the reality of the 'fluid, and downward, mobility' of what is usually considered as a stable, or upwardly mobile, class of people. The rest of the phrases in quotation marks are taken from Heyward, *Touching Our Strength*, p. 7.

23. Heyward, *Staying Power*, p. ix (italics added).

24. Heyward, *Staying Power*, p. 120.

25. Heyward, *The Redemption of God*, p. 15 (emphasis in original). See also p. 14, where Heyward notes that the values she affirms 'form the interpretive framework within which I make whatever claims I do to theological knowledge'. From this statement it is evident that Heyward considers value judgments to be an integral part of the theological paradigm within which she works.

There are two points that I need to discuss with regard to Heyward's hermeneutical norm. The first has to do with the phrase 'right-relation'. In Heyward's work the concept of 'right relation' (in her later works she does not use the hyphen) is the touchstone to which she returns again and again, and the cornerstone on which she constructs her entire theology. Right relation, according to Heyward, is 'mutual relation', and mutual relations are just or loving relations. However, and this is the second point I need to mention, by 'love' she does not mean a private, individualistic feeling, but an openness to action: 'a willingness to participate with others in the healing of a broken world and broken lives'.[26] Therefore, with regard to her hermeneutical norm, it is by the physical presence and absence of right relations (or justice, or love) between neighbours that Heyward evaluates human and creaturely existence. Importantly, while she appropriates from Christian scripture the phrase 'love one's neighbour as oneself', she does not claim that her model of 'right relation' has thus always been a Christian theological norm. Rather than claim authority *from* the Christian tradition, she confronts the tradition with the value judgments of her communities of accountability.[27] In other words, it is not upon the authority of scripture or tradition or the ostensibly unmediated Word of God that Heyward grounds her theology. Nonetheless, the concept of 'God' is a central component in Heyward's theological pattern. This is the case precisely because she defines 'God' as 'our power in mutual relation'.[28]

Given the tightly woven nature of Heyward's writings, it is not possible to make clear Heyward's understanding of God as our power in mutual relation, or as the 'resource and power of relation',[29] without also discussing her understanding and use of the metaphor 'sacred', an effort that involves discussing again her understanding and use of the

---

26. Heyward, *Our Passion for Justice*, p. 187. See also p. 92: 'To really love is to topple unjust structures, bringing down the principalities and powers of domination and control at all levels of human social relations'. It is significant that Heyward uses the language of 'powers and principalities' in the same way that Ruether does.

27. A theological aside: for Heyward, there is nothing inherently better about the Christian tradition than any other religious tradition—it is simply one among others, and ought not be considered as more inherently authoritative than any other tradition, although she acknowledges the powerful influence the Christian tradition has had on shaping in particular the symbolic universe wrapped around Euroamerican societies. See Heyward, *Speaking of Christ*, pp. 64-65.

28. Heyward, *Touching Our Strength*, p. 188.

29. Heyward, *The Redemption of God*, p. 31.

metaphors 'love' and 'justice'. Simply put, Heyward allows of no distinction in her thought between notions of 'love' and notions of 'justice'; to love is to make justice in the world, to do justice is to enact (or make incarnate) love. Further, *to do either is to participate with others in 'godding', or the sacred work and play of making God-as-love/justice incarnate in the world*.[30] Put differently, there is absolutely no *qualitative* difference in her thought between 'justice', 'love', 'God' and the 'sacred' at all. She herself removes any such distinction when she describes 'love and justice in human life as the only sacred—godly, right, and normative—dimension of our life together'.[31] Or, again, when she writes, 'the pattern of the Sacred in our life together is justice. The shape of God is justice'.[32]

Heyward's steadfast refusal to allow any qualitative difference between human acts of love and justice and her understanding of 'God' or the 'sacred' is, in my opinion, one of the most distinctive contributions she makes to feminist Christian theology. Her avowal that human beings, through our actions, do or do not make God incarnate in the world is a profoundly innovative theological move. In making it she is not merely criticizing a hierarchical, dualistic understanding of 'God' and 'humanity', which is, as Ruether noted, arguably *the* ontological (and value-laden) assertion most central to traditional Christian theology.[33] Rather, she is presenting a radically transformed understanding of both 'God' *and* 'humanity': a vision in which human activity *is* divine activity, whenever and wherever it is just and loving.

While there is no *qualitative* distinction, there is, however, a crucial *quantitative* difference between Heyward's understanding of love/justice/God/the sacred as made incarnate by human beings and her understanding of God/the sacred/justice/love as it exists apart from

30. Heyward, *The Redemption of God*, p. 9: 'The human act of love, befriending, making justice is our act of making God incarnate in the world'.
31. Heyward, *The Redemption of God*, p. 222.
32. Heyward, *Touching Our Strength*, p. 22.
33. See Heyward, *The Redemption of God*, p. 192. In 'Appendix B: Chalcedon's Ontology', Heyward describes the decisions reached by the council of Chalcedon (451 CE) regarding 'the relation between the divine and human in Jesus Christ' as reaching the following metaphysical conclusion: '*that all life exists within an ontological structure of hierarchical dualism, in which the higher essence is the valuable essence*' (emphasis original). Of particular importance in Heyward's thought is that this ontological dualism plays itself out in traditional theological anthropology in the form of 'divine activity over human passivity'.

humanity. As insistent as she is on humanity's responsibility for doing the work of love and justice, for making God/the sacred incarnate, she is equally insistent on 'the "more-ness" of God beyond simple humanity'.[34] For example, Heyward writes of 'the whole inhabited earth as sacred space'.[35] Likewise, she characterizes 'the ground we share in this world as holy ground'.[36] While most of her theological attention is devoted to human relations and human activity, she never identifies 'God' (or the sacred, or the holy) solely with humanity, or with any single human being. This point is important; it is not simply as a corrective to the sexism of the church, but is also the 'more-ness' of God that Heyward emphasizes when she refuses to identify 'God' 'with any one person in any time or place', i.e. with God the Son in Jerusalem two thousand years ago or God the Father in heaven:[37]

> To focus messianically on any one person, to try to locate and establish God in any single figure, to insist that relational tension and ambiguity be broken and that the definition of 'God' be handed to us as a package in the person of a lone messiah, is to deny the movement of power in relation through many incarnations in history.[38]

It is also, implicitly, the 'more-ness' of God that sustains Heyward's vision of a theology of mutual relation, a vision she plants solidly in a world of 'alienation', a world replete with badly broken relations (usually of domination and subordination) among human beings, between humans and other earth creatures, and between humans and the very air, water and soil all earth creatures need to survive.[39] When in those fleeting instances genuinely mutual, loving, enabling relations are experienced, the knowledge that there is more to life than domination and oppression, suffering and death is realized. Such knowledge is literally made incarnate in the very bodies of those who have

---

34. Personal correspondence, 17 April 1997.
35. Heyward, *Speaking of Christ*, p. 24.
36. Heyward, *Speaking of Christ*, p. 69.
37. Heyward, *The Redemption of God*, p. 43. Heyward is sharply critical of theological systems that posit the realm of 'God' as existing only in another time or in another place—because such a move undermines *the responsibility of human beings* to effect good, and can serve to sanction present evils in the name of future ('God'-given, heavenly) salvation. See also pp. 2-5, and pp. 107-26.
38. Heyward, *The Redemption of God*, p. 164.
39. See Heyward, *Our Passion for Justice*, pp. xiii-xv. She discusses the 'structures of alienation', or the structures of the social world, into which all of us are born.

experienced moments of mutuality in their lives. Such knowledge leads, according to Heyward, to yearning, the physical, sensual, sacred, erotic yearning for more mutual relation.[40] This concept is a critical one in her work; she demands that bodies, flesh-and-blood desiring bodies, be taken with utmost seriousness, as embodying the sacred, sexual 'yearning for meaningful relationship'.[41] This sacred, embodied, erotic yearning is simultaneously 'our passion for justice' (which is always an embodied passion) and our passion for and with a lover. The sacred demand for involvement, that yearning for mutual, meaningful, just and loving relationships in all aspects of our lives, is always a *physically embodied* yearning, and the justice/love we make together in, through and with our bodies *is* the power of God.

Again, this power of God cannot be the property of any single individual, but is the 'wellspring', the source and resource from which individuals draw the power (as strength) to enact justice (love, God) in the world.[42] I believe Heyward would say also that it is this same power or love that set the planets spinning in their courses—the power that enabled the universe to *be* at all.[43] Importantly, accompanying Heyward's understanding of God as the source or wellspring of the universe is a sense of wonder that creation in all its shapes and sizes exists in the first place. At the conclusion of a talk in which she was speaking of 'the sanctity and the value of the body', Heyward said,

> Finally, acknowledging, as I believe we must, and bowing, as I believe we must, before the *mystery* and the *wonder* of all that is created, we go, aware of our own limitations and boundaries, beginning with those of our own skins.[44]

---

40. See Heyward, *Touching Our Strength*, p. 187, for a concise statement of her understanding of the erotic as 'our yearning to be involved'.

41. See Heyward, *Our Passion for Justice*, p. 35.

42. Heyward, *Our Passion for Justice*, p. 240. Regarding the metaphor of the 'wellspring', Heyward has used this metaphor when writing of her understanding of compassion and the transcendence of God. 'Compassion is a wellspring of transcendence, or the movement of God not only between and among human beings, but also in and through the heights and depths of all that is.'

43. In personal correspondence (17 April 1997) and conversation (late January 1997) Heyward emphasized a growing 'ecological/cosmic awareness' and a belief in the 'purposive nature of the universe'.

44. See Heyward, *Our Passion for Justice*, p. 146 (italics added).

7. The Theology of Carter Heyward

There are two issues intertwined in the metaphors Heyward uses regarding creation and God. First, when she writes of 'mystery' and 'wonder' in the face of creation, or existence as experienced by human beings, she strongly echoes Heidegger's use of the metaphor of 'Being' as expressive of the wonder that anything is at all. Secondly, her use of the metaphors 'wellspring' and 'source' with relation to the more-ness of 'God' seem to correspond almost exactly with Ruether's use of the model of the 'divine matrix', and is also closely aligned with Paul Tillich's model of god as 'the ground of being'. As with Ruether (and in continuity with elements of process thought), Heyward utterly rejects the notion of a transcendent (in both the senses of 'above' and 'wholly other than') and omnipotent God.[45] It is precisely this sort of understanding of God from which, writes Heyward, 'God' needs to be redeemed. And it is frail, finite and fearful human beings who must do the work of redemption, over and over again, in every different corner of our lives.

The metaphor of 'redemption' figures largely in Heyward's theology. Perhaps more vehemently than any other feminist Christian theologian, Heyward insists on human responsibility for doing whatever is redemptive in the world. The work of redemption is the work of making love and justice incarnate in the world wherever love and justice are absent; it is the effort to establish and maintain mutual relations with one another, with other earth creatures, and with the earth itself. In Heyward's thought 'redemption' is the purpose of theology. Importantly, just as she rejects as inadequate any *single* theological paradigm, Heyward does not offer, nor would she accept, a single recipe for redemption. The shape realized justice might take, as opposed to a theoretical notion of justice, differs with every context, every situation. In this regard Heyward is an uncompromising relativist. The shape of redemption depends on the shape of the evil from which real people need to be redeemed. Where there is not enough food, justice/love demands there be more food; where there are not enough schools,

---

45. See *The Redemption of God*, pp. 64-65, for a discussion of Heyward's affinity with process theology's consequent (relational and constantly changing) nature of god, but rejection of process theology's immutable (absolute and unchanging) primordial nature of god. Heyward writes, 'It seems to me that if *God* has a primordial, unchanging, and absolute nature, it is in the same sense that *humanity* does: we are unchanging, or constant, in our changing; we are absolutely, or constantly, relative to one another and the rest of creation' (p. 65, emphasis in original).

justice/love demands there be more schools; where there is violence against women, or lesbians and gaymen, justice/love demands there be no violence. The notion of 'redemption', as Heyward uses it, cannot be understood in a static, single, or once-and-for-all sense, as it is in the traditional Christian paradigm.[46] Instead, it is an 'open' theological concept that must take on different concrete forms relative to different concrete needs. According to Heyward, 'We tend to confuse a recognition of the relativity of all that is with a moral acceptance of all that is, as if our intellectual appreciation of reality's complexities demands passive moral response'.[47] Her antidote to this passivity is found in her use of the metaphor 'redemption'. If this metaphor does not come with a single set of instructions for use in her thought, it does convey a single theo-ethical imperative: to actively love one's neighbour. Accordingly, I suggest that 'redemption' is the theological manifestation of Heyward's hermeneutical norm. As such, it is a concept central (perhaps the most central) to her theological pattern.

This brief overview of Heyward's theology of mutual relation has not, of course, done justice to the intricacy and subtlety of her thought, nor have I managed to convey the importance of human embodiment in Heyward's theology. However, with an understanding of the absolute centrality in her theological pattern of human responsibility for making incarnate love/justice, it is now possible to explore more fully her theological anthropology, an effort that is simultaneously an exploration of her epistemological presuppositions concerning human beings as knowing agents.

Heyward's Theological Anthropology

'In the beginning is the relation'.[48] With this quotation from Martin Buber's *I and Thou*, Heyward begins chapter 1 of *The Redemption of God*. Throughout this work, as well as in all her other books, Heyward elaborates on the implications of this metaphysical presupposition as it relates to her theological anthropology, or conception of human beings. As she noted when reflecting back on the process of writing the book,

---

46. Traditional understandings of redemption are inextricable from traditional understandings of the atonement, according to which Jesus' God-ordained suffering, death and resurrection were necessary (for various reasons) to redeem (some members of) humankind.

47. Heyward, *Our Passion for Justice*, p. 208.

48. Heyward, *The Redemption of God*, p. 1.

'I was trying to articulate a relational *ontology* as a companion piece to the profoundly *moral* motives and commitments of liberation theology'.[49] Her ontology, or her conception of the essential nature of all that is, is grounded on a single presupposition: that 'being' is utterly relational. By extension, for good and ill, human beings are in relation with the rest of creation and with one another—whether we choose to be or not, whether we feel as though we are in relation or not, whether we admit we are or not.[50] 'Whether we experience ourselves this way or not, we are inherently relational. This is the metaphysics of all that is created. From a philosophical perspective, this is our ontological (essential) state'.[51] Heyward grounds her theological anthropology, her claim that humans are inherently relational, on an analysis of the limits of existence given with existence. As she bluntly states, 'We do not grow in incubators. We are not alone in the world. We are in relation'.[52] As I read it, Heyward's understanding of relation includes a critical, usually implicit component: within her thought *relation always involves change*, process.

Importantly, Heyward *never* characterizes the ontological state of relationality as being either inherently idyllic or inherently evil. Nor does she confuse an understanding of 'relationality' with an assumption of 'oneness'. Rather, *in her thought the fact of relation is inherently ambiguous, inherently tense*. Each creature, human and non-human, each aspect of the created universe is different from all others, with different and sometimes conflicting needs and desires: 'In the beginning is the relation, not sameness. In the beginning is tension and turbulence, not easy peace'.[53] This point is critical. Heyward locates her theological anthropology in a society and culture in which the real

---

49. *Staying Power*, p. 17 (italics in original).

50. See Heyward, *The Redemption of God*, p. 164. 'We may *feel* alone, but we are not' (emphasis in original).

51. Heyward, *Touching Our Strength*, p. 12.

52. Heyward, *The Redemption of God*, p. 134. It is important to note that, on a metaphysical level, there is no distinction between Heyward's ontology (as it applies to non-human creation) and her anthropology. All that is, including human beings, is in relation.

53. Heyward, *Touching Our Strength*, p. 100. See also *idem*, *The Redemption of God*, p. 159: 'in relation we are immersed in ambiguity, tension, shifting foci: between self and self, present and past and future, memory and hope, gain and loss, freedom and destiny, what we know and what we dream, what we welcome and what we fear'.

relations between individuals, between groups or categories of people, and even within individuals themselves are most often *not* characterized by mutuality (or love/justice). She refuses to speak of relationality in the abstract, and instead grounds human relations in their social setting: 'no relation happens in isolation from its social milieu. Thus, no relation is asocial and no act is politically neutral (irrelevant to the dynamics of *power* in social relations)'.[54] Insofar as Heyward refuses to discuss 'human beings' apart from the world in which we live, it is impossible to discuss her theological anthropology without also discussing her conception of the social world. While I must therefore elaborate briefly on her understanding of the nature of the world as it has been socially constructed, I shall give this topic more attention in the next section of this chapter.

Elsewhere, rather than use the phrase 'social milieu', Heyward writes of the *alienation* into which all of us are born, albeit born into differently structured relationships to this alienation. Through her use of the metaphor 'alienation' she is clear that she does not mean only or primarily a *feeling* or sense of estrangement, *qua* Paul Tillich. Instead, she defines alienation (in a Marxist sense) as:

> a primary consequence of unjust power relations in which particular groups of people are held systematically over other groups—white, economically privileged people, for example, over others, alienated from others and others from us... As a liberation theologian, I am interested in economic, racial, sexual, and other patterns [of alienation] into which we are born and in which our psycho-spiritualities are being shaped probably *in utero* and surely within the first hours and days of our lives on planet earth. We are, in this sense, born alienated, born into Augustine's *massa damnata* and original sin...[55]

It is a fundamental assumption in Heyward's thought that 'we live in a praxis of alienation, or wrong relation, from which we cannot escape'.[56] And again, the praxis of alienation of which Heyward writes consists of 'the social structures' into which we are born and within which we live our lives.[57] These social structures shape to a large extent the nature of

---

54. Heyward, *The Redemption of God*, p. 135 (emphasis in original). Heyward's concern with the politics of power resonates strongly with Lorraine Code's discussion of power with regard to social institutions and ideologies.
55. Heyward, *Staying Power*, p. 80.
56. Heyward, *Touching Our Strength*, p. 105.
57. Heyward, *Our Passion for Justice*, p. 77. The entire quotation is as follows:

our relations with one another, as well as the shape of our own 'becoming', our own never-static identities.[58] According to Heyward, 'our social situations are so fully the arenas of our becoming that we cannot lift ourselves, as individuals, outside of our communities in the exploration of who we are'.[59] To the extent that our communal 'social situations' are located within unjust social structures, Heyward agrees with Augustine's claim that ' "we cannot not sin" (*non posse non peccare*)—not in a world in which structures of injustice constitute the foundation upon which we all stand together'.[60] Moreover, she asserts that these unjust social structures cannot be understood adequately if they are studied in isolation from one another. Their impact is felt on human lives (and thus they are *known*) only through their 'dynamic interaction':[61]

> For each injustice in our common life is held in place in the everyday lives of women and men on the basis of race *and* class *and* gender *and* sexual preference *and* religion *and* age *and* national/ethnic/cultural heritage *and* a willingness or unwillingness to conform to the ideologies and practices of those (usually Euroamerican men) who deny that *they* are alienated and, rather, perceive the rest of us as prisoners of our own alienation and ideological suspicions by which we are said to bring violence on ourselves.[62]

There are a number of paradigmatic and epistemological elements both explicitly touched upon and implicitly supporting the statements made in the preceding paragraph, all of which need to be examined further. First, regarding her paradigmatic metaphysical presuppositions, Heyward assumes, but never attempts to prove, the full, unqualified humanity of every woman, man and child without exception. According to Heyward, 'we have more compelling tasks than to attempt to "prove" ourselves to anyone'.[63] In a sermon on humility, however, she makes clear her understanding of the worth of every individual: 'To be

'We are in some significant part creatures of the social structures in which we participate...'
    58. See Heyward, *The Redemption of God*, p. 217 and idem, *Touching Our Strength*, p. 40 regarding her understanding of personal identities as non-static, ever-changing.
    59. Mud Flower Collective, *God's Fierce Whimsy*, p. 24.
    60. Heyward, *Touching Our Strength*, p. 208.
    61. See Heyward, *Our Passion for Justice*, p. xiv.
    62. Heyward, *Our Passion for Justice*, p. xv (italics in original).
    63. Heyward, *Our Passion for Justice*, p. 12.

humble means to know ourselves as no more or less valuable than anyone else in the world'.[64] Although she discusses it so rarely, the value judgment that accompanies Heyward's affirmation of the full humanity of every human being is of fundamental significance in her theology. She has written that human 'liberation from injustice in the world is dependent upon the theological value we give to our shared humanity'.[65] Within her work the theological value she gives to every human body is a vital, yet tacit component. Heyward's rarely named presupposition of the full humanity of every human body without exception parallels, in my opinion, Ruether's rarely named presupposition of the embodied nature of every human being. Both theologians must take both assumptions for granted; their theology makes no sense apart from them, but Heyward's emphasis is on redeeming embodiment while Ruether's emphasis is on redeeming the conceptual category of 'women'.

More precisely, Heyward's notion of 'humanity' is *centred* on embodiment; 'the body is to be taken with ultimate seriousness. There is nothing higher, nothing more holy'.[66] It is as *embodied* creatures that we live and act in the world. It is our *bodies* that are affected, scarred, and shaped by the social structures within which we live and from which we cannot escape;[67] and it is *through our bodies* that we know everything we know about ourselves and the world in which we live. On this epistemological point, that it is through our bodies that we know everything we know, Heyward quotes feminist ethicist Beverly Harrison at great length, drawing from 'The Power of Anger in the Work of Love', one of the most important feminist Christian theological essays ever published. The following is an excerpt of what Heyward quotes from Harrison:

> If we begin, as feminists must, with 'our bodies, ourselves', we recognize that all our knowledge, including moral knowledge, is body-mediated knowledge. All knowledge is rooted in our sensuality. We know and value the world, *if* we know and value it, through our ability to

---

64. Heyward, *Speaking of Christ*, p. 57. Heyward does not limit her value judgment concerning the worth of every individual to individuals currently alive.

65. Heyward, *The Redemption of God*, p. 16.

66. Heyward, *Our Passion for Justice*, p. 140.

67. Heyward, *Our Passion for Justice*, p. 171. She writes of 'the folly of the illusion that any of us can simply up and leave the patriarchal structures that surround and fill us'.

touch, to hear, to see. *Perception* is fundamental to *conception*. Ideas are dependent on our sensuality.[68]

This is the foundation upon which Heyward constructs her 'epistemology of embodiment'.[69] It is always through the lived experiences of bodies-in-relation that knowledge is made—and for Heyward knowledge is most certainly made and made again, not simply 'found'.[70] This epistemological assumption is, I suggest, almost identical to Kathryn Pyne Addelson's conception of 'truth' as enacted (discussed in Chapter 5). In keeping with the notion of 'truth' as relationally enacted, or made incarnate, Heyward insists that it is *not* as individual, isolated bodies through which we know the world, but as particularly situated bodies always participating in complex, tension-filled, ambiguous relations with other bodies. Heyward is thus in complete agreement with those feminist epistemologists who insist that situated knowledge is necessarily communal, or, in Donna Haraway's words, that 'situated knowledges are about communities, not about isolated individuals'.[71] In Heyward's thought, there simply are no isolated bodies, thus, as I quoted her earlier, 'we cannot lift ourselves, as individuals, outside of our communities in our explorations of who we are'.

Moreover, Heyward's understanding of 'body' is as a constantly *changing* subject-in-relation. Such change is both physical ('will we resist believing what our bodies know: that whatever is not changing and growing is dead?'[72]) *and* social, in that institutionally sanctioned meanings laid upon various bodies also change over time. As she notes in a footnote appearing in a discussion of bodies, sexuality and power,

---

68. Heyward, *Our Passion for Justice*, p. 172 (italics original). She is quoting from Beverly Wildung Harrison, 'The Power of Anger in the Work of Love', in *idem, Making the Connection*, pp. 3-21.

69. Heyward, *Staying Power*, p. 116: 'I am speaking of an epistemology of embodiment as the basis of both our understanding of ourselves as our church (who we are as a corporate body) and our theological anthropology (who we are in right relation to one another as sisters and brothers and friends and lovers)'.

70. See Heyward, *Touching Our Strength*, pp. 5-6 and p. 160 n. 5: 'Both [Paulo] Freire and the Mud Flower collective start with the presupposition that knowledge is socially constructed and restricted'.

71. Haraway, 'Situated Knowledges', p. 590. See also Heyward, *The Redemption of God*, p. 9: 'Every particular theological expression is peculiar to the theologian and to the community, time, and place which she represents.'

72. Heyward, *Staying Power*, p. 120.

> physiology does not supply motives, passion, object choice, or identity. These come from 'somewhere else', the domains of social relations and psychic conflict. If this is correct, the body can no longer be seen as a biological given which emits its own meaning. It must be understood instead as an ensemble of potentialities which are given meaning only in society.[73]

Again, Heyward has consistently affirmed an ever-changing, never fixed or static understanding of human bodies, human subjectivities. Like Ruether's, her metaphysical assumption of the full humanity of every woman, man and child without exception and without qualification is an open-ended assertion based on a value judgment. That is, she values all human lives equally, but does not and cannot offer a definite, unchanging essence of humanity to accompany her value judgment. Instead, and in keeping with elements of process thought, she affirms that human beings, including herself, are creatures who are constantly changing, whose identities are never fixed:

> My understanding of myself continues to evolve—often very roughly, sometimes abrasively even to myself, peppered with surprises about myself and others. I do not understand myself primarily in categories that suggest that anything about me is static, unchanging, finished. Even those categories that most of us assume to be basic—such as female or male gender, such as racial identity, such as the *Homo sapiens* species itself—seem to me more elusive, less static, than we often assume. I am tempted to say, and will for now, that nothing is fixed; nothing in the world is so essentially what it is today that tomorrow may not surprise us with something new...[74]

The epistemological presuppositions accompanying Heyward's relational, communally situated, physically embodied yet socially defined (and continually redefined), constantly changing subjects are extensive. Heyward rejects the notion that knowledge is ever properly ascribed to any single individual, is ever universal in scope, or is ever static, unchanging, or final; rather, for her 'knowledge is both relational (born in dialogue with others) and relative (contingent upon the difference it makes to our own lives and the lives of others)'.[75] Further, because

---

73. Heyward, *Touching Our Strength*, p. 166 n. 3.
74. Heyward, *Our Passion for Justice*, p. 83.
75. Mud Flower Collective, *God's Fierce Whimsy*, p. 25. Regarding her rejection of static, unchanging knowledge claims, see Heyward, *The Redemption of God*, p. 161. 'Our co-creative task is to see...more fully what we are doing in the world.

Heyward deliberately writes against a liberal, individualistic understanding of epistemic agency,[76] rejecting both a god's-eye view from nowhere and the idea that any knowledge claim is ever value neutral, or can ever be separated from its ethical implications, she must redefine the notion of 'objectivity'. Like the feminist epistemologists discussed in Chapters 4 and 5, Heyward rejects a distant, dispassionate, or abstract approach to knowledge. Instead, she combines an insistence on particularity and situatedness with an insistence on the *ethical* dimensions of knowledge claims. 'Objectivity is knowledge of what is happening in the actual life experiences of people-in-relation—what is, in fact, true or *good* for these real people'.[77] Elsewhere Heyward writes of 'co-subjectivity' as a better way to express the process of making and gaining knowledge:

> With many feminist and liberation analysts, I understand genuine objectivity to be *radically honest co-subjectivity*, in which we are clear and upfront about our biases and experiences and are working together with one another, as co-subjects, toward fuller understandings of what may be more nearly 'objectively' true.[78]

Importantly, while this quotation can be read as pointing in the direction of an immutable 'truth' that can, with effort, be discovered by human beings, Heyward's insistence on the relational and relative nature of all knowledge renders such a reading impossible. For Heyward, knowledge is *never* unchanging. As I read it, the emphasis of the above quotation should be on the notion of 'radically honest co-subjectivity', which is the *sine qua non* of Heyward's epistemological framework, and is also the link between her epistemology and her theology. A relationship of radically honest co-subjectivity is a *mutual*

To see not only what we are looking for, but also what is, in fact, happening. And what is happening is *dynamic*. There is no stasis' (emphasis in original).

76. See Heyward, *When Boundaries Betray Us*, p. 146. She asserts that an individualistic understanding of epistemic agents, in combination with a hierarchical, dualistic symbolic universe, has resulted in a 'fundamental epistemological problem', an epistemological problem that 'has been the basis' of her critique (with others) 'of white Western patriarchal Christian theology'. I discuss her critique of a hierarchical, dualistic symbolic universe in the next section.

77. Heyward, *Touching Our Strength*, p. 7 (italics added).

78. Heyward, *When Boundaries Betray Us*, p. 134 (italics in original). Heyward cites Beverly Harrison's *Making the Connections* and Donna Haraway's *Simians, Cyborgs, and Women* at the end of this quotation.

relationship, in which all participants are mutually *present* to one another, even as they are affected, and thus changed, by that relationship. In Heyward's thought it is only to the extent that we are truly present to one another that knowledge (as understanding, not control) is possible. She is explicit about the relationship between presence and knowledge: 'When we are really present with someone, we know and are known by this person'.[79]

But again Heyward defines all relations as inherently ambiguous, tension-filled. In her thought perfectly loving, perfectly just, or purely 'good' relational presence with another is simply impossible, even as it is the theo-ethical goal of all relations.[80] Whatever knowledge is co-created out of any relationship, even the most mutual, will fall short of 'perfect' knowledge. Thus I suggest that Heyward's understanding of the ambiguous, dialogical process of making knowledge is remarkably similar to Donna Haraway's assertion of

> surprises and ironies at the heart of all knowledge production; we are not in charge of the world. We just live here and try to strike up *noninnocent* conversations... [W]e give up *mastery* but keep searching for fidelity, knowing all the while we will be hoodwinked.[81]

The similarities between their thought go beyond a shared appreciation for the non-innocent nature of conversation/relation. Heyward writes of *'a theology of mutual relation, of knowing and being known, of struggling to know and be and do what we will never "master"'*.[82] Mastery is, in her thought, the goal of those who hold to one 'truth', and use that 'truth' to construct the world according to their (socially and politically powerful) will. To equate knowledge with mastery leads to the imposition of one's knowledge claims upon the lives of others. It does not lead to epistemic responsibility, which is for Heyward no less than for Addelson, Code and Ruether, the primary epistemological issue. In her words, 'The basic issue is relational responsibility'.[83] Given the primacy of 'responsibility' in Heyward's epistemological

---

79. Heyward, *Touching Our Strength*, p. 147.

80. See Heyward, *The Redemption of God*, pp. 160-61. She writes that 'no one of us, nor all of us together, can choose to effect good without also experiencing, and maybe choosing to participate in, evil—destruction of the good, the breaking apart of the relation... We who co-create must acknowledge our own evil effects.'

81. Haraway, 'Situated Knowledges', p. 594 and pp. 593-94 (italics added).

82. Heyward, *Staying Power*, p. 120 (italics added).

83. Heyward, *The Redemption of God*, p. 134.

presuppositions, I suggest that she is in complete agreement with Kathryn Pyne Addelson's words: '*the measure of any epistemology lies in how well it allows knowledge makers to be responsible*. It does not lie in how well it gives us certified knowledge or the route to the truth of the one reality'.[84]

To conclude this discussion of Heyward's theological anthropology and presuppositions regarding humans as epistemic agents, and to prepare the way for a discussion of her conception of the world as it is known, I turn again to an examination of her understanding of the *communal* nature of all knowledge claims. The point I wish to stress is that, while she explicitly characterizes the co-creation of knowledge as inherently relational, dialogical, her emphasis on responsibility and accountability, as well as her conception of the social world, *requires* that she locate knowledge-creating relations within social communities—social communities whose knowledge claims and actions affect and are affected by *other* social communities. In other words, her epistemological presuppositions fit within the conceptual category of standpoint epistemology, with a critical difference. Heyward's use of the concept of accountability underscores the inseparability in her thought of ethics and epistemology, but it also underscores the communal and inescapably relative nature of all knowledge claims:

> If, as the context of theology, praxis is to be anything other than a person's or a group's thinking about interesting abstract ideas, there must be at the outset of the conceptual effort a sense of to whom, *in addition to ourselves*, we are accountable. Otherwise, even at our personal best, we are laboring under the assumptions of a liberal epistemology, in which each person authorizes herself to idealize her subject matter—whether feminism, theological education, God, or the world—and for which she is accountable to no one but herself.[85]

Insofar as Heyward regards all knowledge as 'grounded in human experience',[86] and insofar as she conceives of all human experience to be relational, and insofar as all human relations take place in social worlds comprised of different communities, then all knowledge claims are shaped and formed in the context of specific communal experiences.[87] However, and this is where Heyward's thought extends

---

84. Addelson, 'Knower/Doers', p. 288 (italics original).
85. Mud Flower Collective, *God's Fierce Whimsy*, p. 24 (italics added).
86. Heyward, *The Redemption of God*, p. 6.
87. Heyward, *The Redemption of God*, p. 223. Writing of coming out as a

standpoint theory, 'insofar as anyone, or any group, theologizes *solely on the basis of its own experiences of reality—and takes no care to listen to anyone else*—its theology ought to lack credibility'.[88] It ought to lack credibility precisely because the epistemological community responsible for that knowledge claim is not being accountable to other communities affected by that knowledge claim.

Further, an absence of accountability, in the sense that Heyward uses the term, leads to the universalizing of one epistemological community's knowledge claims, and, by implication, the rejection of other knowledge claims about the same subject matter. An epistemological community that refuses to acknowledge any accountability for its knowledge claims refuses to acknowledge its own 'relational particularity', or the fact that its knowledge claims are situated in relation to other communities' knowledge claims.[89] That is, it denies the fact that its knowledge claims are located relative to, and have relatively larger or smaller impacts on the lives of, bodies located in other epistemological communities. Put differently, Heyward is concerned with discerning which epistemological communities deny any accountability to other communities and then use their political power to structure the social world according to their (usually universalized) knowledge claims.[90] For Heyward, the most credible knowledge claims are neither univocal nor universal; rather, they arise out of '*a praxis of relational particularity and cooperation*', co-operation not just between individuals, but between epistemological communities.[91]

Not surprisingly, the question of which standpoint/community is the *most* epistemically privileged simply cannot arise in Heyward's

---

lesbian priest, Heyward expresses this experience as one of 'craziness'. She says, 'To feel crazy is to wonder if I am concocting a reality meaningful only to me and to a few folks who are crazy enough to agree with me. It is to feel *as if I have stepped outside the arena of what is not only acceptable, but also intelligible—even to myself*' (italics added). I suggest that the significance of this quotation is found in her insistence that more than just 'a few folks' must be in agreement before a knowledge claim concerning the nature of reality is intelligible, or can be acknowledged as a knowledge claim. Again this points to the existence of epistemological communities rather than individuals as the agents of knowledge production.

88. Mud Flower Collective, *God's Fierce Whimsy*, p. 25 (italics added).

89. See Heyward, *Speaking of Christ*, p. 21, for her use of the phrase 'relational particularity'.

90. Heyward, *Speaking of Christ*, p. 20.

91. Heyward, *Speaking of Christ*, p. 21 (italics in original).

thought. Implicit in her work is the assumption that many epistemological communities are able to create responsible, justice-oriented knowledges, and that knowledge can be shared between communities. For example, she writes, 'we must help one another to see that the patient has much to teach the doctor, the Palestinian has much to teach the Jew, the gayman or lesbian has much to teach the heterosexual man or woman'.[92] Importantly, this quotation reveals Heyward's understanding of the power-riddled nature of knowledge claims. In each of the examples she uses, the latter epistemic agent belongs to a more socially or politically powerful epistemological community than the former. Her point is that it is precisely because the knowledge claims of the more powerful epistemological communities are felt to a greater extent by the bodies of those in less powerful communities that the less powerful are epistemically advantaged.[93] The following quotation exemplifies Heyward's understanding of various epistemic (standpoint) communities and their relation to the social world: 'We almost have to be poor, sick, old, differently abled, gaymen or lesbians, women raising kids alone, or people of color to know for a fact that the social fabric of our life together is rotten'.[94] And for Heyward, it is the social fabric of our life together that constitutes, to a large extent, the world in which we live.

Heyward's Understanding of Creation and the World

As is already evident, Heyward's work does not lend itself to systematic, point-by-point analysis. This is especially the case when considering her conceptions of creation and of the world as it is known, for she insists that it is only as particularly located humans that we know creation and the world at all, and that no necessarily situated, humanly constructed knowledge about creation or the world is ever absolute or final. Her insistence on this point is both personal and pointed: 'I, Carter Heyward, don't know for sure, and never will, and you can quote me'.[95] However, there are several paradigmatic assumptions concerning *creation* (in the sense of the physical or material stuff of the

---

92. Heyward, *Speaking of Christ*, p. 66.
93. See Heyward, *Our Passion for Justice*, pp. 224-25. Heyward discusses 'the epistemological privilege of the oppressed'.
94. Heyward, *Touching Our Strength*, p. 127.
95. Heyward, *Staying Power*, p. 10.

world) that she does take for granted, beginning with an assumption of 'normative realism', to use Lorraine Code's expression, i.e., she assumes that creation really does exist apart from human thoughts about it. I suggest that she would also agree with Evelyn Fox Keller's understanding of physical reality as being curiously 'intractable', or stubbornly 'what it is' even in the face of human attempts to define it otherwise. Further, Heyward does not assume that creation exists solely for the benefit of human beings. In ethical terms, she presupposes the inherent value of non-human creation *apart* from any use humans might make of it.[96] Put theologically, that all non-human creation is sacred or holy (in Rudolph Otto's sense of awesome *and* terrifying, i.e., wonderful but not benign) is axiomatic in her thought. In Heyward's work these assumptions concerning creation function as deep background assumptions, and they are for the most part implicit.[97] She is explicit, however, regarding her central ontological presupposition. Creation, being, all that exists, is in relation.

But Heyward does not write often of creation. At the forefront of her thought is her understanding of *the (Western) world* (in the sense of human societies and cultures) as it has been shaped in the image of the symbolic universe constructed primarily by ruling-class, economically and educationally privileged, Christian Euroamerican men. In this regard Heyward's work is similar to Ruether's, although Heyward never explicitly accentuates the difference in her thought between 'creation' and 'the world', as Ruether does. What Heyward does is insist upon the social, political and economic effects—on human bodies as well as on non-human aspects of creation—of a symbolic universe structured according to what she terms 'patriarchal logic'. She uses the expression 'patriarchal logic' to refer 'to the systematic, pervasive ordering of our bodies/minds/souls/selves in relation to one another through a hierarchical construction of unchanging power-relations'.[98] Like Ruether (in fact she cites Ruether as a source informing her own analysis),[99] Heyward characterizes 'the prevailing symbolic

---

96. Heyward, *Staying Power*, pp. 101-11.
97. Most of Heyward's explicitly creation-oriented thoughts appear in Chapter 11 of *Staying Power*, entitled 'Turning to the Animals: Another Conversion'.
98. Heyward, *When Boundaries Betray Us*, p. 4.
99. See Heyward, *Speaking of Christ*, p. 14, and p. 87 n. 5.

7. The Theology of Carter Heyward 207

universe of Christian theology' as structured according to a series of hierarchical dualisms.[100] She writes:

> Dualism is steeped in an assumption of opposition: whether in relation to the knowledge of God or Christ, of ourselves or the world, we can know something only insofar as we are *unlike* it. Man is unlike woman. Spirit is unlike flesh. Light is unlike darkness. Heaven is unlike earth. God is unlike humanity. In a dualistic praxis, 'the other' is always better or worse, more or less, than oneself or one's people. Identity is forged and known by contrast and competition, not by cooperative relation. Dualism is cultivated in a praxis of alienation between men and women, rich and poor, light and dark, and, in the image of such oppositions, divinity and humanity.[101]

Heyward's point is that a symbolic universe structured according to these dualisms (1) provides and sanctions a particular conception of humanity, specifically the division of humanity into categories of people occupying unequal places in social and 'divine' worlds, and (2) is inextricably related to a 'dualistic epistemology', or an epistemological framework structured around metaphysical assumptions of opposition and domination rather than relationality. Further, this epistemological framework has in turn sanctioned the construction of 'cultures of death and despair', or social worlds of domination and oppression.[102] Importantly, Heyward perceives the hierarchical structure of the Christian symbolic universe to be premised on the value-laden assumptions that: 'God is more valuable than humanity; heaven, more valuable than earth; the future realm of God, more valuable than present relation'.[103] According to Heyward such a set of assumptions render it impossible to take 'with *ultimate* seriousness' this world, here and now: the social and political worlds in which real people live and die, in which animals are slaughtered for sport, in which gay men are mutilated just because they are gay, in which women are raped and beaten just because they are women, in which Jews and Muslims and Blacks are murdered just because they are Jews or Muslims or Blacks.[104] In a word, Heyward characterizes most social, political and

---

100. Mud Flower Collective, *God's Fierce Whimsy*, p. 154.
101. Heyward, *Speaking of Christ*, p. 18 (italics in original).
102. Heyward, *Speaking of Christ*, p. 19, re dualistic epistemology; idem, *Staying Power*, p. 105, re cultures of death and despair.
103. Heyward, *The Redemption of God*, p. 131.
104. Heyward, *The Redemption of God*, p. 131 (emphasis in original). See also *Staying Power*, pp. 101-102.

economic relations in this world as *unjust*. They are relations of domination and subordination, and they are a structural feature of 'late monopoly capitalism', of 'white racism and male gender superiority and compulsory heterosexuality and Christianity's claim, implicit or explicit, to possess spiritually the final, supreme, religious truth'.[105] Because she does try to take with ultimate seriousness 'this world', 'the world' of which Heyward writes is a world in which the bodies of many are used as disposable labour forces, playthings, sex toys and cannon fodder by the few.

Heyward uses concrete examples to convey the point that the social and political structures of this world bear a striking resemblance to the prevailing Christian symbolic universe, always stressing the *felt* effects, the *embodied* social and political consequences in *this* world of a hierarchical, dualistic metaphysics and epistemology. The following quotation exemplifies this insistence on her part. In an essay entitled 'Latin American Liberation Theology: A North American Perspective', given as a talk in 1980, Heyward writes:

> The revolution in Latin America seeks to change the structures of society which, with financial and military backing of the United States and other Western capitalist countries, are perpetuated on the economic (capitalist) tenet that for the rich to get richer, the poor must get poorer; that, in fact, the upward mobility of the rich...is dependent on the resignation of the poor to their poverty. In short, the Latin American revolution is rooted in informed analysis of social reality: namely, that the ruling classes and families in Latin America, together with us—their economic and political allies in North America and Europe—*feed ourselves, clothe our bodies, run our cars, buy our houses, invest our money, enjoy our work and leisure time, elect our politicians, and worship our god over the dead bodies of increasing numbers of human beings throughout the world.*[106]

Heyward's ontological assumption of (ambiguous and tension-filled) human relationality is here evident in her perception of *the nature of the relations* between rich and poor people, between Euroamerican governments and ruling class Latin Americans, and between the everyday activities of the economically privileged who benefit as participants in Euroamerican nations and the everyday struggle for survival of the (distant) destitute. She alludes as well to relations between the

---

105. Heyward, *Staying Power*, p. 104.
106. Heyward, *Our Passion for Justice*, pp. 106-107 (italics added).

theological affirmations of the socially and politically powerful and the ongoing crucifixions of the socially and politically marginalized. It is not difficult to discern how the affirmation of an omnipotent God in Heaven, one who causes everything to happen for a reason, could be used to support the unchallenged acceptance of unequal, abusive relationships—interpersonal, social and political—as these occur here and now. Such a theological affirmation leads to the impossibility of taking with ultimate seriousness *either* the full, unqualified humanity of every human body without exception *or* lived experiences of oppression and injustice. It is, moreover, this very theological affirmation that is an integral part of the symbolic universe Heyward is trying to transform.

Writing on behalf of the Mud Flower Collective, she notes that they 'perceive a radical, terrifying disjuncture between the prevailing symbolic universe of Christian theology and our well-grounded senses of identity as women in struggles for justice'.[107] Her point, I believe, is that their 'struggles for justice' in this world are actively hindered by the metaphysical presuppositions concerning 'women' inherent within the 'prevailing symbolic universe of Christian theology'. In addition, a 'terrifying disjuncture' appears with the realization that, within the dominant Christian symbolic universe, no struggle for this-worldly justice can be valued as highly as a passive acceptance of 'God's will'. Indeed, any demand for justice on earth can be interpreted as a rejection of God's assurance of justice in heaven or assurance of heavenly justice brought to earth by God in the future.[108]

Again, it is to the extent that features of the dominant symbolic universe, such as a conception of 'women' as naturally or essentially inferior to 'men', are enacted in *this world*, in the real relations between sexes, classes, races and nations, that Heyward considers the symbolic universe to be a part of the world. That is, a symbolic universe is not known as a disembodied theory, but by its felt effects. And Heyward perceives the cumulative effects of social and political relations as these *do* embody the dominant Christian symbolic universe to be threatening the fabric of creation. In her opinion, the survival of human and non-human life is increasingly under threat. As she bluntly puts it, 'as far as we humans can tell, time is not on "our side" in relation to the survival of life, human and other, on this planet'.[109] Unless

107. Mud Flower Collective, *God's Fierce Whimsy*, p. 154.
108. See Heyward, *Staying Power*, pp. 103-105.
109. Heyward, *Staying Power*, p. 105.

there is a radical shift in the way social, political and economic relations between peoples, nations and human and non-human earth creatures are structured and enacted, there may well be no social worlds in the future at all. In this regard Heyward is in complete agreement with Ruether.

It is fitting to conclude this discussion of Heyward's conception of creation and the world with a brief description of her own vision for the future. Strikingly, when positing her 'goal and vision' for creation and future social worlds, Heyward explicitly refers to the work of Donna Haraway. Quoting Haraway, she writes of working for a world 'that can be partially shared and friendly to earth-wide projects of finite freedom, adequate material abundance, modest meaning in suffering, and limited happiness'.[110] Or, to put it simply, Heyward advocates the ongoing co-creation of a world in which love and justice are made incarnate far more often than hatred and injustice.

Conclusion

Within Carter Heyward's theology are many of the paradigmatic presuppositions inherent within the feminist Christian theological paradigm as described in Chapter 3. She affirms the full, unqualified humanity of every woman, man, and child without exception; she affirms the inherent integrity and value of all non-human creation; she rejects as unloving and unjust the notion of a wholly other-than, transcendent, immutable and omnipotent God; and she rejects as well a value-laden preoccupation with a heaven above this world or a future new creation, brought into being by God above, that would supersede this flawed creation. However, Heyward *is* noticeably silent when it comes to affirming the blessedly finite character of existence. While she does accept that creaturely finitude is an unavoidable fact, she does not (seem to) go as far as Ruether in the sense of positively evaluating this fact, nor does she draw an anthropological-cosmological relation between life-energy and matter (or the constancy of the 'stuff' of the universe)—as Ruether explicitly does.[111]

110. Heyward, *Staying Power*, pp. 97-98, citing Haraway, *Simians, Cyborgs, and Women*, p. 187. I cited the same quotation above; see Chapter 4, n. 48.

111. In fact, as an epigraph to *Touching Our Strength*, Heyward quotes from Edna St Vincent Millay's poem, 'Conscientious Objector': 'I shall die, but that is all that I shall do for death'. I find it deeply intriguing that Heyward has not (or at least

7. The Theology of Carter Heyward

Regarding the epistemological elements in her thought, Heyward's work fits beautifully within the feminist epistemological paradigm outlined in Chapters 4 and 5. She insists on the situatedness and particularity of all knowledge claims; she affirms the relational and communal character of all knowledge production; she explicitly disavows the possibility of any absolute or unchanging 'truth'; she redefines the concept of 'objectivity' in a manner quite similar to Donna Haraway's formulation of this notion; like all the feminist philosophers discussed, she characterizes the production of knowledge as an always value-laden and power-riddled process; and she insists on the centrality, in any knowledge-making effort, of epistemic responsibility. I conclude this chapter with a quotation from Heyward, which, while not explicitly epistemological in focus, does convey, I believe, the core of the epistemological emphasis present throughout all her work. This quotation also provides her answer to the question, 'why does knowledge matter?'

> [W]e must help one another learn to walk more confidently along the boundaries of good and evil. It is a matter of learning to tolerate ambiguity without allowing ourselves to be duped into either the passivity of apathy and indifference, or the panic which seeks final solutions.[112]

---

has not yet) connected more fully her theological anthropology to her cosmological perceptions, particularly given the pastoral strength of such a connection, i.e., it does allow one to claim that the dead are always with us, which is a claim that Heyward has made with reference to the Latin American concept of '¡Presente!', a concept that carries with it the affirmation that '*resurrection is a relational movement*, the revolutionary carrying-on of a spirit of love and justice that does not and will not die' (Heyward, *Touching Our Strength*, p. 20, italics in original).

112. Heyward, *The Redemption of God*, p. 161.

Chapter 8

PARADIGMATIC AND EPISTEMOLOGICAL ELEMENTS IN THE
THEOLOGY OF SALLIE MCFAGUE

In this chapter I shall identify and examine the metaphysical assumptions, value judgments and epistemological presuppositions present, both explicitly and implicitly, in Sallie McFague's work. McFague, who identifies herself as a White, middle-class, Protestant feminist, is the Carpenter Professor of Theology and former Dean of Vanderbilt Divinity School in Nashville, Tennessee.[1] While I have neither met nor communicated with her in any way, she, like Ruether and Heyward, has had a considerable influence on my own theological development. Her book *Metaphorical Theology* was, as far as I can remember, my first introduction to an implicitly (for the most part) feminist Christian theological text. More importantly, it was the first analysis I ever read of the world-shaping power of both theological language and conceptual paradigms. Its impact on me was immediate and profound; it was as though McFague had put into words my own not yet expressible feelings about the relationship between images, concepts, language and 'truth'. She provided what seemed to me to be a brand new window through which to view a brand new world: a window of metaphors living and dead, looking out upon a world in which 'truth' lies as much in human imagination as it does in the 'stuff' of creation.[2] She was not cowed by reified or petrified metaphors; indeed, she argued passionately against the absolutizing of any metaphors, cautioning that 'we do

---

1. Sallie McFague, *Models of God: Theology for an Ecological, Nuclear Age* (Philadelphia: Fortress Press, 1987), p. xiii.
2. McFague, *Metaphorical Theology*, p. 29. Referring to a statement made by the novelist Ursula Le Guin, McFague paraphrases her words: 'truth lies in the imagination. This may be only half a truth, but it is the half we most often forget'. See also p. 32: 'We will not relinquish our idolatry in religious language unless we are freed from the myth that in order for images to be true they must be literal'.

8. *The Theology of Sallie McFague* 213

not so much use language as we are used by it'.[3] Having thus caught my attention McFague continued to speak these most provocative words:

> If language always stands between us and reality, if it is the medium through which we are aware of both our relationship to 'what is' and our distance from it, then metaphor is both our burden and our glory...[4]

'Used by language', 'our burden and our glory'—with expressions such as these McFague spoke to, and in the process helped to free, my theological imagination. It was from McFague that I learned the extent to which our imaginations shape our conceptual frameworks, and vice versa. In short, if not for McFague I would never have written a book having something to do with paradigms, metaphors and models. My intellectual debt to her is significant, to put it mildly.

At this point, however, I need to identify a critical difference between my understanding of theological paradigms and McFague's views on the subject. In the context of this study I have already drawn upon McFague's work with metaphors and models, and have characterized her theology as feminist Christian theology, or as theology that fits within the feminist Christian theological paradigm I am examining. However I need to be clear that, although McFague identified herself in 1982 as a 'feminist reformer' of the Christian tradition and, in 1993, as a 'feminist theologian', she herself does not acknowledge the existence of a feminist Christian theological paradigm in the way that I have presented and am using the concept.[5] Rather McFague maintains that each religious tradition, Judaism, Christianity, Islam, etc., constitutes a single theological paradigm, each paradigm comprised of a host of models built up around a single 'root-metaphor'.[6] In the case of Christianity, she believes this root-metaphor is embodied somehow by the event of Jesus of Nazareth.[7] McFague allows of different *emphases*

---

3. McFague, *Metaphorical Theology*, pp. 8-9.
4. McFague, *Metaphorical Theology*, p. 34.
5. Regarding McFague as a feminist reformer, see *Metaphorical Theology*, p. 165; regarding McFague's self-characterization as a feminist theologian, see Sallie McFague, *The Body of God: An Ecological Theology* (Minneapolis: Fortress Press, 1993), p. 13.
6. McFague, *Metaphorical Theology*, p. 110.
7. See Sallie McFague, 'An Epilogue: The Christian Paradigm', in Hodgson and King (eds.), *Christian Theology*, p. 378. She writes of 'the transformative *event* of new life, a new way of being in the world that is grounded in the life and death of Jesus of Nazareth' (italics in original).

within a single Christian paradigm, but insists, at times quite strongly, that while 'old interpretations are cast aside...the basic assumptions of the religion remain, since they are not after all settled theories'.[8]

I should note that in her work McFague makes what I believe to be a highly questionable distinction between scientific paradigms and theological paradigms. She states that in the case of a scientific paradigm shift there is 'a revolution in basic assumptions...everything is seen from a new perspective'.[9] She then states that this does not happen in theology (i.e. 'the basic assumptions of the religion remain'), but, and I suggest that this is one of the *rare* internal contradictions in her thought, she insists strongly that when a major scientific paradigm shift takes place, theology must take it into account or risk being irrelevant to its time and place, if not idolatrous and actively opposed to the fulfilment of life on earth.[10]

To be more specific, McFague explicitly acknowledges (1) that all theological constructions are built upon on an implicit worldview and (2) that a scientific paradigm shift results in a changed worldview—to which theology must attend. Indeed, she has proposed that 'the question for theology is not worldview or not but *which* worldview?'[11]. She states that 'the reason many Christian doctrines are considered obsolete is that they are based on a very different picture of the world than the current one'.[12] As I argued in Chapter 1, when a basic set of assumptions shifts, when a group of people start doing theology on the basis of a new set of assumptions about humankind, the world and God, they are no longer working within the old theological paradigm. Their worldview has changed; they perceive reality from a new perspective—one informed by a new set of metaphysical presuppositions

---

8. McFague, 'The Christian Paradigm', p. 380.

9. McFague, 'The Christian Paradigm', p. 380.

10. See McFague, *Models of God*, p. 6: 'The constructive character of theology must be acknowledged, and this becomes of critical importance when the world in which we live is profoundly different from the world in which many of the traditional metaphors and concepts gained currency'. See also *idem*, *The Body of God*, p. 74. 'When the picture of reality undergoes a major paradigm shift, theology must attend to it'. See also *idem*, *Metaphorical Theology*, pp. 8-9 (on idolatry and irrelevance broadly) and pp. 185-86 on the irrelevance and destructive consequences of a traditional view of atonement and salvation.

11. McFague, *The Body of God*, p. 74 (italics in original).

12. McFague, *The Body of God*, p. 235 n. 23, referring to the work of Hanbury Brown.

and value judgments. Given that McFague agrees that 'a paradigm constitutes the most basic set of assumptions within which a tradition, in this case a religious tradition, functions', and given that she agrees that all theological constructions presuppose a basic worldview, I find her distinction between scientific and theological paradigms implausible.[13] A theological paradigm shift, *especially* one that takes seriously a scientific paradigm shift, results in a new perspective on the world, a changed set of core assumptions, *not* simply a different set of interpretations concerning an unchanging set of core beliefs.

Further, her own arguments concerning the metaphysical implications of metaphors and models (and the need to stop using metaphors and models that support an ancient worldview) support my contention. She writes of 'the crucial importance of models in theology. They are comprehensive and *at base metaphysical*, and a theologian is not able to operate without them'.[14] Later in the same book she notes: 'The price paid for the hegemony of the hierarchical, monarchical model [of God the Father]...is a heavy one indeed: not only has God been removed from us as a distant being in some other world but, also, apparent licence has been arrogated by "man" to dominate and destroy the natural environment'.[15] My point is that McFague believes that different theologies are grounded upon and project different worldviews; she argues that theologians must take seriously current scientific worldviews; she assumes the metaphysical implications of theological models—and advocates changing them when their metaphysical implications are contrary to current and commonly held scientific understandings of reality—yet she simultaneously insists that various liberation theologies are simply reinterpretations of *the same* 'basic assumptions'.[16] Her own presuppositions, in my opinion, contradict this assertion.

I do want to acknowledge, however, the fact that McFague's insistence on a single Christian theological paradigm may well be motivated in part by political reasons. She has insisted that *all* forms of Christian theology, including but not limited to liberation, Black, and feminist theologies, are simply theology full-stop; and I suggest that this insistence on her part is partly motivated by an unwillingness to ghetto-ize

13. McFague, *Metaphorical Theology*, p. 108.
14. McFague, *Metaphorical Theology*, p. 105 (italics added).
15. McFague, *Metaphorical Theology*, p. 105 and p. 144.
16. McFague, 'The Christian Paradigm', pp. 379-80.

any theological approach by qualifying and perhaps diminishing its worthiness with a label such as 'liberation', 'Black', or 'feminist'.[17] Nonetheless, again, I understand each of these theological approaches to be structured around a different worldview—a different conceptual framework with a different set of underlying assumptions about human beings, God, and the nature of reality. As I shall demonstrate in this chapter, McFague's own worldview, or her metaphysical and epistemological presuppositions, fits perfectly within what I have described as the feminist Christian theological paradigm.

Before I examine her anthropological, ontological and epistemological assumptions, however, I must address another curiously problematic issue: that of the models of God for which she is best known.[18] To some extent in *Metaphorical Theology*, and to a large extent in *Models of God* and *The Body of God*, McFague attempts what she calls a 'thought experiment'. In this thought experiment she self-consciously presents various models of God. At the end of *Metaphorical Theology* she presents the model of God the friend, while in *Models of God* she presents the models of God the mother, God the lover and, again, God the friend. Finally, in *The Body of God* she presents an extended reflection on the model of the cosmos as God's body, and, in conjunction with this model, examines the model of God the spirit, 'the divine wind that 'swept over the face of the waters' prior to creation'.[19]

In this chapter, however, I shall not include within my examination of McFague's overarching theological system the models of God the mother, lover, friend or spirit, although I will examine the metaphysical and ethical implications of the model of the cosmos as God's body. Given the centrality in her thought of these models it is imperative that I explain and justify my rationale for this. The issue as I perceive it is that McFague's conceptual analyses of these models quite often run counter to their inherent imagistic metaphysical implications, contradict her explicitly stated theo-ethical and political agenda, and undermine her theological anthropology. For example, as I shall discuss in greater detail below, she is insistent that human beings need to live, move and have our being in the world as *responsible adults*, 'responsible for all

17. See McFague, *Models of God*, p. 47.
18. McFague received the American Academy of Religion's Award for Excellence for *Models of God*, the book in which she discusses her conception of god as mother, lover and friend.
19. McFague, *The Body of God*, p. 143.

8. *The Theology of Sallie McFague*   217

the rest upon which we are so profoundly dependent'. She asserts, 'no longer should we speak of ourselves as children, especially in a religious context, as the passive, needy children of a loving, all-powerful father who will take care of us and our planet'.[20] While this quotation rejects only a paternal image for God, eleven years earlier she wrote that '*parental* images...cannot express mutuality, maturity, cooperation, responsibility, or reciprocity'.[21] Given the great weight she places on human responsibility, as well as her own critical evaluation of parental images, I find her model of God the mother to fit—at the level of image—not at all with the rest of her thought.

Regarding the model of God the lover, in her analysis of this model she denies what I perceive to be the inherently individualistic and privatistic connotations of this image, i.e., lovers are two individuals who love each other specifically and in some ways exclusively and, at least early on in their relationship, tend to be oblivious to what is happening around them. McFague, however, interprets the model of God as lover 'in the context of the world as God's body'.[22] Accordingly, she perceives that 'the lover is God and the beloved the world'.[23] At the level of image, I suggest, this is simply theological narcissism, a picture of God loving nothing but Godself.[24] To be fair, McFague is attempting to provide a reason for *humans* to love the world and live in it responsibly, but the model of God the lover seems to me to work, at the level of image, against such an effort. As much as she argues against interpreting this model as reflective of a one-to-one relationship between oneself and God, such is the power of the image of God as lover that such an interpretation is almost unavoidable.

---

20. McFague, *The Body of God*, p. 109.
21. McFague, *Metaphorical Theology*, pp. 178-79 (italics added).
22. McFague, *Models of God*, p. 128.
23. McFague, *Models of God*, p. 128.
24. 'Of critical importance, neither her interpretation of God the lover loving God's body nor my interpretation of God the lover focusing on loving and being loved by individual humans can be used to address, in anything other than a superficial way, the suffering of the innocent or humanly caused ecological destruction. In other words, I believe it is theologically reprehensible to say to a woman who has been raped or a child who is dying of AIDS or a species threatened with extinction, 'well, God loves you, and that's the main thing...' Let me be clear that I do not believe McFague would use the model of God the lover in this way, but that does not negate the fact that it is a theological implication of this model.

Her conceptual analysis of God as spirit is similarly problematic, although for a different reason. At the level of image she suggests that it conveys an awareness that 'God is not primarily the orderer and controller of the universe but its source and empowerment, the breath that enlivens and energizes it'.[25] McFague even goes so far as to say that 'one of the great assets of the model is precisely its amorphous character in contrast to the highly human, personal, and androcentric nature of Father and Son: spirit is not necessarily human, personal (though it is relational), or male'.[26] In this instance I quite agree with her analysis of the imagistic connotations of the model. The problem is that she prefaces her discussion of the model of God the spirit with the insistence that it *is* a *personal* model.[27] Again, I would suggest that at the level of image God the spirit, that divine wind that blew across the face of the waters, is not a personal image—as, paradoxically, McFague herself notes. Lastly, if it is to be interpreted as a personal model for God, and if, as is always the case in Christian theology, humans are understood to be made in the image of God, then I do not perceive a way to avoid the problem of a hierarchical, dualistic, value-laden split between spirit and matter, spirit and human bodies. Given McFague's unwavering rejection of any sort of spirit–body or mind–body split (to be discussed in the section on her theological anthropology), her understanding of God the spirit as a personal image does not fit with her anthropological presuppositions.

Finally, there is God the friend, another self-consciously constructed model of God to which I shall not be referring simply because the *metaphors* she most often uses to describe her understanding of God— when she is not engaged in self-conscious, constructive 'thought experiments'—are *not* personal metaphors. Rather, she writes beautifully of God as the source and divine matrix of all that is, as the power

---

25. McFague, *The Body of God*, p. 145.
26. McFague, *The Body of God*, p. 147.
27. McFague, *The Body of God*, pp. 142-43. One of McFague's endearing and exasperating theological quirks is her insistence that to speak of god in the Christian paradigm one *must* use personal metaphors, although one can and should also use impersonal metaphors to accompany them. It is my contention that whenever she tries to use personal metaphors for god, or to interpret impersonal ones as personal images, she contradicts the rest of her otherwise incredibly consistent and elegant theological system.

8. *The Theology of Sallie McFague* 219

enlivening and sustaining creation in all its diversity and intricacy.[28] Source, matrix, power: these metaphors are the only ones that fully support her suggestion that humans ought to turn to the cosmos to glimpse divine transcendence, to experience the mystery and wonder and awe that she believes characterizes a religious sensibility.[29] As I shall demonstrate when discussing her understanding of the world and creation, this understanding of divine transcendence is of central significance in her thought; accordingly, it is noteworthy that, rather than personal metaphors, she uses the metaphors 'source', 'power' and 'matrix' when writing of the transcendence of God in relation to the cosmos. That these particular metaphors are the metaphors for God used by Ruether and Heyward is also rather significant, particularly in the context of this study.[30]

For these reasons I believe it is justifiable to set aside McFague's models of God when examining her theology for her metaphysical and epistemological presuppositions. As I shall demonstrate, she is exceedingly clear about which presuppositions she values and adheres to. It is

---

28. See McFague, *Metaphorical Theology*, p. 187: 'God is part of our being as the source of power, of love, of endurance, of insight. But God is also the source of our life'; or p. 192, 'God as the source and depth of our being'. See also McFague, *Models of God*, p. 111: 'God's body, that which supports all life, is not matter or spirit but the matrix out of which everything that is evolves'. Also p. 139: 'the matrix of being from whom all life comes'. See also McFague, *The Body of God*, p. 20, where she refers to God as 'the source, power, and goal—the spirit—that enlivens (and loves) the entire process and its material forms'. Also p. 100: 'we all exist together in one space, our finite planet or, in terms of our model, within the nurturing matrix of God's body'.

29. See McFague, *Metaphorical Theology*, p. 192: 'Ecstasy and awe cannot be contained in models of God as parent or friend—the ocean, the sky, and the earth express them more fully'. See also *idem*, *Models of God*, p. 186: 'And in fact, does not the universe provide us with far more awesome images of transcendence than the political arena?... If one can say that the basic religious apprehension is the wonder at being, wonder that there is something rather than nothing, then the ecological, evolutionary sensibility is in this sense religious'. She continues by stating that she is 'imaging the transcendence of God in a worldly way...in the mythology or images of our own day that inspire feelings of awe, reverence, wonder'. See also McFague, *The Body of God*, p. 21: 'the cosmos is the picture we turn to when we try to imagine what divine transcendence is'.

30. In fact, McFague's second use of the metaphor of 'matrix' (that I have found, at least) occurs when she is describing Ruether's conception of God/ess as matrix. See *Models of God*, p. 116.

her clarity on these foundational assumptions, as well as her consistent use of metaphors compatible with these assumptions, that, paradoxically, contradict the implications of her own models of God.

Having named what I am not going to explore in this chapter and why, it is time to outline briefly what I am going to examine. In the next section I shall trace McFague's (changing) understanding of the nature and purpose of theology. Following this I shall identify her theological anthropology, or her assumptions about human nature, and discuss at some length her assumptions concerning humans as knowing agents, in particular her understanding of humans as linguistic animals. I shall then turn to an examination of her metaphysical presuppositions concerning the world, or creation and the cosmos. As in Heyward's thought, however, there is a great deal of overlap between McFague's anthropological and epistemological assumptions and her ontological assumptions. That is, the sorts of knowledge claims McFague considers it possible for humans to make about the world and creation are predicated to a large extent upon her understanding of what sort of (creaturely) epistemic agents humans are.

The Nature and Purpose of 'Theology' in McFague's Thought

McFague's understanding of the nature and purpose of theology has undergone, on one level, a profound shift since the mid-1970s. At that time, in keeping with the neo-orthodox tradition, she affirmed Gerhard Ebeling's assertion that 'hermeneutic is the whole of theology'.[31] In other words, she considered theology to be nothing other than an *interpretive* response to 'God's word' to the world.[32] Further, her understanding of this interpretive response was both dependent on a wholly-other-than God *and* individualistic, in the sense that she considered each interpretive encounter to take place between 'God's word' and an

---

31. Sallie McFague, *Speaking in Parables: A Study in Metaphor and Theology* (Philadelphia: Fortress Press, 1975), p. 30. In 1993 McFague characterized herself as an 'erstwhile Barthian', and this characterization is certainly in keeping with her earliest understanding of the nature of theology. See *idem*, *The Body of God*, p. 208.

32. McFague, *Speaking in Parables*, p. 41: 'the task of theology is to serve the hearing of God's word'. It is important to note that McFague did believe that 'God's word' could and did come, indirectly, through human words.

individual—who did not so much do the interpreting but was interpreted by and responded to the Word.³³

By 1982, however, McFague's perspective on theology had changed significantly. She stated then that 'the ultimate goal of theology is *comprehension* of all reality by means of a root-metaphor and its dominant models'.³⁴ To this end she proposed that the question with which theology was most concerned was, 'What is the meaning of life in the world?'³⁵ She herself was far more concerned with collective human attempts to make sense of and value *this* life than she was concerned with individuals being interpreted by and responding to 'the unmerited grace of God', although this was still an identifiable factor in her thought.³⁶ However, McFague's concern with making sense of the world in a way that would allow and encourage humans to live responsibly in it had become pronounced by 1987. By that time she had rejected the notion that theology is hermeneutics, and was insisting instead that 'theology must be self-consciously constructive'.³⁷ The purpose of her own theology, according to McFague, was to 'remythologize' the 'relationship between God and the world'.³⁸

The assumption underlying and supporting her project of remythologizing the relationship between God and the world, and in particular the relationship between humans and the world, is one that she has, I believe, held consistently since at least 1975: that human beings understand ourselves, construct and live in the world according to the *stories* we tell about ourselves and the world. 'We know who we are through the stories we embrace as our own—the story of my life is structured by the larger stories (social, political, mythic) in which I understand my

33. McFague, *Speaking in Parables*, p. 71.
34. McFague, *Metaphorical Theology*, p. 104 (italics in original).
35. McFague, *Metaphorical Theology*, p. 107. The influence of existentialist thought is evident in this quotation: she is concerned with the meaning of being-in-the-world.
36. McFague, *Metaphorical Theology*, p. 108.
37. McFague, *Models of God*, p. 21. The entire quotation is as follows: 'Christian theology, in our time at least, cannot be merely or mainly hermeneutics, that is, interpretation of the tradition, a translation of ancient creeds and concepts to make them relevant for contemporary culture. Rather, theology must be self-consciously constructive…'
38. McFague, *Models of God*, p. xi. In using the term 'remythologize' McFague is (deliberately, I believe) playing against Bultmann's project of *demythologizing* Christian scripture.

personal story to take place'.[39] It is crucial to note McFague's *consistent* affirmation of this epistemological (and anthropological and metaphysical) claim. In 1993, in the preface to *Models of God*, she at last applies this point to her understanding of the nature of theology: 'theology is mostly fiction'.[40] This truly is one of McFague's central insights, and I cannot over-emphasize how *profoundly* aware she is of the world-shaping influence of the stories, narratives, myths into which humans are born and by means of which humans perceive, interpret, and order the world. As she succinctly puts it, 'we live our lives according to our constructions of the world'.[41]

Thus her understanding of theology as 'mostly fiction', an understanding that I take to be McFague's most important contribution to feminist Christian analyses of the nature of theology, is no facile dismissal of past or present theological pronouncements. In her thought they matter greatly, precisely because they are human 'stories' that contribute to shaping human relations with other humans and with the rest of creation. However, McFague is exceedingly forthright in her assessment of the 'certainty' of Christian theological assertions:

> I begin with the assumption that what we can say with any assurance about the character of Christian faith is very little and that even that will be highly contested. Christian faith is, it seems to me, most basically a claim that the universe is neither indifferent nor malevolent but that there is a power (and a personal power at that) which is on the side of life and its fulfillment.[42]

From this statement I take it that McFague understands the *purpose* of theology to be, quite simply, to promote the fulfilment of life. And indeed, in her analysis of those elements any theology ought to include if it is to be relevant to the current historical and ecological context, she notes that 'a credible theology for our time...accepts responsibility for nurturing and fulfilling life in its many forms'.[43] In a note to the same chapter she reiterates her point: 'the main criterion for a 'true' theology is pragmatic, preferring those models of God that are most helpful in

---

39. McFague, *Speaking in Parables*, p. 140.
40. McFague, *Models of God*, p. xi. This is one of my favourite theological quotes of all time.
41. McFague, *Models of God*, p. 28.
42. McFague, *Models of God*, p. x.
43. McFague, *Models of God*, p. 32.

8. *The Theology of Sallie McFague*

the praxis of bringing about fulfillment for living beings'.[44] I suggest that McFague's understanding of the purpose of theology as promoting fulfilment for living beings is, if not precisely the same, extremely compatible with Heyward's understanding of the purpose of theology as the effort to make incarnate love and justice in the world. Further, both McFague and Heyward take for granted Ruether's conception of theology as providing a mediating point between the 'is' and the 'ought' of human life.

Just as Heyward's theological pattern is centred on her understanding of the need for humans to do the work of *redemption*, i.e., to bring love/justice to those people and places from which it is absent, at the heart of McFague's theological system is her understanding of *salvation*—salvation defined 'as the well-being and fulfillment of all that lives'.[45] She explicitly places 'salvation' at the core of her theological system:

> The formal criterion for theology...is that it reflect, in tough-minded, concrete ways and in the language and thought forms of one's own time, about what salvation could, would, mean now, to us... What the formal criterion does not allow, however, is resting in an interpretation of God's salvific love from some bygone time, for this will invariably be escapist and, finally, destructive: that gospel will be good news not for our time but for another.[46]

Importantly, to understand fully the radical implications of this theological move on her part one must know the context in which McFague locates all her theological claims. McFague's understanding of salvation depends for its radicality upon her theological standpoint, which is, and is exclusively, this earth as it exists *within the universe*—of which humans are inextricably a part and upon which humans and all 'earth others' are dependent for life.[47] Her rejection (like Ruether's) of

---

44. McFague, *Models of God*, p. 196 n. 13.

45. McFague, *Metaphorical Theology*, p. 187. See also *idem*, *Models of God*, p. 7. She writes that 'the principal insight of liberation theologies—that redemption is not the rescue of certain individuals for eternal life in another world but the fulfillment of all humanity in the political and social realities of this world—must be further deprivatized to include the well-being of all life'.

46. McFague, *Metaphorical Theology*, p. 45.

47. See McFague, *The Body of God*, p. 40. She writes of 'attempting to take the cosmos as the context for doing theology. We are trying to take the context of the whole within which we exist, rather than merely a psychological or political context, as our theological standpoint in a way that emphasizes rather than sacrifices

a heaven above and of an other-worldly afterlife is total, thus her assertion that 'creation is the *place* of salvation' must be interpreted literally.[48] For example, McFague writes scathingly of 'any notion of salvation which presumes that individuals can be rescued *from* the world', and ironically of 'the strange illusion that we are other than our bodies, that we and those we love can and will exist apart from them, that our spirits will live on, here or "in heaven", after death'.[49] Further, because all earthly life forms exist only in a state of interdependence, McFague asserts that 'in our time, salvation must be understood to extend to all, or it will apply to none'.[50] Her definition of sin, which is perfectly consistent with her understanding of salvation, further clarifies her meaning and use of the metaphor of 'salvation'. 'Sin is the turning-away not from a transcendent power but from interdependence with all other beings, including the matrix of being from whom all life comes'.[51]

McFague's theological extension of the scope of salvation beyond individual human souls to the well-being of the entire creation is in perfect accord with two value judgments underlying all her work since 1982. On the one hand she believes that 'the moral issue of our day—and the vocation to which we are called—is whether we and other species will live and how well we will live', and on the other she refuses to value human life above non-human earth others.[52] The second of these value judgments is critical: in positing all earth others as inherently worthy of salvation, or deserving of whatever constitutes their own well-being and fulfilment, she is not advocating that seals and whales and rivers and rainforests be saved either for the sake or the enjoyment of ongoing human life, *but for their own sakes*, because

diversity'. Regarding the expression 'earth others', see Sallie McFague, *Super, Natural Christians: How We Should Love Nature* (Minneapolis: Fortress Press, 1997), p. 151.

    48. McFague, *The Body of God*, p. 180 (italics in original).

    49. McFague, *Metaphorical Theology*, p. 185 (italics in original), and *idem*, *The Body of God*, p. 16.

    50. McFague, *Models of God*, p. 53.

    51. McFague, *Models of God*, p. 139.

    52. McFague, *The Body of God*, p. 9. See also p. 108, 'we are not the center of things'. See also *idem*, *Metaphorical Theology*, p. xi, where she speaks of 'delight in the other, not domination of the other'. And all of *Super, Natural Christians*, which is an extended reflection on what it might mean to perceive *all* earth others as subjects rather than objects.

8. *The Theology of Sallie McFague* 225

these earth others are as valuable and irreplaceable as any aspect of creation. For McFague it is a fortunate consequence that caring for (trying to save) the earth in its ecological and evolutionary diversity contributes to enabling human life, but this consequence is just that, a consequence, and not the *theological* reason for such activity.[53] Moreover, regardless of its consequences—in the sense of direct, measurable outcomes—activity on behalf of the well-being of particular aspects of the earth (including the health and fulfilment of human earth creatures) is the 'vocation' to which she perceives that humans no less than God (as the source of and power enlivening all that is) are called.

However, regarding outcomes, in McFague's thought neither humans nor God can ever bring about a state of perfect salvation for all. As with Heyward's conception of redemption, McFague's understanding of salvation is that it is always imperfectly achieved where it is achieved at all, and, given her metaphysical stress on process rather than stasis, it can never be achieved once and for all.[54] McFague is, if not exactly a pessimist, a hard-core pragmatist. The issue, in her thought, seems to be twofold: first, 'most life-forms, including human beings, live in a world characterized by brutal, deep, as well as subtle forms of oppression;' and secondly, she notes that 'even when we are motivated by the best of intentions, our efforts to be sensitive to the needs of some parts of God's body, some species of flora and fauna, will inevitably mean the deterioration and demise of others'.[55] As I shall discuss in greater detail below, McFague's conception of reality as relational and interdependent is, again like Heyward's, inherently ambiguous and tension-filled. The salvation or well-being and fulfilment of some aspects of creation requires the destruction and demise of other aspects. Given her assessment of all that hinders the fulfilment of life (in broadest terms, 'the decay of our planet is probably

---

53. See McFague, *Models of God*, p. 7. On a practical level she does assert, with Ruether and Heyward, that unless humans do change our ways of relating to the earth and all earth others we will probably destroy ourselves and most other life forms.

54. McFague, *Models of God*, p. 8: 'Relationship and interdependence, change and transformation, not substance, changelessness, and perfection, are the categories within which a theology for our day must function'. See also p. 10: 'process, change, transformation, and openness replace stasis, changelessness, and completeness as basic descriptive concepts'.

55. McFague, *The Body of God*, p. 72 (first quotation), and *idem*, *Models of God*, p. 137 (second quotation).

inevitable'[56]), how does she answer the question, 'why bother?'

Her answer to this question is, I suggest, three-fold—in an inseparable, trinitarian sense—with discernibly ethical, theological, metaphysical and epistemological dimensions. First, in bleak, stark words she notes that 'one has to get up in the morning and look in the mirror. It may come to nothing more than that.'[57] But this response to the question 'why bother?' is incomplete and too anthropocentric to stand alone in McFague's thought. The second element in her response corrects this anthropocentrism. Quoting Iris Murdoch, McFague conveys her understanding of love: 'Love is the extremely difficult realization that something other than oneself is real. Love...is the discovery of reality'.[58] Love, then, not in a warm fuzzy sense but as acknowledgment of the fact of existence apart from oneself, existence indifferent to, even opposed to one's own existence: the sheer fact of existence beyond oneself is reason to work for the fulfilment of 'what is'. But still not reason enough. The third element in McFague's 'why' is simultaneously epistemological and theological:

> Over the years I have learned that the closer attention I pay to whatever piece of the world is before me—the more I know about it, the more open I am to its presence, the closer I look at it or listen to it or touch it or smell it—the more amazed I am by it. It is not that I 'see God in it' in any direct or general way; rather, it is the specialness, the difference, the intricacy of each creature, event, or aspect of nature that calls forth wonder. And that wonder helps sustain me; it helps me stay the course.[59]

Wonder: in McFague's thought a religious sensibility informed by attention to the presence of the other leads finally to a sense of wonder tinged with awe.[60] Trying to express the implications of such a sentiment, McFague draws on a quotation from feminist lesbian philosopher Marilyn Frye which combines both McFague's understanding of love

---

56. McFague, *The Body of God*, p. 207.

57. McFague, *The Body of God*, p. 208. Whenever I read these sentences I imagine a scrap of paper attached to the mirror containing a quote from Kant including the words 'moral imperative'.

58. McFague, *The Body of God*, p. 50 and *Super, Natural Christians*, p. 35. Citing Iris Murdoch, 'The Sublime and the Good', *Chicago Review* 13 (Autumn 1959), p. 51.

59. McFague, *The Body of God*, p. 210.

60. Regarding attention epistemology see *The Body of God*, pp. 49-50: 'An attention epistemology assumes the *intrinsic* value of anything, everything, that is not the self' (p. 50, italics in original).

and her theological/epistemological bent toward attentive wonder. She quotes: 'The science of the loving eye would favor the Complexity Theory of Truth...and presuppose The Endless Interestingness of the Universe'.[61] From this theological and epistemological standpoint she affirms that this little bit of creation, as spatially and temporally insignificant as it appears to be in the cosmic scheme of things, is inherently wonder-full, intrinsically interesting, and thus inherently worthy of care for as long as any part of it exists. This faith claim/value judgment lies beneath her understanding of salvation, extending outwards from the very core of her theological system.

With this overview of the nature and purpose of 'theology' in McFague's thought (and brief introduction to her theology) in place, I turn now to an examination of her theological anthropology and epistemological presuppositions concerning humans as knowing agents.

McFague's Theological Anthropology

On one level McFague's theological anthropology is inseparable from her ontology, or her understanding of the nature of all reality as 'part and parcel' of an evolutionary process begun billions of years ago and continuing to this day.[62] In keeping with the current scientific view she affirms that human beings, like all earth entities, are nothing more than collections of elements formed when the first stars exploded. In this regard there is nothing uniquely individual about any human being: every atom and molecule of all our bodies comes from the same cosmic smorgasbord as everything else.[63] As she writes, 'All things living and all things not living are products of the same primal explosion and evolutionary history and hence *interrelated* in an internal way right from the beginning'.[64] The ontological fact of relationship is a foundational assumption for McFague. Like Heyward, she quotes from

---

61. McFague, *The Body of God*, p. 52, citing Marilyn Frye, *The Politics of Reality* (New York: The Crossing Press, 1983), p. 76.

62. McFague, *Models of God*, p. 9: 'To feel in the depths of our being that we are part and parcel of the evolutionary ecosystem of our cosmos is a prerequisite for contemporary Christian theology'. See also *idem, The Body of God*, pp. 99-129.

63. See McFague, *Models of God*, pp. 7-8: 'we belong, from the cells of our bodies to the finest creations of our minds, to the intricate, constantly changing cosmos'.

64. McFague, *The Body of God*, p. 104 (italics added).

Martin Buber's *I and Thou*: 'In the beginning is relationship'.[65] That humans are related, connected through the very stuff of our bodies to every other physical entity in the cosmos is of crucial significance in McFague's theological anthropology—as it is in Ruether's as well.

In no way are human beings 'other than' a product of universal evolution, and such evolution is, according to McFague's interpretation of 'the common creation story', a spatio-temporal process characterized by relationship, chance and change.[66] Importantly, this aspect of McFague's thought—which is highly influenced by process philosophy—is present to some degree in all her work since at least 1975.[67] Her emphasis on evolutionary process and relationality, however, must always be read through 'earth lenses'. That is, McFague firmly locates human beings as beings not in the cosmos generally, but as earth creatures, creatures '*in* and *of* the earth'—and again, on this earth, life is characterized more often by brutal, oppressive relationships than by pleasant, nurturing ones.[68] Likewise, the spatio-temporal process in which all relationships are formed is neither, according to McFague, utterly random, disconnected from what *in particular* has happened and is happening to specific earth creatures, nor does it flow along harmoniously, proceeding seamlessly toward some final state of perfection. As she puts it, 'The future is never an abstraction totally unrelated to our particular and familiar presents and pasts; it is the sometimes subtle, sometimes violent renovation and fulfillment of what is familiar to us.'[69] In sum, humans are earth creatures inextricably related to the same evolutionary process as all else in the cosmos, but this process, while of a piece, is at least as random and as violent as it is sustaining and enabling of life.[70] Thus human existence is, in its very nature, relative, ambiguous, tense, and open to the unexpected. In McFague's thought this point is, I suggest, simultaneously an ontological and

---

65. McFague, *Super, Natural Christians*, p. 21.
66. See McFague, *The Body of God*, pp. 38-47.
67. See McFague, *Speaking in Parables*, pp. 55-56; *Metaphorical Theology*, p. 96 and p. 221 n. 95; *Models of God*, pp. 8, 10, 14; *The Body of God*, pp. 20, 31, 74, 111, 140; and *Super, Natural Christians*, p. 2.
68. McFague, *Super, Natural Christians*, p. 6 (italics in original).
69. McFague, *Speaking in Parables*, p. 57.
70. See McFague, *The Body of God*, p. 43. 'The process of evolution is through chance (random errors) operating at the local level; thus, any overall purposive direction, whether divine or of another sort, is highly problematic'.

anthropological affirmation, and it is one of her fundamental metaphysical presuppositions.

Having thus set the stage for the rest of her theological anthropology, McFague's thought becomes rather more focused when she discusses what particular sort of earth creatures humans are. Specifically, she begins from an understanding that 'human beings are organisms'.[71] Further, human beings are particularly *embodied* organisms. McFague's stress on the physically embodied nature of human life cannot be overemphasized. As she says,

> Whatever more or other we may be, we *are* bodies, made of the same stuff as all other life-forms on our planet, including our brains, which are on a chemical continuum with our physical being. We do not *have* bodies, as we like to suppose, distancing ourselves from them as one does from an inferior, a servant, who works for us (the 'us' being the mind that inhabits the body but does not really belong there). We *are* bodies...[72]

I suggest that McFague intends these words to be interpreted as literally as she believes any words *can* be interpreted, but (and this is where her theological anthropology becomes thoroughly epistemological), she understands language no less than our bodies to be our 'house of being', and for McFague language is, at root, always metaphorical, or 'tentative, open, relative, indirect, and tensive'.[73] (In this regard McFague's understanding of language is commensurate with her understanding of the nature of being—her ontology—as inherently relational, ambiguous, open-ended and tensive.) According to her, humans are 'born into a world which is already linguistic', thus we *never* experience our own bodies or any other bodies 'as they are' apart from relative and indirect interpretations of them—that is, interpretations relative to specific times and cultures, and taught to us by others.[74] In her words, just as we cannot live outside our bodies, 'we can only live within the confines of our language', yet 'language always stands between us and reality...it is the medium through which we are aware of both our relationship to "what is" and our distance

---

71. McFague, *Speaking in Parables*, p. 58.
72. McFague, *The Body of God*, p. 16 (italics in original).
73. See McFague, *Metaphorical Theology*, pp. 8-10 and p. 116. She draws the 'language is the house of being' quotation (p. 8) from Martin Heidegger.
74. McFague, *Metaphorical Theology*, pp. 8-9.

from it'.[75] Or again, 'language is the mediation of raw experience (which we never have) and complete intelligibility (which we never have)'.[76] In other words, while McFague would agree (I think) that a human being is just another sort of critter or animal, she would qualify this description: in her thought *humans are linguistic animals*. Thus, in addition to insisting on the body as a physical entity she stresses that

> 'the body' is a social construction... What we mean by body is a set of associations and stereotypes that are often assumed to be 'natural' or 'obvious' but are, of course, complex, highly nuanced networks of values and interests controlled implicitly (and at times explicitly) by those in power.[77]

I take this to mean that McFague understands bodies to be swaddled from birth in power-riddled linguistic constructions—socially 'given' assessments and interpretations of the meaning and value and potential and proper place of 'bodies like that'. Indeed, McFague seems implicitly to assume that the social 'conception' of any particular body occurs prior to the physical conception of that body.[78] Human babies are born into pre-existent, linguistically shaped conceptual bodies— associations and stereotypes that never wash off. Further, with Ruether and Heyward, McFague agrees that these different associations and stereotypes, while theoretically distinguishable, for example as 'white', 'black', 'lesbian', 'heterosexual', 'Muslim', 'disabled', etc., combine *inseparably* when they converge on different, particular bodies.[79] (That is, the conception of a particular Muslim lesbian body is not formed by gluing a stereotype of 'woman' together with a stereotype of 'Muslim' together with a stereotype of 'lesbian'—the 'meaning' of each of these cultural metaphors is transformed when it is associated with the other two metaphors.) I suggest that both of her understandings of 'body'— as physical entity and as power-riddled linguistic construct—come together in the following quotation, in which McFague addresses the extent to which all our lives-in-relationship are shaped by 'both' of the bodies we are born with:

---

75. McFague, *Speaking in Parables*, p. 22 (first quotation), and *idem*, *Metaphorical Theology*, p. 34 (second quotation).
76. McFague, *Metaphorical Theology*, p. 122.
77. McFague, *The Body of God*, pp. 24-25.
78. McFague, *Metaphorical Theology*, pp. 8-9.
79. See McFague, *The Body of God*, p. 48 and pp. 53-54.

8. The Theology of Sallie McFague

> The body is not a discardable garment cloaking the real self or essence of a person (or a pine tree or a chimpanzee); rather, it is the shape or form of who we are. It is how each of us is recognized, responded to, loved, touched, and cared for—as well as oppressed, beaten, raped, mutilated, discarded, and killed.[80]

Just as there are two discernible yet inseparable strands to McFague's understanding of human bodies, I believe there are two discernible yet inseparable elements in McFague's epistemology, each element consistent with and further developing one strand of her anthropology. Accordingly, I shall examine first her understanding of 'metaphorical knowing', which corresponds to her emphasis on the linguistic nature of human animals, and shall then discuss her understanding of 'attention epistemology', which corresponds to her emphasis on the physically embodied nature of all earth entities. Let me be clear, however, that these emphases in her thought are emphases within a single epistemological framework; they are inseparable elements of one approach.

As I shall be drawing primarily from her book *Speaking in Parables* (1975) in the discussion of metaphorical knowing, I should note that McFague may have distanced herself from this work, as she wrote in 1997—of her 'series of four books on religious language'—that '*Metaphorical Theology* laid the groundwork'.[81] In fact she has written five books on religious language, and characterized *Metaphorical Theology*, when it was published, as a sequel to *Speaking in Parables*.[82] It may be that she no longer mentions it simply because it is out of print (which is unfortunate), or she may be trying to distance herself from the particular model of God she accepted without question at the time. What I find most significant, however, is that her latest book, an extended meditation on humans relating to all earth others as subjects rather than as objects, is simply an approach from the perspective of attention epistemology to the same subject McFague approached via metaphorical epistemology in *Speaking in Parables*—the theological and philosophical problem of a hierarchical, value-laden, subject-object/knower-known split.

'Language, all language, is ultimately traceable to metaphor—it is the foundation of language and thus of thought'.[83] '[M]etaphor is a way of

---

80. McFague, *The Body of God*, p. 16.
81. McFague, *Super, Natural Christians*, p. 2.
82. McFague, *Metaphorical Theology*, p. vii.
83. McFague, *Speaking in Parables*, p. 50.

knowing, not just a way of communicating. In metaphor knowledge and its expression are one and the same; there is no way *around* the metaphor, it is not expendable.[84] McFague grounds her analysis of metaphorical knowing, and of humans as linguistic epistemic agents, on these two assumptions: *that language is at root metaphorical and, hence, that shared human knowledge too is metaphorical*. It is therefore imperative to try to be clear about how she understands and uses the metaphor 'metaphor'. However, given that an understanding of all human knowledge as metaphorical is, in my experience, strangely difficult to convey, and in keeping with her assertion that '*there is no way now or ever to have strange truth directly*', I shall be presenting my interpretation of McFague's understanding of metaphor via an indirect route.[85]

First, McFague's understanding of the epistemological function of metaphor is premised on her assumption that *no words* correspond directly to 'what is'.[86] In other words, she assumes that language is never precisely reflective of, or never corresponds directly to a reality that exists independently of human action and reflection. She does not deny the existence of reality apart from human beings, but McFague is insistent on two points: that of the *interdependence* of all reality (although she does write of the relative indifference of many aspects of reality to human existence)[87] and that of the *constructive* character of human knowledge claims. One implication of McFague's metaphysical presupposition of the interdependence of all reality is that, when this presupposition is carried over into one's epistemology, there is no longer the possibility of a strict subject–object split—knowers cannot avoid affecting and being affected by whatever it is they are trying to know, for they are part of the same interrelated whole.[88]

Regarding the second point, with Kant and Paul Ricoeur McFague agrees that humans *construct* and/or *create* the reality in which we live—through our linguistic conceptions of the world.[89] Further, quoting Philip Wheelwright, she believes we do so in a metaphorical manner, that is, by having 'something—whether a body, an image, a

---

84. McFague, *Speaking in Parables*, p. 4 (italics in original).
85. McFague, *Speaking in Parables*, p. 41 (italics in original).
86. McFague, *Speaking in Parables*, p. 29.
87. McFague, *The Body of God*, p. 50.
88. McFague, *Speaking in Parables*, p. 56 and p. 58.
89. McFague, *Speaking in Parables*, p. 52 and p. 56.

8. *The Theology of Sallie McFague* 233

sound, or…a written word—stand as surrogate for something else'.[90] In her words:

> Reality is created through this incredibly complex process of metaphorical leaps, of seeing this as that; we use what we notice about one thing to 'name' (describe, call up, evoke, elicit) another thing when we notice something of the same, and hence for the first time we *see* it that new way.[91]

According to McFague it is through this metaphorical process that humans make sense of, know, the world.[92] Importantly, this metaphorical process must begin concretely, with a 'this' with which to compare, contrast and connect with 'that', with a 'here' from which to move to 'there'. There are thus always two aspects to every metaphor, or two 'terms'—one of which is physically embodied and particularly located. Specifically, in McFague's thought metaphorical knowing *begins* with the fact of human embodiment. This point is so important that I shall quote McFague at length:

> Human beings…take themselves, their bodies, and where those bodies are and what they are, in all their particularity and concreteness and richness, as the 'figure', the image, in terms of which they 'understand', learn about, fathom *whatever* it is they are concerned to fathom. The unknown lies all about us and we 'figure' it all with ourselves—the human metaphors. Our movement, of whatever sort, is always metaphorical, with ourselves as one term of the metaphor.[93]

Elsewhere she reiterates the particular, embodied character of metaphorical knowing:

90. McFague, *Speaking in Parables*, p. 50, citing Philip Wheelwright, *Metaphor and Reality* (Bloomington: Indiana University Press, 1962), p. 19.
91. McFague, *Speaking in Parables*., pp. 52-53 (italics in original). On p. 56 she quotes Paul Ricoeur as saying, 'When we ask whether metaphorical language reaches reality, we presuppose that we already know what reality is. But if we assume that metaphor redescribes reality, we must then assume that this reality as redescribed is itself novel reality… With metaphor we experience the metamorphosis of both language and reality'. Citing Paul Ricoeur, 'Creativity in Language: Word, Polysemy, Metaphor', *Philosophy Today* (Summer 1973), pp. 110-11.
92. McFague, *Speaking in Parables*, p. 59: 'metaphor…is *the human method of investigating the universe*' (italics in original).
93. McFague, *Speaking in Parables,* p. 59 (italics in original). In this passage McFague is presenting her analysis of Elizabeth Sewell's work on metaphor. She cites Elizabeth Sewell, *The Human Metaphor* (Notre Dame, IN: University of Notre Dame Press, 1964), p. 11.

> [M]etaphorical language not only connects this with that, here with there, but demands that one partner of the association, at least, be concrete, sensuous, familiar, bodily. It will abide no abstractions, no head without a body, no mystical flights, but because it is the method of *human* movement it insists on taking along the whole human being in all its familiarity, messiness, and concreteness.[94]

McFague's insistence on the particularly embodied character of metaphorical knowing, that is, on the specifically familiar, or the 'messiness' and 'concreteness' of the lives and locations of particularly embodied human knowers, is in keeping with the claims made by the feminist epistemologists discussed in Chapters 4 and 5. She explicitly proposes 'a view of meaning and truth that takes seriously the diversity of embodied sites from which human beings make such claims: the sites that take into account race, class, gender, sexual orientation, handicapping situations, and so forth'.[95] However, while metaphorical knowledge is inescapably situated knowledge, it is never so situated as to be inescapably trapped knowledge. In other words, metaphorical knowing is never static; it is always a process, a movement. McFague expresses this point beautifully as she relates her understanding of metaphorical knowing to her conception of humans as products of evolution:

> [H]uman knowing, at its most profound, is not disembodied, abstract, or conceptual; the analogy for human knowing is not the Cartesian machine but the evolutionary organism—*the stretching of the whole creature beyond itself into the unknown*.[96]

Metaphorical knowing is thus, in imagistic language, journeying knowledge; it is rather like trying to find your way about an unfamiliar environment in dim light. You begin with your senses, listening, looking, smelling, stretching out your hands to feel your way around, and you cannot help but associate seemingly familiar sounds, sights, smells and feels with your understanding of other places you have been. But neither the sounds and sights and smells nor the material, physical entities you touch are 'the same' as any you have ever known. Nonetheless you must begin to make sense of your physically embodied experience of new surroundings by associating different aspects of it

---

94. McFague, *Speaking in Parables*, p. 61 (italics in original).
95. McFague, *The Body of God*, p. 48.
96. McFague, *Speaking in Parables*, p. 60 (italics added).

8. *The Theology of Sallie McFague* 235

with that place from whence you have come. You borrow from what you have known and apply that borrowed understanding, borrowed interpretation to the new, wherever and whenever the new seems, in one or more ways, to be sort of like the old. Such knowing is, in McFague's words, 'a highly risky, uncertain, and open-ended enterprise—a maneuver of desperation, if you will—in spite of the straightforward grammatical structure of a metaphorical statement'.[97]

It is risky and uncertain because no matter how well the analogies from 'there' seem to fit 'here' they never correspond directly to 'what is', nor are they ever the only analogies that might fit, might make sense of what one is experiencing.[98] Nonetheless 'all that we *know* prior to the metaphor is, at most, inchoate and confused…it is *only* in and through the metaphor that we can speak of it at all'.[99] However, once humans have spoken of something in one way we tend to treat it as though it *is* that way, forgetting what McFague calls 'the underside of all our constructions, the "is not", the incompleteness, the partiality, the uncertainty, that must accompany all our creations lest we reify them into absolutes'.[100] McFague's stress on the 'is-not' side of all linguistic constructions is, I suggest, fuelled by her desire both to keep limited and fallible humans from standing in awe of the emperor's new clothes (dazzling linguistic constructions), and to keep limited and fallible humans aware of our own creaturely limitations and fallibility.[101] Moreover, because humans tend to live and act in the world (treat each other and other entities) in accordance with the ways 'we' (meaning

---

97. McFague, *Speaking in Parables*, p. 44.
98. McFague, *Speaking in Parables*, p. 51: 'we cannot say our metaphors "correspond" to "what is"; at best, we can say only that they seem appropriate to our experience, they "fit" or seem "right"'. See also *idem*, *Metaphorical Theology*, p. 214 n. 37, where she summarizes Dorothy Emmet's metaphysical understanding of 'critical realism' as an epistemological stance.
99. McFague, *Speaking in Parables*, p. 44 (italics in original).
100. McFague, *Models of God*, p. 25.
101. McFague, *Models of God*, p. 25: 'By seeking security through our constructions, we refuse to step outside the house of language we have erected to protect us from the emptiness and terror we cannot control. Our safe havens, called dogma and orthodoxy, become absolutes, giving the illusion of being certain, being "on the inside", having the truth'. See also *idem*, *Speaking in Parables*, p. 29: 'The days of supposing we are free of finite limitations, of supposing that we have some direct access to "Truth", that there might be words that correspond to "what is"… such a time is over (if it ever existed except in the most rationalistic circles)'.

those few with the power to do so) name the world, McFague affirms that great care must be taken when naming any aspect of the world.[102] She states, 'We live our lives according to our constructions of the world; as Eric Heller said, "Be careful how you interpret the world; it is like that".'[103] In this regard McFague's work corresponds closely with Kathryn Pyne Addelson's conception of truth and meaning as enacted by human agents, rather than being 'discovered' as something that was pre-existent.

Metaphorical knowing, as embodied human knowing, is therefore a kind of 'groping' along, the human way of getting from here to there and trying to make sense of, or make ourselves at home, where (and with whom else) we find ourselves.[104] Such an epistemological journey, according to McFague, 'has certain characteristics: it is tentative, relativistic, multi-layered, dynamic, complex, sensuous, historical, and participatory'.[105] In addition, the possibility of any individual even setting out on such a journey depends on that individual's relationships with others—both human and earth others. McFague's understanding of metaphorical epistemology is dependent on her explicit assumption of the thoroughly relational and relative character of human knowledge claims. Within her thought it is taken for granted that human beings are epistemic agents 'only in relationship—relationships with the world of which we are a part and with other selves who respond to us as well as influence us'.[106] But again, particular human beings are related to particular places and communities on this earth. 'To the extent that we know ourselves, our world, and our God, that knowledge is profoundly relational and, hence, interdependent, relative, situational, and limited.'[107]

While this statement is in close accord with statements made by feminist epistemologists such as Addelson, Code and Haraway, McFague's

---

102. See McFague, *Metaphorical Theology*, pp. 8-10 and p. 63. McFague is profoundly aware of the power of naming, of the effects of oppressive and devalued linguistic constructions on entire categories of people and other earth entities. She writes of 'the oppressive cultural structures [language] may mask as absolutes' (p. 63).
103. McFague, *Models of God*, p. 28.
104. See McFague, *Speaking in Parables*, p. 58.
105. McFague, *Speaking in Parables*, p. 62.
106. McFague, *Metaphorical Theology*, p. 96.
107. McFague, *Metaphorical Theology*, p. 194.

8. *The Theology of Sallie McFague* 237

conception of the profoundly relational, situated character of knowledge includes as well Lynn Hankinson Nelson's and Elizabeth Potter's insistence that humans, in order to develop into epistemic agents, are dependent on close interactions with pre-existent human linguistic communities. But McFague extends the scope of human epistemic dependence to include not only other humans, but specific attributes of the 'natural' world. She states:

> [H]uman development is both culture- and nature-dependent. Infants have brains, but the human mind depends not only on other human beings in order to develop the distinctive characteristics of human existence but also on the stimuli of nature such as light, sound, smell, and heat: without the 'warbling birds, blossoming cherry trees, sighing wind, and speaking humans, there would be no sources of signals—and thus no intellects'.[108]

Or, writing in more abstract terms, she asserts that 'the individual achieves being, its ontological status, through its acts in relationship to the network in which it exists'.[109] This 'network' necessarily includes not only other human beings, but also non-human physical reality.

Thus, while it is comprised of linguistic constructions, hence always uncertain and indirect, metaphorical epistemology is also a profoundly participatory and relational form of embodied knowing, and in McFague's thought it is only through *attention* to the relations we have with others that our knowledge claims have a hope of enabling the fulfilment of life. Importantly, this ethical affirmation is a central component of her epistemology, just as it is at the core of her theological system. She asserts that 'our function as human beings on this planet is not mainly to think correct thoughts that correspond to some eternal set of verities, but to live appropriately and responsibly'.[110] Again this corresponds to Lorraine Code's understanding of responsibility as an epistemic virtue, and to Kathryn Pyne Addelson's understanding that

---

108. McFague, *Models of God*, p. 8. Citing Harold K. Schilling, 'The Whole Earth is the Lord's: Toward a Holistic Ethic', in Ian Barbour (ed.), *Earth Might Be Fair: Reflections on Ethics, Religion, and Ecology* (Englewood Cliffs, NJ: Prentice–Hall, 1972), p. 102.

109. McFague, *Metaphorical Theology*, p. 125.

110. McFague, *The Body of God*, p. 89. See also p. 48, where she stresses the integral relationship between knowing and doing, and see also *idem, Super, Natural Christians*, p. 149, where she writes of the integral relationship between 'being, knowing, doing; ontology, epistemology, ethics'.

the goal of all knowledge seeking endeavours is to enable knowers to live more responsibly in the world. McFague puts it in more theological terms (which are highly reminiscent of Ruether's words): 'The goal is not utopia, but sustainability and livability: not the kingdom of God, but a decent life in community for all life-forms and the ecosystem on which they rely'.[111] McFague's understanding of the ethical dimensions of all knowledge claims, her affirmation of responsibility as a core epistemic virtue, and her vision of 'a decent life in community for all' resonate with the epistemological presuppositions of Ruether and Heyward, as well as with those of Addelson, Code, Harding, Haraway and Keller, among others. Like Heyward she further describes her theo-ethical and epistemological agenda (or bias, or standpoint) by drawing on a quotation from Donna Haraway—the same quotation as used by Heyward, in fact. She advocates a stance that would be, quoting Haraway, 'friendly to earthwide projects of finite freedom, adequate material abundance, modest meaning in suffering, and a limited happiness'.[112] But again such projects have no chance of succeeding unless the participants attend, and attend closely, to the 'others' with whom they share their surroundings. McFague characterizes such an approach to knowledge as 'attention epistemology'.[113]

In simplest terms, attention epistemology is about 'the kind of knowledge that comes from paying close attention to something other than oneself'.[114] It is, says McFague, 'listening, paying close attention to another, the other, in itself, for itself'.[115] That the other is, in itself and not as a means to one's own ends, intrinsically valuable—this is a fundamental presupposition associated with attention epistemology. As I understand it, attention epistemology begins, as does metaphorical knowing, with physical embodiment, and again there are two terms to the knowing. One attends with one's embodied self, with all one's physical senses, to that which is physically embodied before one, accepting that it is utterly distinct from oneself, or uniquely 'other-than'. One begins by accepting the other in its otherness, and learns from it by listening, looking, touching, tasting, smelling—but always

111. McFague, *The Body of God*, p. 68.
112. McFague, *The Body of God*, p. 96. Citing Haraway, 'Situated Knowledges', p. 579. See also above, Chapter 4, n. 48.
113. McFague, *The Body of God*, pp. 49-54.
114. McFague, *The Body of God*, p. 49.
115. McFague, *The Body of God*, p. 49.

through an engagement with the other *as a subject* in its own right and its own way. The goal is understanding the other subject in its own in-itself-ness.[116] Drawing on Evelyn Fox Keller's work, McFague refers to Barbara McClintock's efforts to develop 'a feeling for the organism' rather than to impose her own presuppositions concerning how the organism ought to be.[117] In McFague's words, attention epistemology insists that 'one must set dogmas aside and pay attention to differences, even the differences among individual corn plants'.[118]

Attention epistemology is based on the assumption of radical difference and seemingly endless diversity; it is neither a homogenizing nor a reductionistic approach to knowledge.[119] To quote Marilyn Frye again, it presupposes 'The Endless Interestingness of the Universe'. Without denying the interdependence of all aspects of the universe, attention epistemology 'takes with utmost seriousness the differences that separate all beings: the individual, unique site from which each is in itself for itself'.[120] Again drawing upon Iris Murdoch's understanding of love as 'the extremely difficult realisation that something other than oneself is real: love [as] the discovery of reality', McFague characterizes attention epistemology as 'the loving eye'.[121] She explains herself by stating:

> The loving eye is not the sentimental, mushy, soft eye; rather, it is the realistic, tough, no-nonsense eye, acknowledging what is so difficult for us to recognize: that reality is made up of *others*. Love, then, is no big deal or a specific virtue reserved for Christians; it is simply facing facts. It is, in a nice twist, being 'objective'.[122]

Just as Donna Haraway and Carter Heyward both redefine 'objectivity' in their work, so too does McFague—in a manner that combines, I suggest, both Haraway's and Heyward's perceptions. Objectivity as loving attention to the other in its otherness includes (as per Haraway) the presupposition of the other as a subject (or agent) in its own right and in its own way, as well the demand (as per Heyward) that the other

---

116. See McFague, *Super, Natural Christians*, pp. 35-36 and pp. 75-76.
117. See McFague, *The Body of God*, p. 51, and *idem*, *Super, Natural Christians*, p. 76.
118. McFague, *The Body of God*, p. 51.
119. See McFague, *Super, Natural Christians*, p. 76.
120. McFague, *The Body of God*, p. 50.
121. McFague, *Super, Natural Christians*, p. 35.
122. McFague, *Super, Natural Christians*, pp. 35-36 (italics in original).

subject be known within its own context, that knowledge of the other include the attempt to discern what is right or true or good for that subject as it is, not as a human knower might want it to be.

Importantly, just as the cosmos, and in particular the bit of the cosmos known as 'earth', is the standpoint for McFague's theology, this earth, this world teeming with human and non-human earth others is the standpoint for an attention epistemology. McFague writes of 'our place *in* nature along with and close to all the others whom we rub up against, smell, reach out to touch, hear calling us, and see beside us'.[123] By stressing physical relations among earth creatures and earth entities McFague emphasizes the physical, sensate rather than linguistic character of attention epistemology. Aware of the barriers linguistic constructions often place between knowers and that which they are trying to know, she is trying, I believe, to find a way underneath those barriers and see what might happen. It is significant that she quotes at length from a short story by Ursula Le Guin, entitled 'She Unnames Them'. In the story Eve unnames the animals, and this is what happens:

> They seemed far closer than when their names had stood between myself and them like a clear barrier: so close that my fear of them and their fear of me became one same fear. And the attraction many of us felt, the desire to smell one another's smells, feel or rub or caress one another's scales or skin or feathers or fur, taste one another's blood or flesh, keep one another warm—that attraction was now all one with the fear, and the hunter could not be told from the hunted, nor the eater from the food.[124]

Having begun her explanation of attention epistemology by insisting on radical differences between subjects, McFague concludes by holding such differences in creative tension with a deep and abiding *similarity* between all subjects. What she does is extend the notion of 'subjectivity' to all earth others—not in an anthropomorphic sense, but in the sense of respecting the ineluctable otherness, the fullness of presence, the indwelling grace of all earth entities. She uses 'the language of intentions, goals, purpose, direction—even of health and flourishing' with regard to mountains, trees, even the AIDS virus.[125] She does so with the understanding that such language does, in the first instance, refer to human beings, to human experience. But, to bring her

---

123. McFague, *Super, Natural Christians*, p. 77 (italics in original).

124. McFague, *The Body of God*, p. 247 n. 30. Citing Ursula Le Guin, 'She Unnames Them', *The New Yorker*, 21 January 1985.

125. McFague, *Super, Natural Christians*, p. 109 and p. 157.

8. *The Theology of Sallie McFague* 241

epistemology full circle, she insists that 'we use it *metaphorically* of the earth others, not knowing how it applies but finding it better and more appropriate than its opposite'.[126] In perceiving all earth others as 'like humans' insofar as they are subjects in their own right and manner, McFague is emphasizing that 'their raison d'être is not to be objects for us'.[127] She continues:

> They are agents with intentions, albeit often unconscious ones, oriented to their own well-being; they also, as agents, influence, often in broad and deep ways, human well-being. This means, among other things, that both for ethical and political reasons we should take the earth others seriously: we *ought* to because they are centers of value in themselves and we *need* to because as subjects they can and do alter human goals.[128]

McFague does not shy away from the epistemological implications of affirming the subjectivity or agency of all earth entities. She explicitly affirms that the sort of knowledge a knower may come to have about another earth entity/subject is precisely the sort of knowledge that a knower may come to have about another human person.[129] It is situated, relational, relative, incomplete, uncertain, risky, participatory, and both subjects are changed, affected by their relationship. Further, drawing on Lorraine Code's work (as well as, I believe, on her own model of God the friend) she suggests that such epistemological relationships be approached by human knowers as a relationship between potential friends;[130] Or, in Buber's words, as an I–Thou relationship rather than an I–It relationship.[131] Such an epistemological stance, I suggest, is summed up perfectly in Carter Heyward's description of her own theology; it is both a theology and an epistemology 'of knowing and being known'.[132]

To conclude this extended discussion of McFague's anthropological and epistemological presuppositions and value judgments, I would like

---

126. McFague, *Super, Natural Christians*, p. 109 (italics added).
127. McFague, *Super, Natural Christians*, p. 111.
128. McFague, *Super, Natural Christians*, p. 111 (italics added).
129. McFague, *Super, Natural Christians*, pp. 95-97.
130. McFague, *Super, Natural Christians*, pp. 34-38.
131. McFague, *Super, Natural Christians*, p. 35. In the section discussing her understanding of 'subject–subjects' relations she refers to Buber's well-known phrase and Iris Murdoch's conception of love as the realization that others actually exist.
132. Heyward, *Staying Power*, p. 120.

to highlight two points. First, McFague discusses the epistemological implications of her work in greater depth and detail than any other feminist Christian theologian that I am aware of, and she has done so since 1975 at least. Further, the epistemological presuppositions she named in 1975 (her metaphorical assumptions) are in perfect accord with the direction her later work has taken (toward attention). Whether she approaches the subject of human knowledge from a 'metaphorical' or 'attention' perspective, in her thought embodied perception precedes conception; however, she insists that from both perspectives (which I have already suggested are better understood as emphases within the one epistemological framework) *what is initially perceived may well be the conceptions of others*. This follows from her emphasis of the fact that all human knowers are born into pre-existent linguistic systems for structuring and comprehending the world.[133] Thus in her thought it is as true to say that conception precedes perception as it is to say that perception precedes conception. The point I am trying to make is that McFague manages to insist on knowledge as physically embodied while also taking with utmost seriousness the presence in all our lives of various textual 'bodies', or linguistic constructions that shape our relationships with one another and the world.

Secondly, McFague has written that a recent work, *Super, Natural Christians*, was influenced primarily by process philosophy and feminist epistemology.[134] However, I suggest that although the influence of process thought in her work is undeniable, McFague's epistemological presuppositions are better described as remarkably *consistent* with feminist epistemological claims. It was not until 1993 that she began to refer to the work of theorists such as Harding, Haraway, Keller, Longino and Nelson—but by that time her epistemological framework was already well established, and so too were her accompanying anthropological presuppositions.[135] I say this not to deny the important and original work done by feminist epistemologists, but to stress the fact that McFague's feminist Christian theology includes what I consider to

---

133. See McFague, *Metaphorical Theology*, pp. 8-9. She writes, 'With Ludwig Wittgenstein, feminists would say, "The limits of one's language are the limits of one's world"... Since we are all born into a world which is already linguistic, in which the naming has already taken place, we only own the world to the extent that the naming that has occurred is our naming.'

134. McFague, *Super, Natural Christians*, p. 2.

135. See McFague, *The Body of God*, p. 243 n. 76.

be the richest, most provocative epistemological framework I have come across. In her recent work she engages in focused 'conversations' with feminist epistemologists, but her foundational presuppositions were in place long before 1997. That she acknowledges and draws upon the work of feminist epistemologists makes her recent work that much more fruitful, but she is perhaps being overly modest about the extent of her own original thought. It seems to me that what the recent developments in North American feminist epistemology collectively provide for McFague is a rhetorical space in which her own epistemological presuppositions are fully intelligible; in which, to quote Lorraine Code, McFague's words can be 'heard, understood, taken seriously'.[136]

In conclusion, McFague's epistemological presuppositions include an understanding of human knowledge as embodied, relational, participatory, sensuous, indirect, tentative, complex, multi-layered, relative, tensive and inescapably communal—in the sense that language is always the language, hence the knowledge, of a people and not of a single individual. Further, since 1987 she has insisted that human knowers should be *responsible* knowers, aware that their knowledge claims will have various lived effects on earth others; thus she is concerned to promote knowledge that increases the well-being and fulfilment of as many aspects of creation as possible.

McFague's Understanding of The World and Creation

I have already named one of McFague's fundamental metaphysical presuppositions: that reality is best conceived as an interdependent, relational, sometimes surprising spatio-temporal process.[137] Additionally, I have named one of her fundamental value judgments: that of the intrinsic value of all aspects of creation. Accordingly, in this section I shall focus primarily on McFague's conception of the world or the cosmos as God's body, including a discussion of her understanding of transcendence. To understand McFague's conception of the world or

---

136. Code, *Rhetorical Spaces*, p. x.
137. See for example, McFague, *Models of God*, p. 32: 'a credible theology for our time must be characterized by a sense of our intrinsic interdependence with all forms of life, an inclusive vision that demolishes oppressive hierarchies, accepts responsibility for nurturing and fulfilling life in its many forms, and is open to change and novelty as a given of existence'.

cosmos as God's body, however, it must first be made clear that she accepts the 'fact' of the physical world (or reality) apart from human linguistic constructions about the world—although she insists that human access to this world is at best partial. As she says, 'there is a reality to which our constructions refer, even though the only way we have of reaching it is by creating versions of it'.[138] As in Ruether's and Heyward's thought, there is a distinction—albeit an implicit one—in McFague's work between 'the world' and 'creation'. I suggest that within her thought 'creation' is best understood as that which humans attempt to interpret, while 'the world', or more accurately, 'worlds', are those human constructions in which we live, sometimes firmly rooted in 'creation', and sometimes perched precariously on the side of a cliff. For instance, she has written that 'the animal world is *there*; our worlds are constructed'.[139] Further, some world constructions, some interpretations are 'healthier than others for the entities involved'.[140]

Importantly, McFague is keenly aware that humans do not live in 'creation', or in a reality devoid of any human interpretations of it. Accordingly, she writes most frequently of 'the world'. However, she does so always with the awareness of an underlying physical reality (or creation) upon which worldly constructions are built. Further, in keeping with her epistemological affirmation of the agency or subjectivity of all earth entities, she ascribes to reality or creation at least one peculiarly human attribute. Twice she has written of the *patience* of reality with regard to different human interpretations of it. She first noted that 'the basic epistemological situation of *all* investigators and interpreters is of being *in* a world that we create in our attempt to discover those patterns of which it is most patient'.[141]. Later, writing of the 'organic model' for perceiving reality, she said, 'reality appears to be relatively patient in regard to accepting this construct or grid through which it is seen'.[142] Underlying both of these statements is an implicit affirmation of the 'more-than' character of creation or reality; that is, McFague presupposes that all human constructs about reality leave out, exclude, ignore, or fail to perceive a great deal more than they address in their necessarily limited and indirect ways. This

138. McFague, *Models of God*, p. 26.
139. McFague, *Metaphorical Theology*, p. 33 (italics in original).
140. McFague, *Super, Natural Christians*, p. 179 n. 6.
141. McFague, *Metaphorical Theology*, p. 78 (italics in original).
142. McFague, *The Body of God*, p. 90.

8. *The Theology of Sallie McFague*

assumption comes together with her affirmation of the intrinsic value of all aspects of creation in her model of the cosmos as God's body.

McFague writes: 'God's body, that which supports all life, is not matter or spirit but the matrix out of which everything that is evolves'.[143] The value judgment that accompanies this model is of particular significance in her thought. It is not only an ethical judgment, but a deeply theological one as well. McFague conceives of the cosmos as God's body in part so that humans, in particular North American, middle-class Christians, will come to perceive it as worthy of care and respect, but also in a bid to 'consecrate' the universe—to dedicate it to a divine purpose in order that Christians will come to revere it as a holy place. She writes:

> We do not know in all ways or even in many ways what this [divine] purpose is, but the world is not *ours* to manipulate for *our* purposes. If we see it as God's body, the way God is present to us, we will indeed know we tread on sacred ground.[144]

Such a conception of physical reality calls for more than an attitude of respect or even care. It calls for love. It calls for love not only of human interpretations, human constructions of the world, but for love of that which *is* apart from all interpretations, including that which is and is always a mystery to human beings. Put theologically, McFague calls for love of God's transcendence; not the sort of transcendence she has described as 'that Waterloo of Christian theology, which has pushed God out of the world and into another space', but the sort of transcendence that Dorothy Emmet describes in her book, *The Nature of Metaphysical Thinking*.[145] Emmet's work, which McFague identifies as expressive of many of her own metaphysical presuppositions, contains the following definition of transcendence:[146] 'We should need to understand the word "transcendent" as standing for that which is "other" than our minds—"being" or "existence" apart from our interpretations'.[147] While I do not know if McFague's understanding of

---

143. McFague, *Models of God*, p. 111.
144. McFague, *Models of God*, p. 185 (italics in original).
145. McFague, *The Body of God*, p. 20.
146. McFague, See *Metaphorical Theology*, p. 214 n. 37.
147. Dorothy M. Emmet, *The Nature of Metaphysical Thinking* (London: MacMillan, 1949), p. 13.

transcendence was influenced by Emmet's work, it seems likely that it was, especially given McFague's description of 'divine transcendence'. In McFague's words,

> the model of the universe as God's body is…a way to think about, reflect upon, divine transcendence—a way to deepen its significance to us. It is a form of meditation: the more we contemplate any aspect of the universe and especially our own planet, the more we know about it, delve into it, the more *mysterious and wondrous* it appears.[148]

In characterizing divine transcendence as that which is beyond human interpretation, as that which can never be reduced to or expressed through human linguistic constructs, McFague denies a completely immanent reading of her model of the cosmos as God's body. Paradoxically, she does so by insisting that mystery and wonder, divine transcendence, unknowable other-ness, are known only through attention to what *is* immanent, to what is immediately present to us. While she rejects the possibility of a human being ever comprehending in its *fulness* or entirety the presence of another, nonetheless, in her thought, loving openness to the other is the only way to glimpse God's hindquarters, or to come to know and revere and hold sacred every aspect of the cosmos. In her thought '[l]ove and knowledge go together; we can't have one without the other'.[149] I suggest that McFague, through her model of the cosmos as God's body, is attempting to lure people into love, into 'the extremely difficult realization that something other than themselves is real'—real in an inconceivably awesome, complex, and intricate manner.[150] She writes of 'the specialness, the difference, the intricacy, the 'unutterable particularity' of each creature, event, or aspect of nature that calls forth wonder and delight—a knowing that calls forth love and a love that wants to know more'.[151] I can think of no better way to characterize McFague's model of the cosmos as God's body; through this model she is proposing 'a knowing that calls forth love and a love that wants to know more'.

---

148. McFague, *The Body of God*, pp. 20-21 (italics added).
149. McFague, *Super, Natural Christians*, p. 29.
150. McFague, *Super, Natural Christians*, p. 31: 'We pray to God through knowing and thereby being able to love all the wild and wonderful diversity of creatures.'
151. McFague, *Super, Natural Christians*, p. 31.

Conclusion

As with Ruether's and Heyward's work, to attempt to distil McFague's theology into a short summary of her paradigmatic and epistemological presuppositions is to risk an erasure of the depth and intricacy of her thought. Nonetheless, having set out to identify precisely these presuppositions, I conclude this chapter by reviewing them here. First, McFague takes for granted the full, unqualified humanity of every woman, man and child without exception. This assumption is revealed through her affirmation of the inherent value of *every* aspect of the universe. Because she steadfastly insists on perceiving humankind as just a tiny aspect of the incredibly vast evolution or ongoing creation of the cosmos, rather than as the pinnacle of creation, and because she perceives all of the cosmos to be of ultimate value (the body of God), she must affirm the full and unique value of every individual human. Like Ruether and Heyward, however, she cannot and does not offer an understanding of 'human being' or human nature as based on an unchanging essence of any sort, for, like theirs, her theological anthropology is based on an ontological assumption of relationality, interdependence, process, and change.[152]

McFague also affirms the finite nature of every individual aspect of the universe, but (again similar to Ruether's thought) there is within McFague's theology an explicit anthropological-cosmological connection. That is, her conception of God as the matrix of all that is must be read in combination with her understanding of the universe as composed of a fixed or constant amount of 'stuff'. Creaturely finitude is not only an unavoidable fact, but, ultimately, a blessing. Life in the broadest sense cannot continue becoming incarnate in new and unique forms unless what has been ceases to be, returns to the cosmic or divine matrix from which it came and from which all new life is formed. Again, McFague rejects any notion of a transcendent (as in wholly-other-than) God, eternal life (in the sense of the bodily or spiritual resurrection of specific individuals), and a heaven above. In keeping with this theological shift, what matters most in her theology is *not* divine certainty, not revelation from above, but human responsibility: the ability to respond with respect and care and love to all the earth others with whom we find ourselves for a very short while.

---

152. McFague, *Models of God*, pp. 8, 10.

This theological affirmation of human responsibility is simultaneously at the core of her epistemological presuppositions. For McFague, as for Ruether and Heyward and the feminist epistemologists discussed in Chapters 4 and 5, there is an integral relationship between 'being, knowing, doing: ontology, epistemology, ethics'.[153] As ever-changing, relational, interdependent, embodied, specifically situated creatures, we who co-create (primarily through language) whatever knowledge we share are the ones who are responsible for the world-shaping implications of our knowledge claims. And our knowledge claims, our stories, are never certain, never revelatory of an absolute, unchanging truth. Rather, McFague asserts that what knowledge we necessarily create in communities (through shared language and shared theoretical frameworks) is always situated, relational, relative, tentative and limited.[154] Moreover, the stories we co-create are value-laden and power-riddled; they are not innocent tales, but they do structure the ways in which we understand and relate to the world, God and ourselves. Accordingly, McFague insists that we attend as closely to the implications of the stories we tell, the metaphors and models we use, as we do to the physical presence of another, whether friend, lover, cat, flower, or tree. Having tried to attend closely to the paradigmatic and epistemological presuppositions inherent within the feminist Christian theology of Rosemary Radford Ruether, Carter Heyward and Sallie McFague, it is time now to discuss in greater detail what their work embodies: a theological and epistemological paradigm shift the implications of which, I suggest, have not yet been fully grasped even within the feminist Christian theological epistemological community.

---

153. McFague, *Super, Natural Christians*, p. 149.
154. McFague, *Metaphorical Theology*, p. 194.

Chapter 9

AN EPISTEMOLOGY OF PARTICIPATORY DISCERNMENT

> *It was a grove of trees, not a tidy, two-tree garden. And it was the birds and the squirrels and the chipmunks and the possums who showed them, taught them that the fruit was good for eating. And they had been eating that fruit, sometimes hoarding it and sometimes sharing it with one another, for as long as anyone could remember. It was the tree of life they ate from, it is the tree of life we eat from still.*

Why, in the end, do the metaphysical and epistemological assumptions within one feminist Christian theological paradigm matter? Why did I believe that they are of such importance that I was willing to spend three and a half years immersed in a handful of texts, painstakingly identifying and naming, over and over again, a very few shockingly basic and not particularly new or, on the face of it, earth-shattering assumptions? After all, as I tried to show, individually, the fundamental assumptions held by Ruether, Heyward and McFague are not original. Take elements from Schleiermacher, Ritschl, the Social Gospel movement, Barth, Bultmann, Buber, Tillich, Whitehead and the process theologians, re-combine them a bit, add 'her' and stir, and there you have it, one form of feminist Christian theology. It seems utterly obvious and embarrassingly simple. Everything that exists is in an interdependent, albeit deeply ambiguous, relationship with everything else that is. In other words, interdependence is the ontological given; how we participate in that interdependence, or what sort of relations we form and deform, value or devalue, that's the ethical bit that accompanies an ontology of interdependence. But to complicate things just a bit, everything that is is constantly changing. Next, within the feminist Christian theological paradigm explored in this book, all humans are valued as fully, uniquely, preciously human, though what it means to be a human subject is an open question, for, again, as creaturely beings we are constantly changing. More broadly, every aspect of creation is perceived to have inherent value and to be irreplaceable. However, finitude is both unavoidable and good, in that the perishing of what is is necessary in order for what will be to have the chance to come into being. These are the basic metaphysical assumptions/value judgments within one feminist Christian theological paradigm; what about the epistemological ones?

There never was a tree of knowledge, and we humans couldn't reach an eternal truth if our lives depended on it, which they don't, not at all. What they do depend on is our willingness, our ability to find our way through a vastly confusing, muddled, infinitely complicated and always changing world—together. Our knowledge of the world and of one another is relative to the time and place and cultural assumptions within which we live, and depends in large part on what we need to know in order to survive, to help each other to live as well as we can. And the 'we' is not solely limited to other humans. The 'we' includes trees and ants and squirrels and dogs and corn plants. What 'we' must know about includes computers and pacemakers and machine guns and nuclear missiles, soil erosion and carbon monoxide and antibiotics, all those things that we have created together that shape, enable, and threaten our lives, all together all at once, whether we like it or not. We make our knowledge as we need or want it, and no, the making is not fair. Some people, some of us, get to make more than others. Some knowledge is not used to enable life, but instead is used by some to destroy the lives of others. Ouch. Certainty, impeccably dressed, well-groomed Certainty has slipped out an open door, and a disreputable character named Ambiguity, who is in dire need of a bath and a fresh set of clothes, has moved in with a few friends. Non-innocence, Complexity, Relativity, Interdependence, Change, they've begun re-modelling the place and things are a bit of a mess. Where do we turn, what do we do? We do what we've always done.

Slowly, hesitantly, we start telling each other new stories. We use the same old words of course, for they are the only ones we've got. But we combine them in new ways, stack and mould them, push them together and wrench them apart, trying desperately to create a common ground upon which we can gather together for a short while, where we can each be 'heard, understood, taken seriously' (Code), where we can give thanks, laugh, grieve, struggle, grow and love together. Why do metaphysical and epistemological assumptions matter in the first place? Without them, we cannot tell any stories at all, we cannot understand

9. *An Epistemology of Participatory Discernment* 251

(more or less) any stories we may hear. Without them, we simply cannot communicate different ideas with each other; we cannot share our dreams of what might be. We cannot piece together any understandings of what has been, and we cannot begin to share our perceptions of what is. Without shared metaphysical and epistemological assumptions, we would each live in a private, isolated, lonely universe. While Adrienne Rich's 'dream of a common language' has been criticized in these postmodern, poststructuralist times, what shared metaphysical and epistemological assumptions provide is nothing less than the basis for a common language, common, world-shaping languages. Like it or not, common languages are what we speak together, what we live, together. But we are all multilingual, we all live in several 'worlds', and not necessarily the same ones, at the same time; our capacity for misunderstanding each other is enormous. And misunderstanding is currently a feminist Christian theological problem with potentially significant ramifications. What am I talking about?

From 1996 to 1998 I did not read much new feminist theology. It was not until I had completed a draft of this study that I turned from feminist epistemological texts and the texts of Ruether, Heyward and McFague and began to 'catch up' on feminist Christian theology. To put it as nicely as possible, some of what I read both astonished and worried me. To refer to some of the more blatant examples of what worried and still worries me, I read that, according to Sheila Greeve Davaney, Ruether's theology (among others, including McFague's) promoted 'an essentialist notion of tradition that paralleled [an] essentialist notion of the female self'.[1] While I would be the last to suggest that there is a single correct interpretation of Ruether's work, I would also insist that she clearly understands religious traditions as, in the first place, comprised of various and often conflicting under-

---

1. Sheila Greeve Davaney, 'Continuing the Story, But Departing the Text', in Chopp and Davaney (eds.), *Horizons In Feminist Theology*, p. 201. On a related point, Elisabeth Schüssler Fiorenza asserts that 'Rosemary Radford Ruether's concept of "new humanity" does not challenge the Western cultural sex/gender system' (Elisabeth Schüssler Fiorenza, *Jesus: Miriam's Child, Sophia's Prophet* [London: SCM Press, 1995], p. 47). She does not explain how Ruether's concept of 'new humanity' fails to do so. I suggest that Ruether's concept, riddled as it is with reversals and disruptions, with strong women and men who refuse power over others, with the affirmation of the absolute value of every person without qualification, challenges precisely the Western cultural sex/gender system.

standings of God, humanity and the world, and, secondly, as constantly, albeit slowly, changing, changing as the experiences and needs of the diverse people and communities who comprise that tradition change. Likewise, as I tried to make clear in Chapter 6, Ruether never proposes (nor does Heyward or McFague) that there is an essential, unchanging nature that constitutes 'woman' or 'man'. Reading Davaney's words further, I was, accordingly, stunned to learn that only now, apparently, is it 'argued that there is neither an unchanging core that characterizes individual humans nor some transpersonal nature that is constitutive of humans or, in our case, females as such'.[2] Given their insistence that *change* is one of the fundamental ontological features of everything that is, Davaney's interpretation of early feminist Christian theology (at least work by Ruether, Heyward and McFague) as essentialist is without justification. Yet Davaney is certainly not alone in her assumption of 1970s and 1980s feminist Christian theological essentialism. Susan Parsons, in a recent essay comparing Carter Heyward's work with that of Judith Butler, boldly, if erroneously, characterized Heyward as a voice of 'modern feminist essentialism'.[3] We would all do well, I think, to remember the words that Heyward first wrote in 1979:

> Even those categories that most of us assume to be basic—such as female or male gender, such as racial identity, such as the *Homo sapiens* species itself—seem to me more elusive, less static, than we often assume. I am tempted to say, and will for now, that nothing is fixed; nothing in the world is so essentially what it is today that tomorrow may not surprise us with something new...[4]

Those are not the words of an essentialist, or one who ascribes to the notion that human beings have an unchanging, core essence. To interpret Heyward as an essentialist is to ignore, or to be unaware of, her fundamental metaphysical presuppositions, her basic assumptions of the way reality *is*.

To return to Davaney's assertions, reading her text further I was bewildered to learn that, again apparently only now, some theorists are

---

2. Davaney, 'Continuing the Story', p. 203.
3. Susan F. Parsons, 'The Boundaries of Desire: A Consideration of Judith Butler and Carter Heyward', *Feminist Theology* 23 (January 2000), p. 97.
4. Heyward, *Our Passion for Justice*, p. 83. This quotation is taken from an address entitled 'Love and Sexuality' that Heyward gave at the Integrity Convention (Gay Episcopalians and their Friends) on 7 September 1979 in Denver, Colorado.

9. *An Epistemology of Participatory Discernment* 253

concluding that 'there are no universal forms of experience shared by everyone across temporal and historical boundaries'.[5] Wasn't it precisely this claim that led feminist Christian theologians (and liberation and Black theologians) to insist on the need for theology to be grounded in specific, limited contexts, on the need to name and acknowledge the complex and sometimes conflicting situations of those who write and need such theology?

Finally, my jaw dropped open when I read the following:

> If much credence is given to the importance of contextuality and tradition, a growing number of feminist thinkers, including a significant number outside the dominant intellectual and geographical North Atlantic context, are giving this argument an interesting twist. For they are insisting first that the traditions and contexts that shape female subjectivity and identity are pluralistic, conflictual, and unstable. While subjectivity and identity are always situated and those contexts are always part of larger historical traditions, neither contexts nor traditions are homogeneous or monolithic, but are full of diverse and contending possibilities and limitations.[6]

I thought of Ruether's life work, of the effort she has put into tracing heretical and non-traditional strands of thought throughout the history of the Christian church, tracing as well as the historically changing views of the dominant thought within the tradition. I thought of her locating her own work in continuity with those strands within Christian history that did promote the value judgment but did not define the meaning of the full humanity of women as well as men. I thought of her insistence that without a community (whether contemporary or historical) in which one's beliefs are affirmed one simply cannot criticize the dominant tradition. Alone, one's words go unheard, one's thoughts are unthinkable, one is forced to live in conformity with the dominant views, or be considered mad. I thought about her naming and describing more alternative communities within Christian history than I ever dreamt existed. How on earth, I wondered, could Davaney honestly think that the rejection of an essentialist understanding of human nature, the rejection of a single, unchanging, eternal core of Christianity, and the acknowledgment of plurality and ambiguity within a historical tradition are 'new' or 'recent' developments in feminist

---

5. Davaney, 'Continuing the Story', pp. 203-204.
6. Davaney, 'Continuing the Story', p. 204.

Christian theology?⁷ A close, attentive and responsible look at the theology of Ruether, Heyward and McFague, and in particular at their fundamental assumptions, reveals that the assumptions Davaney lists as 'recent' have been collectively asserted since the beginning of the feminist Christian theological paradigm described in this book. It worries me that some of us seem to be in a hurry to rewrite our own recent past, to distance ourselves from the work that enables us to be feminist Christian theologians in the first place.

It worries me, and it makes me grumpy. It made me grumpy that in the conclusion to *Horizons in Feminist Theology* Rebecca S. Chopp simply reiterated Davaney's points as though they were incontestable facts.⁸ Likewise, when Chopp wrote that 'neither Ruether nor [Karl] Rahner differed from modern theorists in the framing of their theories, except in their insistence on resting the whole foundationalist enterprise *in God's revelation as an epistemological correspondence between theory's aims and God's disclosure*',⁹ I wondered if Chopp had ever researched Ruether's understanding of revelation—revelation as the work that humans do together to discover how our lives are shaped (differently) by the institutions and symbolic universes in which we live. How could Chopp assume, as she implicitly does, that Ruether posits a personal deity who reveals Truth to humans? Ruether's conception of God the divine matrix just doesn't work that way, nor does Ruether affirm a static, unchanging, eternal notion of Truth. She does maintain that we must decide what is most 'true', what is ethically 'best' for our time, with the understanding that this 'truth' will, must,

---

7. Davaney suggests that Ruether's affirmation of 'the prophetic-liberating strand within the Hebraic and Christian traditions' constitutes a claim, on Ruether's part, that this strand of thought *is* the normative 'core' of the Christian tradition (Davaney, 'Continuing the Story', p. 201). I would suggest, however, that Ruether's positive affirmation of the prophetic-liberating elements within the Christian tradition is a theo-ethical move on her part based on her value judgment that this is the most life-affirming approach to take now, in our time and given the current crises facing humanity and the earth. Ruether knows full well, for example, that the Jubilee tradition was never a central, core component of what came to be known as Christianity. She is choosing to emphasize it and make it a normative part of her theology, but this is not the same as claiming that it is and always has been the 'real' core of the tradition.

8. Rebecca S. Chopp, 'Theorizing Feminist Theology', in Chopp and Davaney (eds.), *Horizons In Feminist Theology*, p. 217.

9. Chopp, 'Theorizing Feminist Theology', pp. 217-18 (italics added).

9. An Epistemology of Participatory Discernment 255

change over time, and is at best partial and incomplete. In short, Chopp's is an example of epistemically irresponsible scholarship. It is not what I had hoped would appear in the conclusion of this book, as a kind of after-the-fact justification of the importance of my chosen topic. But I feel it needs to appear here, as does Chopp's equally astonishing assertion that 'poststructuralist theory uncovered the binary structure that regulated all meaning through oppositional thinking'.[10] In Chapter 6 I noted the following:

> Ruether identifies the hierarchical dualisms (God over man, transcendent over immanent, heaven over earth, mind over body, spirit over matter, male over female, master over slave, etc.) inherent within this symbolic understanding of the cosmos, whether presented as salvation myth or metaphysical fact, as the ideological ground and justification for social structures and systems that perpetuate 'patriarchy' and oppression. Of critical importance is the fact that 'these ideologies try to make that social structure look "natural", inevitable and divinely given'.[11] Accordingly, Ruether stresses the epistemological as well as the world-shaping consequences of this hierarchical, dualistic theological and philosophical inheritance. 'Apocalyptic dualism, interpreted as gnostic body-soul dualism, gave to classical Christianity a dualistic mode of moral, epistemological and ontological perception'.[12]

While the metaphors 'hierarchical' and 'dualistic' are not usually a part of poststructuralist vocabulary, I would suggest that it is rather clear that Ruether identified, without the help of poststructuralist thought, the way in which 'binary structures regulate meaning through oppositional thinking'. In short, I am deeply worried about the growing tendency among highly educated feminist theologians, ethicists and biblical scholars to misinterpret *badly* work written by established feminist Christian theologians. I also find it confusing, for I am convinced that most of these women know better.

For example, Sheila Greeve Davaney edited what was, as far as I am aware, the first text in which the strong connections between process thought and feminist theology—more broadly, 'feminism'—were elaborated.[13] In the introduction to *Feminism and Process Thought*,

---

10. Chopp, 'Theorizing Feminist Theology', p. 218.
11. Ruether, *New Woman/New Earth*, p. xiv.
12. Ruether, *Liberation Theology*, pp. 16-17.
13. Sheila Greeve Davaney (ed.), *Feminism and Process Thought* (Lewiston, NY: Edwin Mellen Press, 1981).

published in 1981, Davaney noted that feminism and process thought 'both make common assertions and share fundamental presuppositions'.[14] She went on to say that 'both perspectives begin by affirming the essential [as in fundamental] subjectivity of all that exists. And both suggest that this subjectivity is essentially social, creative, and processive'.[15] In 1981 Davaney would most probably have been shocked to hear or to read that feminist Christian theology posited a fixed or static notion of human (or non-human) subjectivity. Such a claim would not have made sense to her; it would have flown in the face of what she knew to be a new set of fundamental metaphysical presuppositions—a set including the notion that subjects are always in process, changing, that human (and non-human) subjectivity includes no fixed essence.

Similarly mystifying is Chopp's reiteration of the assertions Davaney makes in her 1997 essay. Following Davaney, Chopp writes that 'the first point of this modern feminist theological frame assumes a common and universal character to women's *experience*. Although argued for in a variety of different ways by feminist theologians such as Rosemary Radford Ruether, Judith Plaskow and Elisabeth Schüssler Fiorenza, the strategy was "to assert a universal and common *essence* that somehow defined women as women".'[16] First, there is a vast and critical difference between the terms 'experience' and 'essence', a difference Chopp ignores here; it is highly irresponsible to slide between the two terms as though one led inevitably to the other, particularly when one is describing (in a faintly pejorative way) early feminist theology. Secondly, I strongly suspect that Chopp *would* agree that one experience common to all women is that of having to fit into a 'social-symbolic order' not of their/our own making.[17] This, at any rate, is the thesis with which she introduces her 1989 book *The Power to Speak*. Thirdly, in *The*

14. Davaney, *Feminism and Process Thought*, p. 1.
15. Davaney, *Feminism and Process Thought*, p. 3.
16. Chopp, 'Theorizing Feminist Theology', p. 217 (italics added).
17. See Rebecca S. Chopp, *The Power to Speak: Feminism, Language, God* (New York: Crossroad, 1989), p. 1. In making this statement I am well aware that a number of different social-symbolic orders, or different symbolic universes, co-exist in the world at this time. My point is that none of them were constructed by women, and all women have to live in one or more of them. Whether some women find them comfortable and others uncomfortable is not the point; the point is that there is no 'outside' in which to dwell. Thus living within them is an experience common to all women, even while their interpretations of that experience vary wildly.

9. *An Epistemology of Participatory Discernment*

Power to Speak, after discussing the different methodological approaches of Mary Daly, Sallie McFague, Elisabeth Schüssler Fiorenza, and Rosemary Radford Ruether, Chopp writes, 'All these forms are important and, I want to contend, integral to feminist theology, for feminist theologians proclaim, in a variety of ways, the importance of speaking and hearing the otherness and multiplicity of women'.[18] This statement affirming a feminist theological proclamation of the *otherness* and *multiplicity* of women contradicts rather forcefully the notion of a feminist theological 'strategy...to assert a *universal* and *common* essence that somehow defined women as women'. The question, it seems to me, is, 'why are these women, these theologians who know better, now misinterpreting, badly, early feminist Christian theology?'

While I do not believe there is one single correct answer to this question, I do have a few random thoughts on the subject. In no particular order, I want to say to White, educationally and economically privileged feminist Christian theologians that we do not need to commit matricide, or attempt to kill our foremothers' theology, in order to be taken seriously as feminist theologians in our own right, nor do we need to search desperately for (the God) Theory everywhere but within the White North American feminist Christian theology we read. I also wonder if perhaps we, 'we' being professional feminist Christian theologians, might not be shooting ourselves in the feet in an effort to be taken seriously as Theorists by other, non-theologically-inclined Theorists? The thing is, it is most difficult to be taken seriously by Theorists once you front up and admit to being a Christian theologian. On the one hand, Christianity simply isn't a very trendy religion in Theoretical circles at the moment, and on the other, it is usually assumed that theologians actually believe in God and the sacred and Those Sorts of Things, which most Theorists all know for a Fact are simply human projections and haven't we outgrown that yet?[19] Well, you see the issue; it can be a problem to have a conversation with a Theorist. They don't speak much theology, so if you want to talk with

---

18. Chopp, *The Power to Speak*, p. 12.

19. And the 'stuff' of theological reflection might indeed be simply a bunch of human projections; what is so fascinating to me is that humans are so good at projecting them, can't seem to function well without some version of them, and those same projections have hugely world-shaping, life-shattering and, sometimes, healing implications.

them you must speak in their language. But their language doesn't include many concepts like God, faith, sin, miracle, evil, salvation, atonement, redemption, prophetic, incarnation, revelation, etc.—in other words, the very 'stuff' of theological reflection, imagination, and creation. Consequently, articles and books written in the language of Theory seem to me to be (more or less) highly theoretical, and almost never very theological at all. It's a terribly basic point, but to write theology one does need to use theological metaphors and models. And to try to evaluate feminist Christian theology using theoretical tools that are not sensitive enough to distinguish between, for example, revelation from a God Above and revelation as an ongoing, collective human effort to discern what is affecting the shape and contours of life for some community—well, it doesn't seem to work at all well. Even with tools that work it isn't easy…

Nonetheless, while it may not be easy to compare the metaphors, models, metaphysical assumptions and value judgments within one paradigm with the metaphors, models, metaphysical assumptions and value judgments of a different theoretical paradigm, it is possible. It is possible to identify and name the similarities and differences between them, and in doing so one avoids the trap of dualistic, binary, either/or thinking, that is, assuming that if one theory says one thing another theory cannot possibly say something similar. I believe strongly that we need to read and write about feminist Christian theology far more carefully, that we must read and write about it more carefully in order to be epistemically responsible theologians.

Most of all I want to say that from Ruether, Heyward and McFague I have learned that epistemic responsibility requires *participatory discernment*: slow, painstaking, roll-up-the-shirtsleeves, get-your-hands-dirty work. It requires that I acknowledge the other members of the epistemic communities of which I am a part, that I reflect deeply and seriously on the presence and absence of others within those communities as well as within the rhetorical spaces within which my/our words make sense. It requires of me that I locate myself, acknowledge my own biases and limitations and peculiarities, that I take responsibility for my own words, while at the same time acknowledging my dependence on the words and work of others.

It takes time, a long time, to read and study another's work, to suspend judgment as far as possible and to meet that text as a subject, a complicated subject or 'Thou' in its own right. It takes time and effort

9. *An Epistemology of Participatory Discernment* 259

to discern which assumptions are required for that text to make sense, especially when those assumptions are not made explicit. An epistemology of participatory discernment requires that I take that time, that I make the effort to give every text a thorough, respectful reading—and that I never assume that I have got it thoroughly right. It requires of me that I locate that text within the body of a theorist's thought, take seriously its connections with other texts by the same author, as well as the historical, social and political context within which it was written. An epistemology of participatory discernment requires also that I take the insights found within those texts and put them into practice, take them into grassroots gatherings and find out whether they 'work', whether they are meaningful to the participants in those gatherings. An epistemology of participatory discernment requires that I shut up and listen when I am with others, especially with others who are not professional theologians, listen to what they feel they need from feminist Christian theology. And it requires of me that I act on what I hear.

An epistemology of participatory discernment does not provide a methodology—a study of the methodological *differences* between Ruether, Heyward and McFague could easily be the subject of another book. Nor does it, ever, provide easy answers to anything. In fact, such an epistemology rejects the possibility of final answers to any question. Paradoxically, the epistemological assumptions held by Ruether, Heyward and McFague serve the same purpose as Karl Barth's theological assumption of the wholly-otherness of God. They free us to continue becoming who we might become, learning what we might learn, making the mistakes we will inevitably make, without having to worry about fitting into a predetermined Truth. Just as Barth believed that humans could never reach God on our own, so these feminist Christian theologians reject the possibility of humans ever reaching an absolute Truth. At the same time, they suggest that we make our truths as we go along, and we can, if we pay attention, hear whispers of little truths from time to time.

Taken by themselves, the metaphysical, epistemological and theological assumptions of Ruether, Heyward and McFague are not earth-shattering. But put them together, and you have an alternative, one among others, to the dominant Western Christian symbolic universe. What Ruether, Heyward and McFague have created, what their work collectively provides, is a new symbolic universe in the form of a new discursive universe, one in which others of us can tell, hear, understand

and begin to live new stories. They've given old metaphors and models new life, and have prepared the way for a whole new way of doing theology. And they have been clear that this one new way is not and cannot be the only way to do theology: that their beliefs are not universal or absolute truths. Still, those of us who feel most free (or perhaps simply at home for the first time) in this new symbolic universe can now take up the life-long task of reinterpreting, re-creating every aspect of Christian theology. We do not have to begin this work by naming or justifying our most basic assumptions, for that work has been done. We do not have to define every metaphor we use every time we use it, for that work has been done. What we can do is stop writing about theology, and write theology. We have been given the extraordinary possibility that our words might be heard, understood and taken seriously. We can begin wherever we want, even from the Very Beginning. And this is what could happen if we did.

> *In the beginning, nothing. No space, no time, no material stuff, just nothing. Nothing so tightly wrapped in on itself as to be everything and nothing all at once, everything and nothing both at once. Occupying no space, taking up no time, there was no distinction, no separation of past, present, future; here, there, nowhere, everywhere; something, nothing. All was one. It was nothing, yet it was. Words apply only awkwardly to the everything/nothing that was, that existed before time and space, presence and absence had any meaning at all. There was nothing; all was one.*
>
> *And then, ages and ages ago, nothing changed. Everything, which had been one, became many. Perhaps what was so utterly one became lonely, and in a single, desperate gesture stretched out its arms and sought to embrace all that was not. As this is, after all, theology, I choose to imagine The Beginning as compelled by a wistful, extravagant love: a longing for the company of others so huge and steadfast that yearning itself became incarnate.*
>
> *The physicists, when distracted from their Big Bang, say that energy is neither created nor destroyed. That energy can take the form of matter, and matter the form of energy. The universe, they say, can be understood as an equation. All the energy there is plus all the matter there is always equals one. One universe, though always shifting, moving, changing: now you see a particle, now you see a dash of energy. Though always shifting, there is a constant. The universe, they say, is composed of a fixed amount of stuff. Measure it as energy or measure it as matter or measure it as both, the sum remains the same: nothing ever added, nothing ever subtracted. It is now as it was in the beginning.*

9. *An Epistemology of Participatory Discernment*

But now this one is no single steady thing but everything that is ceaselessly moving, shifting, stretching, yearning. And in the beginning, can you imagine it, the shock, the unexpected speed with which one became separate from itself, had to begin to know itself as other, as many? And with time and space, and more time and space now stretching out beyond imagined bounds, twisting and spinning and racing in all directions...was there not a remnant of that extravagant love that began to mourn lost unity, lost timelessness?

Disconsolate, energy grew slower, drew in upon itself, discovered it could reunite as matter: matter seeking to gather into its arms all that might travel across its path. Gravity attracts, the physicists say. Finally. There is hope for the physicists yet. Attraction. Can you feel it? It is attraction, it is desire, it is yearning, it is love, the force behind gravity, the force holding matter together. In the beginning a wistful, extravagant love, a longing for the company of others. Come unto me, for I desire you.

But is this not the same yearning, the same desire that compels time and space and matter to wrench itself apart, to rush headlong away from all that is familiar: shifting, changing, creating new time and space and matter which to love?

I say it is; I say such wild, extravagant longing is exactly like a passionate embrace. It cannot be contained; it cannot be sustained. So I choose to imagine the nature of the universe. Now wistful, now wild: always extravagant in its gestures, with its love. A love caught now between a reaching out and a drawing in: a love pulled equally in all directions all at once.

Energy is neither created nor destroyed. Now it's wistful, now it's wild. Now it's matter, now it's not. Now it whispers, now it cries out with desire: such is the stuff and structure of the universe.[20]

The end. Which is, of course, in its own way a beginning.

---

20. Slightly modified excerpt from Lucy Tatman, 'Mind the Gap: A Feminist Underground Guide to Transcendence, Maybe', *Feminist Theology* 23 (January, 2000), pp. 79-81.

BIBLIOGRAPHY

Addelson, Kathryn Pyne, 'The Man of Professional Wisdom', in Harding and Hintikka (eds.), *Discovering Reality*, pp. 165-86.
—*Impure Thoughts: Essays on Philosophy, Feminism, and Ethics* (Philadelphia: Temple University Press, 1991).
—'Knower/Doers and Their Moral Problems', in Alcoff and Potter (eds.), *Feminist Epistemologies*, pp. 265-94.
Alcoff, Linda, and Elizabeth Potter (eds.), *Feminist Epistemologies* (New York and London: Routledge, 1993).
Altizer, Thomas J.J., and William Hamilton, *Radical Theology and the Death of God* (New York: Bobs-Merrill, 1966).
Baier, Annette, *Postures of the Mind: Essays on Mind and Morals* (Minneapolis: University of Minnesota Press, 1985).
Barbour, Ian G., *Myths, Models and Paradigms: The Nature of Scientific and Religious Language* (London: SCM Press, 1974).
Barth, Karl, 'The Doctrine of Creation', in G.W. Bromily and T.F. Torrance (eds.), *Church Dogmatics* III (Edinburgh: T. & T. Clark, 1961).
Bonhoeffer, Dietrich, *Letters and Papers from Prison* (ed. Eberhard Bethge; London: SCM Press, 1953).
Bowden, John, 'Word of God', in Allan Richardson and John Bowden (eds), *The Westminster Dictionary of Christian Theology* (Philadelphia: Westminster Press, 1983), pp. 603-604.
Brown, Joanne Carlson, and Carole R. Bohn (eds.), *Christianity, Patriarchy, and Abuse* (New York: Pilgrim Press, 1989).
Buber, Martin, *I and Thou* (trans. Ronald G. Smith; Edinburgh: T. & T. Clark, 2nd edn, 1958).
Butler, Judith, 'Gender Trouble, Feminist Theory, and Psychoanalytic Discourse', in Linda J. Nicholson (ed.), *Feminism/Postmodernism* (New York and London: Routledge, 1990), pp. 324-40.
Canberra Times, 'Let mums abort gay babies', in Monday, 17 February 1997.
Chopp, Rebecca S., *The Power to Speak: Feminism, Language, God* (New York: Crossroad, 1989).
—'Theorizing Feminist Theology', in *idem* and Sheila Greeve Davaney (eds.), *Horizons in Feminist Theology*, pp. 215-31.
Chopp, Rebecca S., and Sheila Greeve Davaney (eds.), *Horizons in Feminist Theology: Identity, Tradition, and Norms* (Minneapolis, MN: Augsburg Fortress, 1997).
Christ, Carol P., and Judith Plaskow (eds.), *Womanspirit Rising: A Feminist Reader in Religion* (San Francisco: Harper & Row, 1979).

Code, Lorraine, *Epistemic Responsibility* (Hanover and London: University Press of New England, 1987).
—*What Can She Know? Feminist Theory and the Construction of Knowledge* (Ithaca, NY: Cornell University Press, 1991).
—'Taking Subjectivity into Account', in Alcoff and Potter (eds.), *Feminist Epistemologies* (New York and London: Routledge, 1993), pp. 15-34.
—*Rhetorical Spaces: Essays on Gendered Locations* (New York and London: Routledge, 1995).
Collins, Sheila D., *A Different Heaven and Earth* (Valley Forge, PA: Judson Press, 1974).
Cox, Harvey, *The Secular City* (New York: Macmillan, 1968).
Crouter, Richard, 'Introduction', in *idem* (ed.), *On Religion* (Cambridge: Cambridge University Press, 1988).
Daly, Mary, *Beyond God the Father* (Boston: Beacon Press, 1973).
—*Gyn/Ecology: The Metaethics of Radical Feminism* (Boston: Beacon Press, 1978).
—'After the Death of God the Father', in Christ and Plaskow (eds.), *Womanspirit Rising*, pp. 53-62.
—*The Church and the Second Sex* (Boston: Beacon Press, rev. edn, 1985).
—*Outercourse: The Be-Dazzling Voyage* (San Francisco: HarperCollins, 1992).
Davaney, Sheila Greeve, 'Continuing the Story, But Departing the Text', in Chopp and Davaney (eds.), *Horizons in Feminist Theology*, pp. 198-214.
Davaney, Sheila Greeve (ed.), *Feminism and Process Thought* (Lewiston, NY: Edwin Mellen, 1981).
DePaul, Michael, 'Coherentism', in Robert Audi (ed.), *The Cambridge Dictionary of Philosophy* (Cambridge: Cambridge University Press, 1995), pp. 133-35.
Donaldson, Mara E., *Holy Places Are Dark Places: C.S. Lewis and Paul Ricoeur on Narrative Transformation* (Lanham, MD: University Press of America, 1988).
Emmet, Dorothy M., *The Nature of Metaphysical Thinking* (London: MacMillan, 1949).
Ferm, Deane William, *Contemporary American Theologies: A Critical Survey* (San Francisco: Harper & Row, 1981).
Friedan, Betty, *The Feminine Mystique* (New York: Dell Publishing Company, 1964).
Fulkerson, Mary McClintock, *Changing the Subject: Women's Discourses and Feminist Theology* (Minneapolis, MN: Fortress Press, 1994).
Gill, Jerry H., *Wittgenstein and Metaphor* (Washington, DC: University Press of America, 1981).
Gross, Rita M. (ed.), *Beyond Androcentrism: New Essays on Women and Religion* (Missoula, MT: Scholars Press, 1977).
Gutiérrez, Gustavo, 'Expanding the View', in Marc H. Ellis and Otto Maduro (eds.), *Expanding the View* (Maryknoll, NY: Orbis Books, 1988), pp. 3-36.
—*A Theology of Liberation* (trans. Sr Caridad Inda and John Eagleson; Maryknoll, NY: Orbis Books, 1988).
Halkes, Catharina J.M., *New Creation: Christian Feminism and the Renewal of the Earth* (trans. Catherine Romanik; Louisville, KY: Westminster/John Knox Press, 1991).
Hampson, Daphne, *After Christianity* (London: SCM Press, 1996).
Haraway, Donna, 'Situated Knowledges: The Science Question in Feminism and the Privilege of Partial Perspective', *Feminist Studies* 14.3 (1988), pp. 575-99.
—*Primate Visions: Gender, Race, and Nature in the World of Modern Science* (London and New York: Verso, 1989).

—*Simians, Cyborgs, and Women: The Reinvention of Nature* (New York: Routledge, 1991).
Harding, Sandra, *The Science Question in Feminism* (Ithaca, NY, and London: Cornell University Press, 1986).
—'Rethinking Standpoint Epistemology: What Is "Strong Objectivity"?', in Alcoff and Potter (eds.), *Feminist Epistemologies*, pp. 49-82.
Harding, Sandra, and Merrill B. Hintikka (eds.), *Discovering Reality: Feminist Perspectives on Epistemology, Metaphysics, Methodology, and Philosophy of Science* (Dordrecht: D. Reidel, 1983).
Harrison, Beverly Wildung, *Making the Connections: Essays in Feminist Social Ethics* (ed. Carol S. Robb; Boston: Beacon Press, 1985), pp. 3-21.
Hartshorne, Charles, *Omnipotence and Other Theological Mistakes* (Albany, NY: State University of New York Press, 1984).
Hartsock, Nancy, 'The Feminist Standpoint: Developing the Ground for a Specifically Feminist Historical Materialism', in Harding and Hintikka (eds.), *Discovering Reality*, pp. 283-310.
—*Money, Sex, and Power: Toward a Feminist Historical Materialism* (New York and London: Longman, 1983).
—*The Feminist Standpoint Revisited and Other Essays* (Boulder, CO: Westview Press, 1998).
Heron, Alasdair, *A Century of Protestant Theology* (Philadelphia: Westminster Press, 1980).
Heyward, Isabel Carter, *The Redemption of God: A Theology of Mutual Relation* (Lanham, MD: University Press of America, 1982).
—*Our Passion for Justice: Images of Power, Sexuality, and Liberation* (New York: Pilgrim Press, 1984).
—*Speaking of Christ: A Lesbian Feminist Voice* (ed. Ellen C. Davis; New York: The Pilgrim Press, 1989).
—*Touching Our Strength: The Erotic as Power and the Love of God* (San Francisco: Harper & Row, 1989).
—*When Boundaries Betray Us: Beyond Illusions of What is Ethical in Therapy and Life* (New York: HarperCollins, 1994).
—*Staying Power: Reflections on Gender, Justice, and Compassion* (Cleveland, OH: Pilgrim Press, 1995).
Hodgson. Peter C., and Robert H. King (eds.), *Christian Theology: An Introduction to its Traditions and Tasks* (Philadelphia: Fortress Press, 2nd edn, 1985).
Keller, Catherine, 'Seeking and Sucking: On Relation and Essence in Feminist Theology', in Chopp and Davaney (eds.), *Horizons in Feminist Theology*, pp. 54-78.
Keller, Evelyn Fox, *A Feeling for the Organism: The Life and Work of Barbara McClintock* (New York: W.H. Freeman and Company, 1983).
—'The Gender/Science System', in Nancy Tuana (ed.), *Feminism & Science* (Bloomington, IN: Indiana University Press, 1989), pp. 33-44.
—'Nature, Nurture, and the Human Genome Project', in Daniel J. Kevles and Leroy E. Hood (eds.), *The Code of Codes: Scientific and Social Issues in the Human Genome Project* (Cambridge, MA: Harvard University Press, 1992).
King, Robert H., 'Introduction: The Task of Theology', in Hodgson and King (eds.), *Christian Theology: An Introduction to its Traditions and tasks*.

Kuhn, Thomas, *The Structure of Scientific Revolutions* (Chicago: The University of Chicago Press, 2nd edn, 1970).
—'Reflections on My Critics', in Imre Lakatos and Alan Musgrave (eds.), *Criticism and the Growth of Knowledge* (Cambridge: Cambridge University Press, 1970).
Kyung, Chung Hyun, *Struggle to be the Sun Again: Introducing Asian Women's Theology* (London: SCM Press, 1990).
LaCugna, Catherine Mowry (ed.), *Freeing Theology: The Essentials of Theology In Feminist Perspective* (San Francisco: HarperSanFrancisco, 1993).
Lehrer, Keith, 'Coherentism', in Jonathan Dancy and Ernest Sosa (eds.), *A Companion to Epistemology* (Oxford: Blackwell, 1993), pp. 67-70.
Longino, Helen E., 'Subjects, Power, and Knowledge', in Alcoff and Potter (eds.), *Feminist Epistemologies*, pp. 101-120.
Lugones, Maria, 'Community', in Alison M. Jagger and Iris Marion Young (eds.), *A Companion to Feminist Philosophy* (Oxford: Blackwell, 1998), pp. 463-68.
MacQuarrie, John, *An Existentialist Theology* (London: SCM Press, 1955).
McFague, Sallie, *Speaking in Parables: A Study in Metaphor and Theology* (Philadelphia: Fortress Press, 1975).
—*Metaphorical Theology: Models of God in Religious Language* (Philadelphia: Fortress Press, 1982).
—'An Epilogue: The Christian Paradigm', in Peter C. Hodgson and Robert H. King (eds.), *Christian Theology: An Introduction to its Traditions and Tasks*, pp. 377-89.
—*Models of God: Theology for an Ecological, Nuclear Age* (Philadelphia: Fortress Press, 1987).
—*The Body of God: An Ecological Theology* (Minneapolis, MN: Fortress Press, 1993).
—*Super, Natural Christians: How We Should Love Nature* (Mineapolis, MN: Fortress Press, 1997).
Merton, Thomas, and Rosemary Radford Ruether, *At Home in the World: The Letters of Thomas Merton and Rosemary Radford Ruether* (ed. Mary Tardiff, OP; Maryknoll, NY: Orbis Books, 1995).
Midgley, Mary, *Wisdom, Information and Wonder: What is Knowledge For?* (London and New York: Routledge, 1989).
Miller, Donald, 'Liberalism', in Allan Richardson and John Bowden (eds), *The Westminster Dictionary of Christian Theology* (Philadelphia: Westminster Press, 1983), pp. 324-25.
Moody, Linda A., *Women Encounter God: Theology across the Boundaries of Difference* (Maryknoll, NY: Orbis Books, 1996).
Morton, Nelle, *The Journey is Home* (Boston: Beacon Press, 1985).
Moulton, Janice, 'A Paradigm of Philosophy: The Adversary Method', in Harding and Hintikka (eds.), *Discovering Reality*, pp. 149-64.
Mud Flower Collective, *God's Fierce Whimsy: Christian Feminism and Theological Education* (New York: Pilgrim Press, 1985).
Nelson, Lynn Hankinson, *Who Knows: From Quine to a Feminist Empiricism* (Philadelphia: Temple University Press, 1990).
—'Epistemological Communities', in Alcoff and Potter (eds.), *Feminist Epistemologies*, pp. 121-60.
Parsons, Susan F., 'The Boundaries of Desire: A Consideration of Judith Butler and Carter Heyward', *Feminist Theology* 23 (January 2000), pp. 90-104.

Plaskow, Judith, *Sex, Sin and Grace: Women's Experience and the Theologies of Rheinhold Niebuhr and Paul Tillich* (Lanham, MD: University Press of America, 1980).
Plaskow, Judith, and Carol Christ (eds.), *Weaving the Visions: New Patterns in Feminist Spirituality* (San Francisco: Harper & Row, 1989).
Potter, Elizabeth, 'Gender and Epistemic Negotiation', in Alcoff and Potter (eds.), *Feminist Epistemologies*, pp. 161-86.
Rauschenbusch, Walter, 'A Theology for the Social Gospel', in Peter C. Hodgson and Robert H. King (eds.), *Readings in Christian Theology* (Philadelphia: Fortress Press, 1985), pp. 317-19.
Richmond, James, 'Existentialism', in Allan Richardson and John Bowden (eds.), *The Westminster Dictionary of Christian Theology* (Philadelphia: Westminster Press, 1983), pp. 201-204.
—'Liberal Protestantism', in Allan Richardson and John Bowden (eds.), *The Westminster Dictionary of Christian Theology* (Philadelphia: The Westminster Press, 1983), pp. 325-28.
Ruether, Rosemary Radford, *The Radical Kingdom: The Western Experience of Messianic Hope* (New York and London: Harper & Row, 1970).
—*Liberation Theology: Human Hope Confronts Christian History and American Power* (New York: Paulist Press, 1972).
—*Faith and Fratricide: The Theological Roots of Anti-Semitism* (New York: Seabury Press, 1974).
—*New Woman/New Earth: Sexist Ideologies and Human Liberation* (San Francisco: Harper & Row, 1975).
—*Mary: The Feminine Face of the Church* (Philadelphia: Westminster Press, 1977).
—'Motherearth and the Megamachine: A Theology of Liberation in a Feminine, Somatic and Ecological Perspective', in Christ and Plaskow (eds.), *Womanspirit Rising*, pp. 43-52.
—*Disputed Questions: On Being a Christian* (Nashville, TN: Abingdon Press, 1982).
—*Sexism and God-Talk: Toward a Feminist Theology* (Boston: Beacon Press, 1983).
—*Womanguides: Readings Toward a Feminist Theology* (Boston: Beacon Press, 1985).
—*To Change the World: Christology and Cultural Criticism* (New York: Crossroad, 1989).
—*Gaia and God: An Ecofeminist Theology of Earth Healing* (San Francisco: HarperCollins, 1992).
—'Women's Difference and Equal Rights in the Church', in Elisabeth Schüssler Fiorenza (ed.), *The Power of Naming: A Concilium Reader in Feminist Liberation Theology* (Maryknoll, NY: Orbis Books, 1996), pp. 208-15.
—*Women and Redemption: A Theological History* (London: SCM Press, 1998).
Ruether, Rosemary Radford (ed.), *Religion and Sexism: Images of Women in the Jewish and Christian Traditions* (New York: Simon and Schuster, 1974).
—*Women Healing Earth: Third World Women on Ecology, Feminism, and Religion* (Maryknoll, NY: Orbis Books, 1996).
Ruether, Rosemary Radford, and Rosemary Skinner Keller (eds.), *Women and Religion in America* (3 vols.;. San Francisco: Harper & Row, 1981–86).
—*In Our Own Voices: Four Centuries of American Women's Religious Writing* (San Francisco: HarperSanFrancisco).
Russell, Letty M., Kwok Pui-lan, Ada María Isasi-Díaz, and Katie Geneva Cannon (eds.), *Inheriting Our Mothers' Gardens: Feminist Theology in Third World Perspective* (Philadelphia: Westminster Press, 1988).

Saiving, Valerie, 'The Human Situation: A Feminine View', in Carol P. Christ and Judith Plaskow (eds), *Womanspirit Rising: A Feminist Reader in Religion* (San Francisco: Harper & Row, 1979), pp. 25-42.
—'Androgynous Life: A Feminist Appropriation of Process Thought', in Sheila Greeve Davaney (ed.), *Feminism and Process Thought* (Lewiston, New York: The Edwin Mellon Press, 1981): 11-31.
Schleiermacher, Friedrich, *On Religion: Speeches to its Cultured Despisers* (ed. and trans. Richard Crouter; Cambridge: Cambridge University Press, 1988 [1799]).
—*The Christian Faith* (ed. H.R. Mackintosh and J.S. Stewart; Edinburgh: T. & T. Clark, 2nd [1830] edn, 1956).
Schüssler Fiorenza, Elisabeth, *In Memory of Her: A Feminist Theological Reconstruction of Christian Origins* (New York: Crossroad, 1986).
—*Jesus: Miriam's Child, Sophia's Prophet* (London: SCM Press, 1995).
Sharpe, Eric J. 'The Kingdom of God', in Allan Richardson and John Bowden (eds), *The Westminster Dictionary of Christian Theology* (Philadelphia: Westminster Press, 1983), pp. 317-18.
—'Social Gospel', in Allan Richardson and John Bowden (eds), *The Westminster Dictionary of Christian Theology* (Philadelphia: The Westminster Press, 1983), pp. 540-41.
Soelle, Dorothee, *The Strength of the Weak: Toward a Christian Feminist Identity* (trans. Robert Kimber and Rita Kimber; Philadelphia: The Westminster Press, 1984).
Solberg, Mary M., *Compelling Knowledge: A Feminist Proposal for an Epistemology of the Cross* (Albany, NY: State University of New York Press, 1997).
Soskice, Janet Martin, *Metaphor and Religious Language* (Oxford: Clarendon Press, 1985).
Suchocki, Marjorie Hewitt, *The Fall to Violence: Original Sin in Relational Theology* (New York: Continuum, 1995).
Tatman, Lucy, 'Mind the Gap: A Feminist Underground Guide to Transcendence, Maybe', *Feminist Theology* 23 (January 2000), pp. 79-84.
Thistlethwaite, Susan Brooks, and Mary Potter Engel (eds.), *Lift Every Voice: Constructing Christian Theologies from the Underside* (San Francisco: Harper & Row, 1990).
Tillich, Paul, *Dynamics of Faith* (New York: Harper and Colophon, 1958).
Trible, Phyllis, *God and the Rhetoric of Sexuality* (Philadelphia: Fortress Press, 1978).
Whitehead, Alfred North, *Process and Reality: An Essay in Cosmology* (New York: The MacMillan Company, 1929).
—'In Defense of Speculative Philosophy', in Donald W. Sherburne (ed.), *A Key to Whitehead's Process and Reality* (New York: The MacMillan Company, 1966).
Wilmore, Gayraud S., and James H. Cone (eds.), *Black Theology: A Documentary History, 1966–1979* (Maryknoll, NY: Orbis Books, 1979).
Wittgenstein, Ludwig, *Philosophical Investigations* (trans. G.E.M. Anscombe; Oxford: Blackwell, 2nd edn, 1958).

INDEX OF MODERN AUTHORS

Addelson, K.P. 13, 21, 23, 101, 128, 132, 137-39, 141, 143, 148-50, 162, 169, 172, 199, 202, 203, 236-38
Alcoff, L. 96-98
Altizer, T.J.J. 61

Baier, A. 130
Barth, K. 51-55, 60, 64, 70, 72, 81, 86, 163, 164, 249, 259
Bonhoeffer, D. 61
Bowden, J. 52
Buber, M. 55, 172, 194, 228, 241, 249
Bultmann, R. 53, 54, 163, 185, 186, 221, 249
Butler, J. 125, 252

Chopp, R.S. 254-57
Christ, C.P. 66, 67, 92, 125
Code, L. 13, 19, 21, 22, 41, 99-101, 120, 126, 128-31, 135, 139-43, 145, 146, 149-51, 158, 163, 167, 172, 178, 196, 202, 206, 236-38, 241, 243, 250
Collins, S. 12, 40, 67, 82, 86
Cone, J.H. 62, 63
Cox, H. 61
Crouter, R. 46

Daly, M. 12, 66, 67, 69, 70, 72, 73, 82-93, 257
Davaney, S.G. 251-56
DePaul, M. 95
Donaldson, M.E. 35

Emmet, D.M. 235, 245, 246

Ferm, D.W. 43, 47, 53
Foucault, M. 139, 142

Friedan, B. 60
Frye, M. 226, 227, 239

Gill, J.H. 32-34
Gilman, C.P. 108
Gross, R.M. 17
Gutiérrez, G. 60-63, 153

Hamilton, W. 61
Haraway, D. 13, 97, 101, 102, 109-20, 122-24, 127, 143, 148, 151, 170, 172, 199, 201, 202, 210, 211, 236, 238, 239, 242
Harding, S. 13, 34, 97, 98, 101, 102, 110, 111, 118-22, 127, 131, 143, 171, 238, 242
Harnack, A. von 47
Harrison, B.W. 40, 198, 199, 201
Hartshorne, C. 59
Hartsock, N. 13, 101-109, 112, 114, 116-18, 120, 122, 123, 127, 143, 172
Heidegger, M. 53, 54, 193, 229
Heron, A. 42, 43, 45, 48, 50-52, 55
Heyward, I.C. 13-15, 41, 49, 93, 101, 151, 181-212, 219, 220, 223, 225, 227, 230, 238, 239, 241, 244, 247-49, 251, 252, 254, 258, 259
Hintikka, M.B. 98

Keller, C. 180
Keller, E.F. 28, 101, 138, 139, 148, 178, 206, 238, 239, 242
Keller, R.S. 154
King, R.H. 40, 43, 45, 48
Kristeva, J. 125
Kuhn, T. 11, 18-20, 25, 56, 67, 72, 73, 92

Le Guin, U. 240

Index of Modern Authors

Lehrer, K. 95
Longino, H. 28, 29, 101, 124, 126-28, 131, 144, 145, 242
Lugones, M. 131, 132

MacQuarrie, J. 53-55
Marx, K. 103-105
McClintock, M.F. 239
McFague, S. 13-15, 18, 36, 37, 41, 93, 101, 151, 181, 212-49, 251, 252, 254, 257-59
Merton, T. 162, 164, 168, 170, 175
Midgley, M. 18, 19, 21, 24-26, 30, 31, 99, 150
Miller, D. 48
Moulton, J. 99
Murdoch, I. 226, 239, 241

Nelson, L.H. 19, 30, 101, 126-28, 132-35, 142, 143, 149, 169, 178, 237, 242

Parsons, S.F. 252
Plaskow, J. 66, 67, 71, 92, 125, 126
Potter, E. 20, 24, 96-98, 101, 128, 132, 133, 135, 138, 142-44, 169, 237

Rauschenbusch, W. 49, 50
Rich, A. 251
Richmond, J. 47, 48, 54
Ricouer, P. 32, 34, 232, 233
Ritschl, A. 47-50, 64, 249

Ruether, R.R. 12, 14, 15, 23, 41, 62, 66, 67, 69, 70, 74-82, 84, 85, 87, 89-93, 101, 108, 151-83, 187, 189, 190, 193, 198, 200, 202, 206, 210, 212, 219, 223, 225, 228, 230, 238, 244, 247-49, 251-59

Saiving, V. 12, 66-73, 82, 84, 85, 90, 92
Schilling, H.K. 237
Schleiermacher, F. 43-49, 53, 55, 59, 64, 161, 186, 249
Schüssler Fiorenza, E. 18, 251, 256, 257
Schweitzer, A. 50
Sewell, E. 233
Sharpe, E.J. 48, 49
Sherburne, D.W. 57
Soskice, J.M. 31, 35, 36
Spivak, G. 125

Tatman, L. 261
Tillich, P. 32, 33, 54, 55, 86, 87, 89, 91, 161, 177, 193, 196, 249
Trible, P. 185
Troeltsch, E. 47

Weiss, J. 50
Wheelwright, P. 232, 233
Whitehead, A.N. 56-59, 71, 86, 249
Wieman, H.N. 59
Wilmore, G.S. 62, 63
Wittgenstein, L. 18-20, 38, 133, 135, 242